WESLEYAN PERSPECTIVES ON HUMAN FLOURISHING

Wesleyan Perspectives *on* Human Flourishing

EDITED BY
Dean G. Smith & Rob A. Fringer

☙PICKWICK *Publications* • Eugene, Oregon

WESLEYAN PERSPECTIVES ON HUMAN FLOURISHING

Copyright © 2021 Wipf and Stock Publishers. All rights reserved. Except for brief quotations in critical publications or reviews, no part of this book may be reproduced in any manner without prior written permission from the publisher. Write: Permissions, Wipf and Stock Publishers, 199 W. 8th Ave., Suite 3, Eugene, OR 97401.

Pickwick Publications
An Imprint of Wipf and Stock Publishers
199 W. 8th Ave., Suite 3
Eugene, OR 97401

www.wipfandstock.com

PAPERBACK ISBN: 978-1-5326-9919-1
HARDCOVER ISBN: 978-1-5326-9920-7
EBOOK ISBN: 978-1-5326-9921-4

Cataloguing-in-Publication data:

Names: Smith, Dean G., editor. | Fringer, Rob A., editor.

Title: Wesleyan perspectives on human flourishing / edited by Dean G. Smith and Rob A Fringer.

Description: Eugene, OR : Pickwick Publications, 2021 | Includes bibliographical references.

Identifiers: ISBN 978-1-5326-9919-1 (paperback) | ISBN 978-1-5326-9920-7 (hardcover) | ISBN 978-1-5326-9921-4 (ebook)

Subjects: LCSH: United Methodist Church (U.S.)—Doctrines. | Happiness. | Theology. | Wesley, John, 1703–1791. | Methodist Church—Doctrines.

Classification: BX8331.3 .W475 2021 (print) | BX8331.3 .W475 (ebook)

Scripture quotations are from New Revised Standard Version Bible, copyright © 1989 National Council of the Churches of Christ in the United States of America. Used by permission. All rights reserved worldwide.

Dedication

To the fellows, members, friends, and partner institutions of the ACWR, thank you for promoting the flourishing of Wesleyan research and scholarship

Table of Contents

Preface – *Dean G. Smith* ix

List of Contributors xi

Chapter 1: Salvation as Flourishing for the Whole Creation: A Wesleyan Trajectory – *Randy L. Maddox* 1

Chapter 2: Health of Soul and Health of Body: Relating Inward and Outward Health to Human Flourishing – *David B. McEwan* 24

Chapter 3: Divine Joy and Human Gladness in Life in Christ – *John Mark Capper* 44

Chapter 4: John Wesley on the State of the Nation and Its People – *Glen O'Brien* 63

Chapter 5: Care of Souls in the Classic Tradition: Revisiting Thomas Oden – *Kate Bradford* 81

Chapter 6: Human Technological Enhancement and Christian Perfection – *Victoria Lorrimar* 103

Chapter 7: Healing our Intellectual Ambivalence: The Salvation Army and the Challenge of Higher Education in the New Millennium – *Dean G. Smith* 114

Chapter 8: Human Flourishing until Death: Living Well until the Very End – *Kirsty Beilharz* 135

Chapter 9: Exploring Salvationist Understandings of Holiness in the Anthropocene – *Matthew D. Seaman* 158

Chapter 10: How Relationality Facilitates Human Flourishing:
A Neurobiological and Christological Conversation
– *Emma E. Moore* 181

Chapter 11: "Let Our Anger Cease":
George Te Ara as a Case Study of the Encounter
between Human Trauma and Gospel Healing – *Peter G. Bolt* 190

Chapter 12: Aspects of Believers' Flourishing
in Paul's Language of Call/Calling – *Rob A. Fringer* 215

Preface

The righteous flourish like the palm tree, and grow like a cedar in Lebanon. They are planted in the house of the Lord; they flourish in the courts of our God. (Ps 92:12–13)[1]

THE BRINGING TOGETHER OF this collection of essays in published form is but one activity conceived of by the executive committee of the Australasian Centre for Wesleyan Research (ACWR) for the purpose of widening the influence of Wesleyan thought throughout our region and beyond. While certainly not the only publication of the ACWR, this is the first edited and published book of essays brought together around a common theme. The impetus for the book was the ACWR's 2018 conference in Sydney, Australia that featured the eminent Wesleyan scholar Dr. Randy Maddox delivering a series of papers on the theme of "Incarnation, Salvation, and Healing: Wesleyan Perspectives on Human Flourishing." We are delighted that Dr. Maddox was willing to contribute a chapter to this book, which includes a range of papers on the above theme, in addition to some of those delivered at that conference. It is hoped that readers will have their horizons expanded as they consider not only John and Charles Wesley's understanding of human flourishing but the broader Wesleyan perspectives on contemporary issues such as calling, creation care, healthcare, education, technological enhancements, death and dying, and more. It is my hope that by way of this publication, and hopefully those to come, more people will come to appreciate the generous orthodoxy of the Wesleyan worldview and continue the challenging work

1. Unless otherwise stated, all Scripture references throughout this book are from the NRSV.

of exploring the implications of our shared faith for life in an increasing complex and challenging world.

Dean G. Smith
14 December 2020

List of Contributors

Kirsty Beilharz, PhD (Music, University of Sydney), PhD (Theology, Sydney College of Divinity), Professor and Program Head of Theology and Integrative Studies, Excelsia College, Sydney; and Director of Lumen Research Institute.

Peter G. Bolt, PhD (University of London), Academic Director, Sydney College of Divinity; and Director of the Centre for Gospels and Acts Research.

Kate Bradford, MA (Theology), MA(Chaplaincy), Anglicare Chaplain and Pastoral Supervisor ministering in a large public hospital; she is completing an MTh at Moore Theological College.

John Mark Capper, PhD (University of Cambridge), Academic Dean and Senior Lecturer in Theology, Stirling Theological College in the University of Divinity.

Rob A. Fringer, PhD (University of Manchester), Principal and Senior Lecturer in Biblical Studies and Biblical Language, Nazarene Theological College, Australia & New Zealand; research supervision faculty member for Sydney College of Divinity and Flinders University; and Honorary Research fellow in the School of Historical and Philosophical Inquiry, University of Queensland.

Victoria Lorrimar, PhD (University of Oxford), Lecturer in Systematic Theology and Academic Dean, Trinity College Queensland; Winifred Merritt Research Fellow, Australian College of Theology; and Honorary Research Fellow in the Institute for the Advanced Study of the Humanities, University of Queensland.

Randy L. Maddox, PhD (Emory University), William Kellon Quick Emeritus Professor of Wesleyan and Methodist Studies, the Divinity School, Duke University; Institute Secretary, Oxford Institute of Methodist Theological Studies; and General Editor of the John Wesley Works Editorial Project.

David B. McEwan, PhD (University of Queensland), Director of Research and Associate Professor of Theology and Pastoral Theology, Nazarene Theological College, Australia & New Zealand; research supervisor for Sydney College of Divinity, University of Queensland, University of Manchester, and Flinders University; and Honorary Associate Professor in the School of Historical and Philosophical Inquiry, University of Queensland.

Emma E. Moore, MA (University of Manchester), Coordinator of Mission and Ministry Formation at Officer Formation Stream, Eva Burrows College, The Salvation Army Australian Territory.

Glen O'Brien, PhD (La Trobe University), Research Coordinator, Associate Professor, and Higher Degree by Research supervisor, Eva Burrows College in the University of Divinity; Research Fellow, Australasian Centre for Wesleyan Research; and Honorary Fellow, Manchester Wesley Research Centre.

Matthew D. Seaman, PhD (University of Queensland), Research Supervisor and Sessional Lecturer, Eva Burrows College in the University of Divinity; Sessional Faculty at Booth University College; and Honorary Research Fellow in the School of Historical and Philosophical Inquiry, University of Queensland.

Dean G. Smith, PhD (University of Queensland), Senior Lecturer in Theology and Philosophy and Dean of Students, Nazarene Theological College, Australia & New Zealand; research supervision faculty member for Sydney College of Divinity and Flinders University; and Director of the Australasian Centre for Wesleyan Research.

I

Salvation as Flourishing for the Whole Creation

A Wesleyan Trajectory

Randy L. Maddox

When the elderly John Wesley contemplated the mediocrity of moral character and the ineffectiveness in social impact of Christians in eighteenth-century England, he listed a major cause as inadequate understanding of doctrine.[1] By this he meant the broad lack of knowledge of Scripture among those claiming adherence to Christianity. But at times he highlighted specifically the inadequacy of the reigning popular understanding of "salvation," insisting that salvation involved "not barely (according to the vulgar notion) deliverance from hell, or going to heaven" but a restoration to health or wholeness.[2] More to the point, he joined his brother Charles in stressing that Christians can "anticipate your heaven below,"[3] or enjoy significant degrees of this health and wholeness *now*.

---

1. J. Wesley, *Works*, 4:86–96; esp. 89.

2. J. Wesley, *Works*, 11:106.

3. This famous line appeared first in C. Wesley, *Hymns and Sacred Poems* (1740), 123; a hymn abridged by J. Wesley in later collections to start with stanza 7 ("O for a Thousand Tongues to Sing").

Background: The "Vulgar" Embrace of a Transcendent and Spiritualized Eschatology

The Wesley brothers' suggestion that authentic Christian salvation involves anticipation of heaven *below* reflects their awareness of—and resistance to—a tendency to transfer much of God's saving work to the realm of heaven above. This tendency permeated Christian circles in their day and remains prevalent today, so it would be helpful to begin by reminding ourselves that the tendency stands in tension with central elements of Scripture and early Christian belief, and tracing how it became prominent in later Christian understanding.[4]

Hebraic Hope for Long Life in an Ideal Creation

One of the most central convictions running through the Old Testament is affirmation of God's "covenant faithfulness"—that the holy and loving God will honor those who live in the ways that make for justice and peace (*shalom*). In the earliest parts of the Old Testament this is expressed in a claim that the just will live long lives and be blessed with prosperity, while the wicked will die young (e.g., Prov 10:22, 27). The focus is on this life, with any suggested afterlife presented as a "shade" or faint image of present existence.

Over time it became clear that immediate blessing and retribution are often not evident in the present age. In the book of Job we see the deep perplexity that this realization created, but we also see Job's refusal to surrender his conviction about God's justice! This same conviction permeates the Old Testament prophets. At times it led them to explain to the Israelite nations that the reason for their current misfortunes was their failure to live within the guidelines of God's covenant. But more deeply it brought the prophets to insist that God would soon act in a new way *in history* to remove current injustices, change people's hearts (Jer 31:31–34; Ezek 36:24–35), and restore creation to its intended state of peace and flourishing. Isaiah 11:6–8 paints a vivid image of such a creation where wolves dwell peacefully alongside lambs, children play harmlessly among snakes, and all manner of plants and animals flourish.

---

4. For more discussion and documentation of the summary that follows, see McDannell and Lang, *Heaven*; Nichols, *Death and Afterlife*, 19–76.

Isaiah 65:18–25 details some of the social-political dimension of God's promised redemption:

> But be glad and rejoice forever in what I am creating;
> for I am about to create Jerusalem as a joy, and its people as a delight.
> I will rejoice in Jerusalem, and delight in my people;
> no more shall the sound of weeping be heard in it, or the cry of distress.
> No more shall there be in it an infant that lives but a few days,
> or an old person who does not live out a lifetime; . . .
> They shall build houses and inhabit them;
> they shall plant vineyards and eat their fruit. . . .
> They shall not hurt or destroy on all my holy mountain, says the Lord.
> (Isa 65:18–20a, 21, 25b)

Apocalyptic and New Testament Vision of Resurrected Life in Renewed Creation

For all of its grandeur, Isaiah's visionary hope remains set in the present age, assuming the current realities of birth and death. One might be blessed with long life, but not eternal life. More importantly, Isaiah's vision does not address how things might be made right for those who suffered unjustly *in the past*. Eventually some of the latest voices in the Old Testament began to express a more dramatic and more inclusive vision of hope—they promised God's cataclysmic judgment of present evil, followed by the resurrection of all persons (past and present) and recreation of *all* things (heavens and earth) in a state of unending life and abiding *shalom*!

This minority voice within the Old Testament witness was endorsed by the resurrection of Christ and became the normative aspect of Christian hope. The New Testament clearly affirms the resurrection of *all persons* for judgment. It also retains the assumption that God's redeeming concern is for *all* creation! Consider the witness of Paul: "We know that the whole creation has been groaning in labor pains until now; and not only the creation, but we ourselves, who have the first fruits of the Spirit, groan inwardly while we wait for adoption, the redemption of our bodies" (Rom 8:22–23).[5]

---

5. The spiritualizing trajectory we will trace next has tended to obscure the cosmic scope of God's anticipated saving work in Scripture. Among recent works helping us to recognize this again are Wright, *Surprised by Hope*; Middleton, *New Heaven and New Earth*.

Alternative Greco-Roman Focus on Immortal (Human) Life

Expectation of a new creation, teaming with life, in which resurrected humanity dwells, carried over from the New Testament to many early Christian writers. But we also see from the earliest years of the church the influence of a rather different model of hope for human afterlife, a model that was at home in the Greco-Roman culture within which the church was taking root. In its popular form this model held that the essence (*geni*) of the human person, or at least of certain heroic persons, was of such inherent value that it simply could not be terminated at death—the *real* person does not die; instead, death marks the point where one's essential nature was freed to enter a transcendent eternal state often pictured as peaceful gardens (the "Elysian fields").

Two characteristics of this alternative vision of hope should be highlighted. First, the state of the person immediately after death was fully conscious and filled with delight. Often there was stress that they are *more fully alive* after death; they were able, for example, to think faster, see more clearly, and feel more deeply than they could in their physical bodies. Second, in this vision hope was focused almost entirely on *human* welfare. These characteristics were heightened as Plato's philosophy, with its counterposing of matter and spirit, permeated Greco-Roman culture. Death was increasingly seen as the time when human spirits were *set free* from our bodies and this earthly existence, to enter into the eternal delights of a *purely spiritual* realm.

Growing Christian Assumption of a Conscious Intermediate State

The emphases of the Greco-Roman model of the afterlife proved attractive to Christians and were increasingly adopted—initially as characterizing the state of humans *between* our death and the resurrection of our bodies. The possibility of such an intermediate state is, at best, hinted at in a few places in the New Testament. But by the Middle Ages popular Christian imagination usually took for granted that humans enter a conscious disembodied state at death. Few echoes continued of biblical texts portraying the dead as "asleep" in the grave, awaiting the resurrection. Although there is even less support in the New Testament for viewing the human state after death as exceedingly better than our present embodied existence, popular belief embraced this aspect of the Greco-Roman model as well. There is no more relevant example than the opening lines of a hymn in John and Charles Wesley's first collection of *Hymns and Sacred Poems* (1739):

> We deem the saints, from mortal flesh releas'd,
> With brighter day, and bolder raptures blest:
> Sense now no more precludes the distant thought,
> And naked souls now feel the God they sought.[6]

Increasing Shift to a Transcendent and Spiritualized Final Hope

As conviction of the ideal nature of our disembodied intermediate state spread among Christians, it created some tension with the traditional hope for future resurrection of the body and reunification of the person. Expectation of such reunification persisted through the medieval period, often portrayed as reclaiming the very body placed in the grave (or its re-gathered parts, when necessary)![7] But this reclaimed body was assumed to be quickly transformed into the most ethereal form of matter, fit to return to the heavenly realm. Dieric Bouts's 1450 painting of the resurrected saints in paradise is representative.[8] Raised in bodily form into a paradisiacal garden, the saints are led by angels to the top of a mountain, where they ascend into heaven, their bodies turning progressively translucent as they rise.

Among elements that this painting captures is the marginalization of restored earthly existence to medieval Christian hope. Dante's *Divine Comedy* is characteristic in ignoring this theme, content to portray the church triumphant existing eternally in a heavenly realm adjacent to the angels. Moreover, there is no suggestion in Dante that earthly creatures other than humans participate in God's final redemption. We see here one result of an emphasis running back to the early church that deemed humans to be *microcosms* of the whole cosmos (containing all forms of being in our nature). This emphasis inclined Western Christians to read biblical imagery of salvation of the animals as more properly about healing of the "animal nature" (i.e., the passions, etc.) of humanity—and to assume that God need only redeem humanity to redeem the "cosmos."

---

6. C. Wesley, *Hymns and Sacred Poems* (1739), 16. This poem was likely written by John Wesley.

7. This topic is covered with fascinating detail in Bynum, *Resurrection of the Body*.

8. https://commons.wikimedia.org/wiki/File:Dieric_Bouts_-_Paradise_-_WGA02965.jpg.

Commitment to the literal meaning of Scripture in the Reformation led some like Luther to reaffirm animal salvation, drawing on Isaiah and Romans 8. Calvin's cautious response was more typical. He allowed that there would be a renewed earth, but resurrected humans (in ethereal bodies) will not live on it—they will merely contemplate it from their heavenly setting. He then cautioned against useless debate over why God would do such a seemingly needless thing. Such cautious affirmation of biblical imagery soon confronted the strong spirit/matter dualism of Enlightenment thinkers like Descartes. With "science" now reducing animals to mere machines, defense of the notion that they (or anything physical) participate in final salvation was increasingly rare. Popular Christian belief in the West came to anticipate final salvation as the deliverance of individual humans at their death from their earthly setting, and from all but the most ethereal of bodies, into an eternal spiritual realm.

The Wesley Brothers' Inheritance of this Transcendent Spiritualized Eschatology

This was as true in eighteenth-century England as anywhere, and the Wesley brothers clearly imbibed this transcendent spiritualized understanding of our final hope (eschatology) in their upbringing and education, as is reflected in their early writings. Consider, for example, the well-known section of John's preface to his first volume of *Sermons* (1746): "I am a spirit come from God and returning to God; just hovering over the great gulf, till a few moments hence I am no more seen—I drop into an unchangeable eternity! I want to know one thing, the way to heaven—how to land safe on that happy shore."[9] Or how it permeates hymns that Charles crafted for Methodists to sing at funerals of their friends, where we find stanzas like:

> Rejoice for a brother deceased,
> (Our loss is his infinite gain,)
> A soul out of prison released,
> And freed from its bodily chain:
> With songs let us follow his flight,
> And mount with his spirit above,
> Escaped to the mansions of light,
> And lodged in the Eden of love.[10]

---

9. J. Wesley, *Works*, 1:105.

10. C. Wesley, *Funeral Hymns* (1746), 3.

The Impact of Transcendent Eschatology on Christian Spirituality

A change in understanding of last things (eschatology) as far-reaching as that which we have just traced was sure to impact other areas of Christian faith and practice. One significant impact of the transcendent emphasis (the distancing of the realm where God's full redemption is realized from this present age) was the prominence in the Wesley brothers' day of the pilgrimage metaphor for characterizing present Christian life.

Patient Pilgrimage—A Spirituality Attuned to Transcendent Hope

While there are strands of the pilgrimage metaphor in Scripture, they do not constitute the dominant pattern of biblical spirituality. The Bible generally presents peaceful human life in a flourishing physical world as God's loving gift in creation. Suffering and evil are portrayed as corruptions of this original ideal, and death (or at least early and unjust death) is considered a curse. God's salvific activity in the present corrupt age is focused on restoring the peaceful and flourishing condition of the whole creation, with humanity in its midst.

This allowed, Scripture does portray life in the present corrupt age as threatened and often short and encourages readers to be prepared for death. These themes resonated strongly with Christians experiencing the repeated conquests and frequent plagues of the unfolding Middle Ages. Some (particularly monastics) began to identify preparation for death as the primary purpose of life. Such suggestions fostered the spread of a model of spirituality that adopted pilgrimage as a dominant metaphor—where Christians understand themselves as currently placed in an alien and dangerous setting, with the task of making their way home.[11] Cast in these terms, the challenge for Christian life is less the need to contend with the *temporary corruption* of God's ideal creation, and more the *temporary endurance* of this probationary setting. Life in this world is less God's blessing than it is our dominant challenge (almost a curse); and death is less a curse than a desired release into a more ideal state (heaven above). Proponents are drawn less to the hope of Isaiah 65:18–25, and more to the conclusion of Ecclesiastes 7:3, "the day of death is better than the day that one was born."

---

11. See the detailed discussion of this model in its Puritan form in Hambrick-Stowe, *The Practice of Piety*, 54–90.

The elaborate tour through the various levels of hell, purgatory, and heaven in Dante's *Divine Comedy* (ca. 1320) provides some sense of this shift; life in the present world is part of the narrative mainly as the implied setting where persons decide their future state. The most developed and well-known articulation of this metaphor for the Christian life is John Bunyan's *Pilgrim's Progress* (1678). In this allegory we watch the pilgrim (named "Christian") negotiate the many wearisome obstacles that comprise life in this world—all of which tend to distract him from his heavenly goal, the Celestial City.

Intertwined with the growing prominence of the pilgrimage metaphor for Christian life was spreading popularity of manuals on the "art of dying" (*ars moriendi*), which offered advice on how to prepare during life for a "good death."[12] Significantly, given the negative undertones of the pilgrimage metaphor, a common theme in these manuals was the importance of enduring the challenges of this life patiently, rather than seeking escape.[13]

The Wesley Brothers' Reflection of the Pilgrimage Metaphor

The pilgrimage metaphor permeated both the Puritan and Anglican strands of the Wesley brothers' ancestry and they were shaped deeply by it in their upbringing. It is apparent in John's early sermons like the claim in a 1725 homily on death: "We all agree in calling life a burden … death is not only a haven, but an entrance into a far more desirable country";[14] and he overtly endorsed it by publishing an abridged version of *Pilgrim's Progress* in 1743. Likewise, Charles wrote a series of hymns in the mid-1740s based on the allegory. The opening stanzas of one of these hymns map well the general contours of the pilgrimage metaphor.

> 1. Leader of faithful souls, and guide
> Of all that travel to the sky,
> Come, and with us, e'en us abide,
> Who would on thee alone rely,
> On thee alone our spirits stay,
> While held in life's uneven way.

---

12. For a good summary of this genre, see Vogt, *Patience, Compassion, Hope*, 15–51. For excerpts from examples in England see Atkinson, *The English Ars Moriendi*.

13. See Vogt, *Patience, Compassion, Hope*, 29, 37–38.

14. J. Wesley, *Works*, 4:208.

> 2. Strangers and pilgrims here below,
> This earth, we know, is not our place,
> And hasten thro' the vale of woe,
> And restless to behold thy face,
> Swift to our heavenly country move,
> Our everlasting home above. . . .
>
> 4. Patient th' appointed race to run,
> This weary world we cast behind,
> From strength to strength we travel on,
> The New Jerusalem to find,
> Our labour this, our only aim,
> To find the New Jerusalem.[15]

The negative undertones of the pilgrimage metaphor rise to the surface in some of Charles's hymns. The present earth can be characterized as a "world of sin and pain" to which we have been banished to suffer until our death. He can glory (prior to his 1749 marriage) that he has no spouse or children that might entice him to "basely pant" for natural things, distracting him from his heavenward pilgrimage.[16] And he can suggest that the sole purpose of life is to prepare for death, which is a blessing when it comes early.

> What would I have on earth beneath?
> Pardon, and an early death:
> Out of the vale of tears
> I long on mercy's wings to fly,
> To leave my sins, and griefs, and fears,
> To love my God, and die.[17]

The Wesley Brothers' Shared Initial Push Back— Affirming Present Spiritual Hope

Charles Wesley's occasional longing for "pardon, and an early death" emulates the focus of the "vulgar" notion of salvation almost entirely on escaping hell and going to heaven. But what was more characteristic of both Charles and John *after their experience of the renewing work of the*

---

15. C. Wesley, *Redemption Hymns* (1747), 51.

16. See C. Wesley, *Hymns and Sacred Poems* (1740), 125; C. Wesley, *Redemption Hymns* (1747), 66–68.

17. C. Wesley, *Redemption Hymns* (1747), 9.

Spirit in 1738 was how they pushed back against the tendency to postpone the divine transformation of our lives until the afterlife. They began to emphasize almost immediately two dimensions of God's salvific work in our lives *here below*.

The Witness of Love—Inspired Assurance of Pardon and Adoption

Ever since Jesus proclaimed that the Kingdom of God was *in the midst* of his hearers (Luke 17:21), Christians have assumed that they can experience some dimension of salvation in their present life. At a minimum this involved a consciousness of pardon (the certification for final salvation). Often it extended to a general sense of spiritual well-being. Notably, both of these are states of the human spirit. A more debated dimension gained prominence in the Wesley brothers' preaching and hymns through engagement with the pietist spirituality of the English Moravians in 1738. They shifted emphasis from the *human* dimension of assurance to the *agency of the Holy Spirit*.

For example, conscious reception of the Spirit became one of Charles's marks of authentic faith:

> The *pledge* of future bliss
> He now to us imparts,
> His gracious Spirit is
> The *earnest* in our hearts:
> We antedate the joys above,
> We taste th' eternal powers,
> And *know* that all those heights of love,
> And all those heavens are ours.[18]

This emphasis drew the critical eye of many Anglican peers, who worried that it verged on enthusiasm. Charles's response was resolute: "It nothing helps them to say, 'We do not deny the *assistance* of God's Spirit, but only this *inspiration*, . . . this *feeling* of the Spirit, this being *moved* by the Spirit, or *filled* with it, which we deny to have any place in sound religion.' But in 'only' denying this you deny the whole Scriptures, the whole truth and promise and testimony of God."[19]

---

18. C. Wesley, *Hymns and Sacred Poems* (1749), Vol 2, 221.
19. C. Wesley, *Sermons*, 222.

John Wesley too, after 1738, emphasized that our human trust in God's pardoning love is possible only as it is awakened by the witness of the Spirit that sheds the love of God abroad in our heart. His comment in a letter to Samuel Walker is characteristic: "I hold a *divine* evidence or conviction that Christ loved *me* and gave Himself for *me* is essential to if not the very essence of justifying faith."[20] Or, as he put it in an earlier letter: "[We affirm] that inspiration of God's Holy Spirit whereby he fills us with righteousness, peace, and joy. . . . And we believe it cannot be, in the nature of things, that a [person] should be filled with this peace and joy and love . . . without perceiving it. . . . This is . . . the main doctrine of the Methodists."[21]

The Indwelling of Love—Power for Spiritual Transformation

If the Wesley brothers' introduction to the emerging pietist revival in England played a positive role in forming their conviction about the nature of saving faith, their second emphasis about truly holistic salvation was framed in resistance to certain tendencies of colleagues in this revival. They came to worry that some of these colleagues focused so much on salvation as God's forgiveness of our guilt as sinners (the theme of Rom 1–3) that they marginalized the equally biblical theme (e.g., in Rom 7–8) of God's Spirit healing our spiritual debilitation resulting from sin. Two of John Wesley's classic comments on salvation capture this concern:

> By salvation I mean, not barely (according to the vulgar notion) deliverance from hell, or going to heaven, but a present deliverance from sin, a restoration of the soul to its primitive health.[22]

> What is *salvation*? . . . It is not a blessing which lies on the other side of death . . . it is a present thing. . . . There is a *real* as well as a *relative* change. We are inwardly renewed by the power of God. We feel the "love of God shed abroad in our heart by the Holy Ghost which is given unto us," producing love to all humankind.[23]

---

20. J. Wesley, *Works*, 27:93.
21. J. Wesley, *Works*, 26:181.
22. J. Wesley, *Works*, 11:106.
23. J. Wesley, *Works*, 2:156–58.

Key English Moravians who helped draw John and Charles Wesley into the revival in 1738 also connected justifying faith with holy living, but in a way that proved problematic. They encouraged the brothers to expect that when they experienced the assurance of God's love they would be immediately and completely renewed—all of their doubts and fears would be gone, and all sinful inclinations would be replaced by Christ-like inclinations. While both brothers found that their deepened assurance of God's love awakened new strength to resist sinful inclinations, they also recognized that the inclinations were still present. This realization did not lead them to forfeit the concern for full spiritual healing. Instead they progressively distinguished between the initial renewing effect that accompanied a sense of pardon and the further transformation of our inclinations that the Spirit makes possible in this life.[24] Charles, for example, crafted a rich set of hymns for believers who were waiting for this full redemption, a longing captured in an early stanza of the first hymn in the set:

> From actual blame
> I am sav'd by thy name,
> But mourn, till thou save me from all that I am;
> Till more than subdued,
> Till entirely renew'd
> Both my heart, and my nature are wash'd in thy blood.[25]

Over the decades of ministry among their Methodist people some shifts and tensions emerged between John and Charles about the dynamics of sanctification, and the nature of its full expression (Christian perfection) in this life. But both continued to affirm that God's Spirit made possible authentic Christian holiness "here below," nurtured in the means of grace.[26]

---

24. The best study of the expectations instilled by the English Moravians, and J. Wesley's later revisions, is Heitzenrater, "Great Expectations." For a parallel consideration of C. Wesley, see Maddox, "Anticipate Our Heaven Below," 23–25.

25. C. Wesley, *Hymns and Sacred Poems* (1749), Vol 2, 148. See also the thirty-seven "Hymns for Those that Wait for Full Redemption," in C. Wesley, *Hymns and Sacred Poems* (1749), Vol 2, 147–95.

26. See the Introduction to J. Wesley, *Works*, 12:15–24; and Maddox, "Anticipate Our Heaven Below," 25–27.

John Wesley's Broadening Precedent for Anticipating the Flourishing of All Creation

While the Wesley brothers remained in general agreement after 1738 about the present possibility—through grace—of anticipating the *spiritual* dimensions of salvation (or "heaven"), John progressively diverged from Charles (and the majority stance of his day) in affirming *other* dimensions in which God called us to "anticipate our heaven below." A good background for highlighting this divergence is again Bouts's painting of the resurrected saints ascending to heaven from the restored paradise.[27] As each saint ascends, note not only that their body dissipates, but they each enter heaven alone, and leave the restored paradise behind (reflecting an assumption that the "new heavens and new earth" were a temporary reality, a setting for the millennium but not eternity). If what God cares about ultimately (i.e., in eternity) is any guide for what we should care about during this life, then there is nothing in Bouts's painting to counter the charge leveled by Ludwig Feuerbach in 1841: "Nature, the world, has no value, no interest for Christians. The Christian thinks only of himself and the salvation of his soul."[28] In another setting I have shown that Charles Wesley also offered little to counter this charge.[29] By contrast, in the remainder of this essay I will highlight three areas in which John Wesley consciously challenged the restriction of a Christian's present concern to spiritual dimensions of salvation.

Anticipation of the Flourishing of Bodies, Not Just Souls!

We noted above that John Wesley imbibed in his upbringing the popular understanding of salvation as the human *spirit* spending eternity in heaven. But through the later decades of his life John took the scriptural imagery of bodily resurrection and of the new heavens and earth ever more seriously. Ultimately (drawing on a suggestion of Charles Bonnet, a prominent Swiss biologist) he was drawn to a model of the afterlife in which humans are embodied and reside in a physical universe, though we are higher on the "chain of being" than in our current setting.[30]

---

27. See n. 8 above.
28. Feuerbach, *Essence of Christianity*, 287.
29. Maddox, "Anticipate Our Heaven Below," 27–34.
30. J. Wesley even republished a translation of an extract from Bonnet titled

While most clear in his later writings, this emphasis on our bodies participating in ultimate salvation was consistent with John Wesley's *life-long* conviction that God's saving concern in the present includes our bodies. To appreciate fully this precedent in Wesley we need to remember the Puritan piety that remained dominant in his day.[31] A good sense of this piety can be gained from Lewis Bayly's *Practice of Piety*, one of the most popular books of its time, which included a section on the "practice of piety in glorifying God in times of sickness."[32] Bayly's most central (and repeated) point was that Christians should recognize that illness and affliction do not beset us by chance; they are sent providentially by God—in part as punishment for our sins, but even more as a type of treatment administered by the divine Physician. The purpose of this divine physic is to draw forth our repentance, and to "wean our hearts from too much loving this world and worldly vanities."[33] The most important response to affliction is to sanctify it, by giving thanks for it and allowing it to have this twofold effect. This is not to say that Bayly, or other Puritans, discounted the help of physicians. As part of their rejection of the *miraculous* efficacy of sacraments and relics, they stressed God's use of "second causes" in effecting providence.[34] Thus Bayly ruled out neither prayers for healing nor solicitation of medical advice. But he cautioned: (1) this concern should be secondary to drawing from our affliction the spiritual benefit of reconciliation; (2) our trust for healing must remain grounded in God, not the human physician or medicine; and (3) we should not desire restored health *over* death, but trust that the eventual outcome is God's providential will.[35]

Charles Wesley's various hymns on illness echo the Puritan stance presented in Bayly, including caution about assuming that God's primary concern is our present health.[36] By contrast, John Wesley was less hesitant to assure sufferers of God's desire to provide healing *now*. His stance is epitomized in advice he gave Alexander Knox in a 1778 letter: "It will be a double blessing if you give yourself up to the Great Physician, that he may

Conjectures Concerning.
    31. For a broader treatment of this topic, see Harley, "Spiritual Physic."
    32. Bayly, *Practice of Piety*, 792–855.
    33. Bayly, *Practice of Piety*, 799, 826.
    34. See Harley, "Spiritual Physic," 112.
    35. Bayly, *Practice of Piety*, 803–5, 815–17, 818.
    36. See Maddox, "Anticipate Our Heaven Below," 27–29.

heal soul and body together. And unquestionably this is his design. He wants to give you . . . both inward and outward health."[37] While Wesley did not underline the word, he surely intended "unquestionably" to be emphatic

If this is God's design, then for John Wesley it was obvious that we should *co-operate* by doing all that we can to restore and preserve our physical health.[38] How seriously he felt about this is evident in his instructions to his lay assistants about their ministry among the Methodist people. As they visited the various societies, Wesley charged them to leave behind books that could provide ongoing guidance, highlighting most often two works that should be in every house: (1) his excerpt of Thomas a Kempis's *The Imitation of Christ*, which Wesley valued as a guide to spiritual health; and (2) *Primitive Physic*, which he had prepared as a guide to physical health.[39]

Most Methodists today are unaware of the second volume, and scholars who come across it often dismiss it as a collection of "home remedies." This seriously misjudges its nature and its centrality to John Wesley's ministry. He read broadly on the topic of medicine throughout his life and gathered many of the remedies in *Primitive Physic* from medical authors of his time. This was as much a use of his scholarly gifts to provide aids for his people as was his collection of theological writings in the *Christian Library*. Moreover, in the preface to this volume (and in other publications) John added advice for preserving health to his suggestions for treating wounds and illnesses. He was interested not simply in offering cures but in promoting wellness.

John Wesley was also clear that Methodist ministry to others should address their needs for physical healing as well as for spiritual healing. This conjunction came naturally, because the Anglican model in which Wesley was trained expected priests to offer medical care as part of their overall ministry, at least in smaller villages. To be sure, he was aware of the efforts of the newly founded Royal College of Physicians to professionalize the practice of medicine by restricting the ranks of those certified to offer treatment. But Wesley recognized that there were simply not enough certified physicians available yet, and the poor were the ones most likely to be left without care. Deep concern about this led him to take

---

37. J. Wesley, *Works*, 32:661.

38. For more details on what follows, see Maddox, "John Wesley on Holistic Health"; and the Introduction to J. Wesley, *Works*, 32:1–65.

39. J. Wesley, *Works*, 10:920.

the "desperate expedient" of opening free clinics in Bristol and London where he offered medical treatment for the poor.[40] It was also led him to include basic medical texts in the readings assigned for his lay assistants, so that they could offer medical advice as they rode their circuits, and to create a lay office of the "visitor of the sick" within Methodist societies.

As all of this reflects, John Wesley longed for his followers to see that anticipation of God's salvific commitment to the flourishing of life involved nurturing not only our souls but our bodies in this life, and addressing both of these dimensions in our outreach to others.

Anticipation of the Flourishing of Society, Not Just Individuals!

A second area in which John Wesley broadened Christian anticipation of God's salvific work beyond the spiritual dimension is suggested by his well-known aphorism: "The gospel of Christ knows of no religion, but social; no holiness, but social holiness."[41] This aphorism is well known because it has been invoked by so many Methodists since the late nineteenth century to warrant their focus on socioeconomic transformation as they embraced the emphases of the Social Gospel movement, Liberation Theology, and the like. In other words, this is one place where his heirs have been ready to claim Wesley's legacy. But few of those making this claim recognized that Wesley's primary focus in the specific text cited is different from the implication they were suggesting.[42]

In the early years of the revival—the context of this quotation—the dimension of the *social* character of salvation on which Wesley focused most attention was corporate support and accountability for our ongoing growth in grace. He inherited this appreciation for "religious society" from his father, who sponsored a small group in his parish at Epworth; and he shared it with his brother Charles, who described such corporate support as the divinely intended way to "nourish us with social grace."[43] The depth of John's appreciation is evident in the multi-layered structure of support groups that he progressively crafted for the benefit of his Methodist people.

---

40. See J. Wesley, *Works*, 9:275.
41. J. Wesley, *Works*, 13:39.
42. On this point, see Thompson, "From Societies to Society."
43. See C. Wesley's hymn written for love feasts, *Hymns*, #507 in J. Wesley, *Works*, 7:698.

While the dimension of corporate spiritual formation is always central in Wesley's affirmations of the social character of salvation, a second dimension can be discerned as well in nearly every case. He took it for granted that those who were being renewed in the Methodist societies would be expressing this change in society at large. Note how this comes through in his longest elaboration of the Methodist understanding of salvation:

> By *salvation* [the Methodist] means holiness of heart and life.... a Methodist is one who has "the love of God shed abroad in his heart by the Holy Ghost given to him"; one who "loves the Lord his God with all his heart, and with all his soul, and with all his mind, and with all his strength." ... [and] this commandment is written in his heart, that "he who loveth God, loves his brother also." ... His obedience is in proportion to his love, the source from whence it flows. And therefore, loving God with all his heart, he serves him with all his strength.... Lastly, as he has time, he "does good unto all men"—unto neighbours and strangers, friends and enemies. And that in every possible kind; not only to their bodies, by "feeding the hungry, clothing the naked, visiting those that are sick or in prison," but much more does he labour to do good to their souls.[44]

This "social service" dimension of salvation as flourishing found its most formal expression in the General Rules, which admonished Methodists (1) to do no harm to others and (2) to do as much good for the bodies and souls of others as they could.[45]

While modern Methodists who invoke the aphorism "no holiness but social holiness" would appreciate such acts of caring for the needy and suffering, their focal concern has been to transform political and economic structures that ignore the poor or cause human suffering. Is there evidence of this focus in John Wesley's affirmation of the social character of salvation? There is indeed, though it emerges only in his later years. The clearest expressions are two tracts: *Thoughts on the Present Scarcity of Provisions* (1773), which proposes several political and economic moves to increase production of basic foods; and *Thoughts upon Slavery* (1774), which focuses on undercutting supposed humanitarian and theological justifications for slavery, but thereby lays the basis for support of political moves to abolish slavery.

44. J. Wesley, *Works*, 9:35–41.
45. J. Wesley, *Works*, 9:69–73.

What accounts for the rareness of emphasis on socioeconomic transformation in Charles Wesley's writings, and in John Wesley's earlier years? Many have assigned it to conservative political commitments which the brothers inherited, that led them to distrust all revolutionary agendas. But few have recognized how these commitments were grounded in a specific Anglican premillennial eschatology expounded by their father—which stressed *passive obedience* to the current (imperfect) king and church, while waiting for Christ (the *true king*) to return and institute the millennial age of earthly peace and tranquility through the *true church*.[46] Both John and Charles reflect this eschatology (and relative political conservatism) in their early ministry, and Charles retained it through his life. By contrast, in his later years John embraced an emerging emphasis on the hope for "latter day glory"—a culminating age of *this world*, effected by the Spirit through the church, where humans enjoy the peace and justice promised in the prophets.[47]

While it is not without its problems, this new emphasis allowed John Wesley to broaden (1) his confidence in the present empowering affect of the Spirit and (2) his conviction that God values human co-operation, such that they applied not only to the personal realm but also to societal realities. But what is most significant is the way he wove personal and socioeconomic transformation together by continuing to highlight the role of small support groups in nurturing both the inclination and the tenacity that sustained service to others in need and the struggle to transform socioeconomic structures.

Anticipation of the Flourishing of all Creation, Not Just Humans!

The final way in which John Wesley broadened Christian anticipation of God's salvific work in his later years is the one that most differed from the spiritualized model he had inherited. It is also likely the one that is least familiar to his present heirs.

If the spiritualized model of "heaven above" found it difficult to admit human bodies to the afterlife (allowing them only in an ethereal form), it struggled all the more with notions of animals or the physical elements having a place in ultimate salvation. But as Wesley continued to

---

46. See Maddox, "Millennial Hopes."
47. See J. Wesley, *Works* 2:490–99.

probe the biblical witness to salvation in his sixties, he decisively shifted the focus of his ultimate hope from "heaven above" to the promised new creation. Indeed, the new creation became one of the most prominent themes of his late sermons. These sermons leave no doubt that this future creation will be a physical place, even as Wesley speculated about how dramatically each of its basic elements would be improved over present conditions. Most importantly, while both his father and his brother Charles assumed that the "new heavens and new earth" were a temporary part of God's blessing (the setting of the millennium), John Wesley came to affirm this biblical promise as God's intention for eternity.[48]

John also became convinced that the range of animals would be present in this renewed creation. He had likely sympathized with the view that animals had souls for some time (a clear minority view in his day), possibly devoting one of the required lectures in his Oxford degree program to this topic. He offered a guarded reaffirmation of this point in 1775.[49] Then in 1781 he boldly affirmed final salvation for animals in his sermon "The General Deliverance."[50] While not unprecedented, this sermon was unusual for its time and is often cited today as a pioneer effort at reclaiming the doctrine of animal salvation in the Western church.[51] Wesley reinforced the point of his sermon two years later by placing in the *Arminian Magazine* an extended extract of John Hildrop's spirited defense of animal salvation, which contested the alternative comments of such notables as John Locke. In the preface to his extract Wesley noted that some might think that this issue was an ingenious trifle, but he considered it central to our confession of the wisdom and goodness of God. As Hildrop had argued, to allow that God did not redeem all that God created and called good would mean that God had not truly overcome the work of Satan.[52]

The connection of the issue of animal salvation to affirmation of God's goodness lies behind what is surely the most unusual element in the aged Wesley's reflections on the cosmic dimension of new creation. He had long doubted the adequacy of a theodicy that justified God's goodness in permitting the possibility of the fall by noting that God would

---

48. See in particular J. Wesley, *Works*, 2:500–510.
49. See J. Wesley, *Works*, 2:382.
50. J. Wesley, *Works*, 2:437–50.
51. See the reference in Linzey, *Christianity and Rights of Animals*, 36.
52. The extract of Hildrop's *Free Thoughts upon the Brute Creation* (1742–43) is scattered through *Arminian Magazine* 6 (1783). Hildrop's reference to Satan is on 598.

eventually restore things to their pre-fallen condition. In Wesley's view, a truly loving God would only permit the present evil in the world if an *even better* outcome might be achieved by allowing this possibility than without it. On these terms, he believed that God would not just restore of fallen creation to its original state, God would recreate it with greater capacities and blessings than it had at first.[53] What all might this entail? Drawing again on the work of Bonnet, Wesley proposed in "General Deliverance" that as compensation for the evil they experienced in this life God would move the various animals higher up the chain of being in the next life—granting them greater abilities, including perhaps even the ability to relate to God as humans do now![54]

Whatever we make of this speculation, the most significant aspect of Wesley's reflection on this cosmic dimension of ultimate salvation is his sense of its relevance for present Christian life. He defended his speculation about God's future blessings of animals on the grounds that it might provide further encouragement for us to imitate now the God whose "mercy is over all his works."[55] Lest this be left in generalities, he frequently exhorted against abusive treatment of animals.[56]

In short, in his later years John Wesley increasingly encouraged Methodists to "anticipate their heaven below" by participating in God's salvific concern for the flourishing of all creation.[57]

A Continuing Wesleyan Agenda

Such is the legacy that John Wesley in particular bequeathed to his ecclesial descendants and—through them—to the whole church. I wish that I could next recount how his descendants fully embraced this legacy and gladly shared it with others. Unfortunately, the historical reality was more mixed than this, particularly in the North American setting where Methodism most flourished through the nineteenth and twentieth century.

---

53. See J. Wesley, *Works*, 2:423–35.
54. J. Wesley, *Works*, 2:448.
55. J. Wesley, *Works*, 2:449.
56. See Runyon, *New Creation*, 202–5, for a convenient collection of such exhortations.
57. For more on this point, see Maddox, "Anticipating the New Creation"; Snyder, *Salvation Means Creation Healed*.

The early circuit riders in North America followed Wesley's instructions to offer medical advice as part of their ministry, until increasing professionalization made this unacceptable. In the nineteenth century Wesley's commitment to this aspect of holistic salvation was honored more by building colleges across the continent that emphasized training physicians and nurses. At the turn of the century this was supplemented by establishment of several church-supported "charity" hospitals.[58] Then came the financial pressures of health care in recent decades, which have largely removed the church from direct involvement, and have again left the poor in danger of inadequate access. Methodists are only beginning to explore how to honor their Wesleyan legacy within this new reality.

While twentieth-century Methodists picked up and elaborated Wesley's emphasis on socioeconomic transformation, most of them had meanwhile abandoned the small groups that Wesley valued for nurturing the inclination and tenacity for consistent engagement in social service and advocacy.

Finally, Wesley's support of animal welfare, and their ultimate salvation, continued in some strands of British Methodism into the nineteenth century.[59] But there is little evidence that this particular emphasis in the Wesley's mature understanding of salvation carried across the Atlantic to the North American church, or that it was consciously echoed on either side of the Atlantic by the later nineteenth century.

In other words, we who stand today in the traditions tracing back to the ministry of the Wesley brothers face much the same challenge as they did—the challenge of reclaiming an understanding and embodiment of the full scope of salvation affirmed in Scripture—the flourishing of *all* creation.

Bibliography

Atkinson, David W. *The English Ars Moriendi*. New York: Lang, 1992.

Bayly, Lewis. *The Practice of Piety; Being the Substance of Several Sermons Preached at Evesham*. London: Andrew Crook, 1613.

Bynam, Carolyn Walker. *The Resurrection of the Body in Western Christianity*. New York: Columbia University Press, 1995.

Feuerbach, Ludwig. *The Essence of Christianity*. New York: Harper and Row, 1857.

---

58. These transitions are traced well in Holifield, *Health and Medicine*.

59. Cf. Turner, *All Heaven in a Rage*, 50, 72, 161; Thompson (a Methodist minister), *Essays Tending*.

Hambrick-Stowe, Charles E. *The Practice of Piety: Puritan Devotional Discipline in Seventeenth-Century New England.* Chapel Hill: University of North Carolina Press, 1982.

Harley, David. "Spiritual Physic, Providence and English Medicine, 1560–1640." In *Medicine and the Reformation*, edited by Ole Grell and Andrew Cunningham, 101–17. New York: Routledge, 1993.

Heitzenrater, Richard P. "Great Expectations: Aldersgate and the Evidences of Genuine Christianity." In *Mirror and Memory: Reflections on Early Methodism*, 106–49. Nashville: Kingswood, 1989.

Hildop, John. *Free Thoughts upon the Brute Creation.* 2 vols. London: R. Minors, 1742–43.

Holifield, Elmer Brooks. *Health and Medicine in the Methodist Tradition.* New York: Crossroad, 1986.

Linzey, Andrew. *Christianity and the Rights of Animals.* London: SPCK, 1987.

McDannell, Colleen, and Bernhard Lang. *Heaven: A History.* 2nd ed. New Haven: Yale University Press, 2001.

Maddox, Randy L. "'Anticipate Our Heaven Below': The Emphatic Hope and Abiding Tone of Charles Wesley's Eschatology." *Proceedings of the Charles Wesley Society* 17 (2013) 11–34.

———. "Anticipating the New Creation: Wesleyan Foundations for Holistic Mission." *Asbury Journal* 62 (2007) 49–66.

———. "John Wesley on Holistic Health and Healing." *Methodist History* 46 (2007) 4–33.

———. "Millennial Hopes in the Wesley Family: Samuel Wesley Sr.'s Bequest." *Wesleyan Theological Journal* 55.1 (2020) 193–213.

Middleton, J. Richard. *A New Heaven and New Earth: Reclaiming Biblical Eschatology.* Grand Rapids: Baker, 2013.

Nichols, Terence. *Death and Afterlife: A Theological Introduction.* Grand Rapids: Brazos, 2010.

Runyon, Theodore. *The New Creation: John Wesley's Theology Today.* Nashville: Abingdon, 1998.

Snyder, Howard A., with Joel Scandrett. *Salvation Means Creation Healed.* Eugene, OR: Cascade, 2011.

Thompson, Andrew C. "From Societies to Society: The Shift from Holiness to Justice in the Wesleyan Tradition." *Methodist Review* 3 (2011) 141–72.

Thompson, Samuel. *Essays Tending to Prove Animal Restoration.* Newcastle: Walker, 1830.

Turner, E. S. *All Heaven in a Rage.* New York: St. Martins, 1965.

Vogt, Christopher P. *Patience, Compassion, Hope, and the Christian Art of Dying Well.* Lanham, MD: Rowman & Littlefield, 2004.

Wesley, Charles. *Funeral Hymns* (1746). https://divinity.duke.edu/sites/divinity.duke.edu/files/documents/cswt/34_Funeral_Hymns_%281746%29_Mod.pdf.

———. *Hymns and Sacred Poems* (1739). https://divinity.duke.edu/sites/divinity.duke.edu/files/documents/cswt/01_Hymns_and_Sacred_Poems_%281739%29_CW_Verse_mod.pdf

———. *Hymns and Sacred Poems* (1740). https://divinity.duke.edu/sites/divinity.duke.edu/files/documents/cswt/05_Hymns_and_Sacred_Poems_%281740%29_mod.pdf

———. *Hymns and Sacred Poems* (1749), Vol 2. https://divinity.duke.edu/sites/divinity.duke.edu/files/documents/cswt/46_Hymns_and_Sacred_Poems_%281749%29_Vol_2_mod.pdf.

———. *Redemption Hymns* (1747). https://divinity.duke.edu/sites/divinity.duke.edu/files/documents/cswt/44_Redemption_Hymns_%281747%29_mod.pdf.

———. *The Sermons of Charles Wesley: A Critical Edition with Introduction and Notes.* Edited by Kenneth G. C. Newport. New York: Oxford University Press, 2001.

Wesley, John. *Conjectures Concerning the Nature of Future Happiness.* Dublin: Dugdale, 1787.

———. *The Works of John Wesley: Volume 1: Sermons I, 1–33.* Edited by Albert C. Outler. Nashville: Abingdon, 1984.

———. *The Works of John Wesley: Volume 2: Sermons II, 34–70.* Edited by Albert C. Outler. Nashville: Abingdon, 1985.

———. *The Works of John Wesley: Volume 4: Sermons IV, 115–151.* Edited by Albert C. Outler. Nashville: Abingdon, 1987.

———. *The Works of John Wesley: Volume 7: A Collection of Hymns for the Use of the People Called Methodists.* Edited by Franz Hildebrandt and Oliver Beckerlegge. Nashville: Abingdon, 1983.

———. *The Works of John Wesley: Volume 9: The Methodist Societies: History, Nature, and Design.* Edited by Rupert E. Davies. Nashville: Abingdon, 1989.

———. *The Works of John Wesley: Volume 10: The Methodist Societies: The Minutes of the Conference.* Edited by Henry D. Rack. Nashville: Abingdon, 2011.

———. *The Works of John Wesley: Volume 11: The Appeals to Men of Reason and Religion and Certain Related Open Letters.* Edited by Gerald R. Cragg. Nashville: Abingdon, 1989.

———. *The Works of John Wesley: Volume 12: Doctrinal and Controversial Treatises I.* Edited by Randy L. Maddox. Nashville: Abingdon, 2012.

———. *The Works of John Wesley: Volume 13: Doctrinal and Controversial Treatises II.* Edited by Paul Wesley Chilcote and Kenneth J. Collins. Nashville: Abingdon, 2013.

———. *The Works of John Wesley: Volume 26: Letters II, 1740–1755.* Edited by Frank Baker. Nashville: Abingdon, 1982.

———. *The Works of John Wesley: Volume 27: Letters III, 1756–1765.* Edited by Ted A. Campbell. Nashville: Abingdon, 2015.

———. *The Works of John Wesley: Volume 32: Medical and Health Writings.* Edited by James G. Donat and Randy L. Maddox. Nashville: Abingdon, 2018.

Wright, N. T. *Surprised by Hope: Rethinking Heaven, the Resurrection, and the Mission of the Church.* New York: HarperOne, 2008.

2

Health of Soul and Health of Body

*Relating Inward and Outward Health
to Human Flourishing*

David B. McEwan

Introduction

For some time now there has been a renewed desire for a more holistic approach to medicine, health, and well-being. Such concerns link a wide range of professions and practitioners with the desire by those who are ill to be treated as a whole person and not just a set of symptoms to be cured. In the eighteenth century the ministry of John Wesley reflected his belief that God's provision of salvation in Jesus Christ was for the whole person, not just their spiritual life. His writings reflect this holistic approach to human flourishing and how he applied it to a wide range of physical and mental health issues. This chapter briefly examines John Wesley's understanding of inward and outward health, and how they impact each other. It then turns to a specific examination of the area of mental health and how this impacted both the physical and spiritual life. The final section utilizes Wesley's extant correspondence with Alexander Knox, a young man who suffered greatly from epilepsy and depression, to examine how he dealt with the relationship of inward and outward health in pastoral practice.

The Human Body and Health

Medical practice from the late seventeenth to the end of the eighteenth century was gradually moving away from the preserve of the herbalist and knowledgeable amateur to that of the professional physician and surgeon. With increasing specialization, came an increase in costs and a corresponding neglect of the poor. Like many Anglican clergy of the period who offered health advice and practical help to their parishioners, John Wesley had a keen interest in medical matters and read extensively on the subject for most of his life. He sought to bridge theology, science and medicine, and believed that medical and scientific research carried out within a Christian framework was an act of piety.[1] In 1746 he began intentionally dispensing free remedies and medical advice, including founding a dispensary in Bristol. This led to his publication of *Primitive Physick* in 1747 and it became his most popular publication.[2] The text went through numerous reprints in his lifetime and throughout the book Wesley carefully used the best scientific and medical knowledge of his day, coupled with his own practical observations and theological insights.[3] The book reflected his interest in health and healing in the broadest possible sense:

> Medical care and practices of preventative health stemmed from Wesley's practical theology, in which salvific restoration of the soul was integrally connected to the body. Christ as the Great Physician heals our woundedness and sin-diseased souls (the Latin term *salvus* means both healing and wholeness of mind/body and spirit) and makes us partakers of holiness, restoring the vitality of life that God intended for us.[4]

---

1. Madden, "Medicine and Moral Reform," 742.
2. Rogal, "Pills for the Poor," 81–82.
3. See for example, Madden, "Contemporary Reaction," 65–378; Madden, "Limitation of Human Knowledge," 163–66; Maddox, "Wesley on Holistic Health," 4–6. It is important to be reminded that Wesley lived in the eighteenth century and not the twenty-first century with its advanced medical knowledge.
4. Hughes, "The Holistic Way," 245.

That meant he saw no real distinction between the power of God delivering us from our sinfulness and healing us from that damage that sin had wrought, both personally and corporately. Such a deliverance was real and extensive, even though complete healing from all illness, disease and bodily limitations awaited the day of resurrection.

This raises the issue of the nature of the connection between the physical body and our spiritual nature. Wesley, like many in the eighteenth century, was Cartesian, drawing upon its image of the body as a "curious machine."[5] However, he did not reduce human beings to "a machine whose action could be explained fully on the basis of mechanistic principles."[6] The critical element here is our spiritual nature or soul, which "encompassed the mind or thinking principle, the affections and the will."[7] This acted upon the body (which was itself passive) and therefore made us responsible for its actions.[8] While his framework was dualistic, in practice Wesley believed that the two elements were so intertwined that it was impossible to separate them, and they both impacted the overall health and wellbeing of the person. This is seen in his sermon on the image of God, where he describes human beings as

> a compound of matter and spirit; and that it was ordained by the original law that during this vital union neither part of the compound should act at all but together with its companion; that the dependence of each upon the other shall be inviolably maintained; that even the operations of the soul should so far depend upon the body as to be exerted in a more or less perfect manner, as this was more or less aptly disposed.[9]

This meant that anything which impacts the physical (outward health) also impacts the mental and the spiritual (inward health).[10] Because human life is essentially bodily life "the animal frame will affect more or less every power of the soul; seeing at present the soul can no more *love* than it can *think*, any otherwise than by the help of bodily organs. If, therefore, we either *think*, *speak*, or *love* aright, it must be

---

5. J. Wesley, *Works*, 3:20.
6. Ott, "Wesley on Mind and Body," 63.
7. Ott, "Wesley on Mind and Body," 62.
8. Ott, "Wesley on Mind and Body," 65.
9. J. Wesley, *Works*, 4:296. See also J. Wesley, *Works*, 2:129.
10. McEwan, *Life of God*, 16.

by power from on high."[11] This theme of wholeness "was central to his theology and structured all of his work, in its written, oral and practical forms."[12]

Inward and Outward Health

Wesley believed that in the original creation there was no need for medicine because Adam knew no sin, pain, sickness, or bodily disorder:

> The habitation wherein the angelic mind, the *Divinae Particula Aura* abode, although originally formed out of the dust of the earth, was liable to no decay. It had no seeds of corruption or dissolution within itself. And there was nothing without to injure it: heaven and earth and all the hosts of them were mild, benign and friendly to human nature.[13]

He goes on to point out that since the human race had rebelled against God, the seeds of weakness, sickness and death are "lodged in our inmost substance—whence a thousand disorders continually spring, even without the aid of external violence."[14] Humanity's fall from grace means that nature itself now conspires against us, with the air we breathe, the water we drink and the food we eat all impacting our health in potentially negative ways. As Wesley says in his sermon, "The One Thing Needful":

> Our nature is distempered as well as enslaved; the whole head is faint and the whole heart is sick. Our body, soul and spirit, are infected, overspread, consumed, with the most fatal leprosy. We are all over, within and without, in the eye of God, full of diseases, and wounds, and putrifying sores. Every one of our brutal passions and diabolical tempers, every kind of pride, sensuality, selfishness, is one of those deadly wounds, of those loathsome sores, full of corruption, and of all uncleanness.[15]

The damage to our physical life consequently impacts our spiritual life: "And by sad experience we find that this 'corruptible body presses

---

11. J. Wesley, *Letters*, 5:4.
12. Madden, *Cheap, Safe and Natural Medicine*, 31.
13. J. Wesley, *Works*, 32:110.
14. J. Wesley, *Works*, 32:110.
15. J. Wesley, *Works*, 4:354.

down the soul'. It very frequently hinders the soul in its operations, and at best serves it very imperfectly."[16] He told Elizabeth Bennis:

> As thinking is the act of an embodied spirit, playing upon a set of material keys, it is not *strange* that the soul can make but ill music when her instrument is out of tune. This is frequently the case with you; and the trouble and anxiety you then feel are a natural effect of the disordered machine, which proportionally disorders the mind.[17]

While he insisted that there was a close connection between physical, mental and spiritual health, it did not lead him to conflating physical and spiritual health or to spiritualize physical symptoms.[18] "Wesley believed that a merciful God provided the antidotes to nature's poisons. Illness and death, the result of man's fall, are unavoidable, but Christ, the ultimate physician, healed the sick and bore the sins of man *bodily* on the cross."[19] Neither did he simplistically link ill-health to God's divine judgement on personal sin. His extensive correspondence and journal entries demonstrate that he always encouraged his people to do all they can to regain their health. While he clearly believed in the importance of self-discipline and self-denial, he did not see sickness as an indispensable help to spiritual growth. He told one of his correspondents that "It is undoubtedly our duty to use the most probable means we can for either preserving or restoring our health. But, after all, God does continually assert His own right of saving both souls and bodies. He blesses the medicines, and they take place; He withdraws His influence, and they avail nothing."[20] It was important for the sick to keep their trust in God even if the healing process seemed very slow; they were not to simply resign themselves to ill-health without seeking God's provision for healing. While he believed that God did heal directly by his grace in answer to prayer, it was most often by the use of the various medicines and remedies that were available to us.[21] As Madden observes, Wesley was convinced that God provided salvation through Christ so that the tension between corruption and renewal could be resolved, providing both spiritual and physical healing.

16. J. Wesley, *Works*, 2:405.
17. J. Wesley, *Letters*, 5:284.
18. Madden, *Cheap, Safe and Natural Medicine*, 185.
19. Madden, *Cheap, Safe and Natural Medicine*, 34.
20. J. Wesley, *Letters*, 7:209–10.
21. J. Wesley, *Letters*, 4:55–56.

However, the healing of the one does not guarantee the healing of the other in this life.[22]

The Impact of Mental Health on Well-being

A healthy body and mind were essential for human flourishing and Wesley was convinced that God was as interested in preventing illness in the first place as he was in curing it after it had developed. This meant taking care of those aspects of daily life that impacted health—and it was why Wesley was as interested in social and economic reform as he was in the spiritual reform of the nation. From Wesley's practical and pastoral perspective, people need to make use of all that God has provided if they are to experience the best health possible. This meant having as good a diet as possible, drinking fresh water, exercising regularly (outside if possible), and sleeping well. He encouraged his people to ensure their persons, clothes and homes were clean, and well-aired.[23] This would go a long way to reducing illness or limiting its severity, as well as minimizing the use of expensive medicines and other treatments. His letters and journals amply demonstrate that he did not see prayer for healing as more spiritual than making use of the remedies and medicines that were available. He did not place them in opposition to each other but believed that they were always to be used together as a God-ordained means of grace. Prayer was particularly important in calming the mind and the passions, which then had a positive effect on the body itself.[24] This inter-relationship of mind, body and soul was particularly important when considering the impact of life circumstances on people presenting with a range of physical symptoms. The danger of dealing only with the physical symptoms is shown in this entry from Wesley's *Journal* for May 12, 1759:

> Reflecting today on the case of a poor woman who had continual pain in her stomach, I could not but remark the inexcusable negligence of most physicians in cases of this nature. They prescribe drug upon drug, without knowing a jot of the matter concerning the root of the disorder. And without knowing this, they cannot cure, though they can murder the patient. Whence came the woman's pain (which she would never have told had

22. Madden, *Cheap, Safe and Natural Medicine*, 34.

23. Madden, *Cheap, Safe and Natural Medicine*, 156–85; McEwan, *Life of God in the Soul*, 114–15, 130–41.

24. Madden, *Cheap, Safe and Natural Medicine*, 186.

she never been questioned about it)? From fretting for the death of her son. And what availed medicines while the fretting continued? Why then, do not all physicians consider how far bodily disorders are caused or influenced by the mind, and in those cases which are utterly out of their sphere, call in the assistance of a minister.[25]

Likewise, physical disorders can impact both the mental/emotional, as well as the spiritual life.[26]

As with "outward" or somatic health, Wesley viewed "inward" health in terms of wholeness or well-being; it is a state of emotional stability, balance, or equilibrium.[27] This is where the writings of George Cheyne (a noted medical practitioner and writer in Wesley's day) were a strong influence and helped him to keep connected the impact of emotional health on both the body and the spiritual life.[28] In particular, Cheyne influenced his understanding of the "passions", which Maddox describes as "the current umbrella term for emotional states that arise naturally in response to events and agents external to the self—such as joy, grief, fear, and love."[29] Wesley abstracted the main points of Cheyne's presentation and presented them in the Preface to his *Primitive Physick*:

1. The passions have a greater influence on health than most people are aware of.
2. Violent and sudden passions dispose to, or actually throw people into, acute diseases.
3. Slow and lasting passions, such as grief and hopeless love, bring on chronical diseases.
4. Till the passion which caused the disease is calmed, medicine is applied in vain.
5. The love of God, as it is the sovereign remedy of all miseries, so in particular it effectually prevents all the bodily disorders the passions introduce, by keeping the passions themselves within due bounds. And by the unspeakable joy, and perfect calm, serenity, and

---

25. J. Wesley, *Works*, 4:191.
26. J. Wesley, *Letters*, 7:52.
27. Ott, "Mind and Body," 71.
28. Maddox, "Holistic Health and Healing," 13.
29. Maddox, "Holistic Health and Healing," 14.

tranquility it gives the mind, it becomes the most powerful of all the means of health and long life.³⁰

This comes to the fore in Wesley's main single work on the subject, "Thoughts on 'Nervous Disorders': Particularly that which is usually termed 'Lowness of Spirits.'" He acknowledges that sometimes minor emotional upset can be a genuine response to the work of God in the soul bringing conviction for sin, an awareness of God's presence and a loss of appetite for the things of this world.³¹ At other times, nervous disorders arise purely naturally and are often connected with a physical illness. Sometimes the disorder precedes the evidence of physical symptoms and sometimes they are the consequence of the illness. There are other cases where the nervous disorder is itself the illness. In particular, he mentions "lowness of spirits," and identifies the symptoms as follows:

> Does not this imply, that a kind of faintness, weariness, and listlessness affects the whole body, so that he is disinclined to any motion, and hardly cares to move hand or foot? But the mind seems chiefly to be affected, having lost its relish of everything, and being no longer capable of enjoying the things it once delighted in most. Nay, everything round about is not only flat and insipid, but dreary and uncomfortable. It is not strange if, to one in this state, life itself is become a burden; yea, so insupportable a burden, that many who have all this world can give, desperately rush into an unknown world, rather than bear it any longer.³²

He identifies a range of causes, including excessive alcohol consumption (particularly spirits) and drinking tea. However, the major causes are "indolence, intemperance and irregular passions."³³ The first is identified as a failure to adequately exercise; the second as poor diet (particularly overeating) and sleeping for too long. Irregular passions are such things as excessive joy, fear, loss of hope, all "foolish and hurtful desires," and excessive sorrow.³⁴ Wesley believes that the treatment for this type of nervous disorder is not the medicine prescribed by a doctor, as it will not deal with the cause. This disease responds only to the work

30. J. Wesley, *Works*, 32:119.
31. J. Wesley, *Works*, 32:616.
32. J. Wesley, *Works*, 32:616. This is a classic description of the disease we now classify as major depression.
33. J. Wesley, *Works*, 32:617.
34. J. Wesley, *Works*, 32:617–20.

of God. By this, he does not mean prayer and miraculous healing. He says the person must:

- drink no more spirits
- drink only a small amount of tea
- take at least an hour exercise every day after breakfast and preferably another hour after supper.
- do this in the open air, riding (if possible) or walking, as well as lifting weights
- if the person does not have the strength to do this for an hour, then do two or three shorter periods over the course of the day
- limit the type and amount of food eaten at each meal
- go to bed early and rise early, and, unless ill, sleep no more than about 7 hours
- above all, discipline the passions—particularly anger, excessive sorrow, fear, foolish and hurtful desires, inordinate affection
- surrender the heart to God and let the peace of God rule.[35]

It is instructive to compare this eighteenth-century document with current practice. We are now able to access the services of a range of health professionals when dealing with depression and have access to a wide range of medical treatments, including behavioral and drug therapy. Nevertheless, medical experts still recommend: regular physical exercise, increasing the amount of enjoyable activities, keeping a regular time for rising in the morning and going to bed at night, limiting the amount of caffeine and alcohol, finding a way to relax before bedtime, avoiding a focus on negative thoughts, keeping the focus on the present, sharing honestly with family and friends, taking steps to avoid anger and irritability, and finding a support network.[36] In all of this, the pastor and church community remain a major source of support and encouragement, while ensuring that the person makes the best use of current medical treatments.

As we have seen, Wesley believes that there is a depression that is healthy if we are to attend to the convicting work of the Spirit in our life.

---

35. J. Wesley, *Works*, 32:620–21.

36. Better Health Channel, "Depression." Similar advice is found on most Australian government health sites and mental health support groups.

The challenge comes in identifying when this is a symptom of a physical illness or mental stress rather than spiritual conviction, and this is where pastoral wisdom and discernment were all-important. As Madden observes, "Wesley assessed each individual's symptoms before deciding the origin of an illness, but even when he felt that a condition was spiritual in its basis, his letters usually recommend that the person apply regimen, medicine and faith."[37] In particular, he sought to clarify the difference between "spiritual darkness" and what he termed "heaviness." The former is almost exclusively a spiritual phenomenon, while the latter has a wider range of causes (often an illness), and usually extends over longer periods.

> The difference between heaviness and darkness of soul (the wilderness state) should never be forgotten. Darkness (unless in the case of bodily disorder) seldom comes upon us but by our own fault. It is not so with respect to heaviness, which may be occasioned by a thousand circumstances, such as frequently neither our wisdom can see nor our power prevent; perhaps, too, it was partly owing to the body.[38]

Spiritual darkness (or dryness) was defined as a believer's loss of a sense of God's love or his presence. He believed that this did not normally last for an extended period and strongly rejected the claims made by many Roman Catholic and mystic writers that it was a necessary spiritual experience to wean us from depending upon a sense of God's presence rather than walking by faith alone. In his opinion, this was not a scriptural understanding: "the Scripture nowhere says that the absence of God best perfects his work in the heart!"[39] A deepening knowledge of our faults and failings may bring "heaviness" but it never brings "darkness." Wesley believed that God increased our experience of his love in the midst of our struggles, as this was the real way to bring about transformation.[40] If a Christian lost the sense of God's loving presence for any extended time, it was far more likely to be a sign of our stubborn persistence in sin, whether outward behavior and speech or inward motives and desires.[41] The cure was this is confession, forgiveness and spiritual renewal.

37. Madden, *Cheap, Safe and Natural Medicine*, 189.
38. J. Wesley, *Letters*, 6:111.
39. J. Wesley, *Works*, 2:219.
40. J. Wesley, *Works*, 2:231.
41. J. Wesley, *Works*, 2:229. See also J. Wesley, *Letters*, 8:138–39.

The Christian's experience of "heaviness" may initially be very similar to that of spiritual darkness. In terms of mental and emotional health, Wesley often writes about the impact of "heaviness' on the life of the Christian. He identifies "heaviness" with experiencing grief and sorrow; it is a strong, settled sorrow that "continues for some time, as a settled temper, rather than a passion—even in them that have living faith in Christ, and the genuine love of God in their hearts," and it may impact the person's affections, behavior and body.[42] This is a description of a deep-settled despair that is not amenable to easily being changed. This may arise from an extended period of temptation as well as from illness and disease (whether brief or protracted).[43] Sometimes it arises from nervous disorders, because "faith does not overturn the course of nature: natural causes still produce natural effects."[44] He notes we may experience it from a range of circumstances, such as personal calamity, poverty, or death of a loved one. Wesley is confident that God "would have our affections regulated, not extinguished," and therefore sorrow and grief can exist without sin.[45] What he is describing fits with what we know today as depression; this is a normal and natural component of human life, though in some cases it can become a severe and debilitating illness. The danger comes when we link our emotional state to our spiritual state and believe that the former is an accurate measure of the latter. For example, he cautions Mrs. Marston about this danger, reminding her that "Undoubtedly as long as you are in the body you will come short of what you would be, and you will see more and more of your numberless defects and the imperfection of your best actions and tempers. Yet all this need not hinder your rejoicing evermore and in everything giving thanks. Heaviness you may sometimes feel; but you need never come into darkness."[46] Similarly, times of low spirits or the absence of feeling are not necessarily due to personal sin but may be caused by bodily weakness. The believer must continue to be faithful to God's call and not judge their spiritual state by the presence or absence of certain feelings.[47] Wesley does not identify depression, whether mild or severe, short term or longer lasting, as sin or

42. J. Wesley, *Works*, 2:225; see also 2:222–23.
43. J. Wesley, *Letters*, 3:230–31.
44. J. Wesley, *Works*, 2:227.
45. J. Wesley, *Works*, 228.
46. J. Wesley, *Letters*, 5:196; see also 5:198.
47. J. Wesley, *Letters*, 4:221; 5:235; 6:241; 7:185.

necessarily a sign of God's displeasure with us. This can most readily be illustrated by Wesley's pastoral dealings with Alexander Knox.

The Correspondence with Alexander Knox

John Wesley had encountered the Knox family during his travels in Ireland and had become a friend to their son, Alexander (1757–1831). Between 1776 and 1785 (when Knox was in his twenties) we have twenty extant letters from Wesley to Knox in which he expresses his personal and pastoral care for the young man. Knox was described as being in delicate health from the beginning of his life and suffering from what would almost certainly be diagnosed today as epilepsy and severe depression. This extended correspondence gives us insight into Wesley's counsel to one dealing with a long-term illness (epilepsy) and its impact (depression) in the light of his spiritual life. It is important to note that we don't have all the correspondence and sometimes we need to use some of the later material to infer what Wesley had advised earlier.

In the first letter (1776) we see Wesley's initial diagnosis of the situation when he refers to Knox's "almost continual depression of spirits, which is a *bodily as well as spiritual malady* [emphasis mine]."[48] Wesley notes that the young man has been greatly blessed by God in his social and economic situation, as well as his family life and friendships. Given our human sinfulness, Knox could easily be induced to find his happiness in the admiration of others rather than in God. This seems to underly the advice to see the illness in a positive light, as an instrument of God's grace: "Your illness will continue just so long as is necessary to suppress the fire of youth, to keep you dead to the world, and to prevent you seeking happiness where it never was nor ever can be found. Considered in this view, it is a great blessing and a proof of God's watchful care over you."[49] Wesley believes that the illness has partly natural causes and partly it is a gift of God to balance the petulance of youth and foolish desires. The reason why this is judged to be God's providential care for Knox is because he did not choose to put himself in a situation where he would inevitably contract the illness. The illness itself has natural causes, therefore, Knox is to actively pursue certain remedies (salt-water bathing

---

48. J. Wesley, *Letters*, 6:212.
49. J. Wesley, *Letters*, 6:204.

is clearly identified) for healing.[50] Believing the illness to be a means of grace to foster spiritual health did not mean that it was to be stoically endured for the rest of his life, and so Wesley holds out the offer of God's grace and mercy: "Is not health at hand, both for soul and body!"[51]

By the following year (1777) there seems to be some improvement in Knox's health and Wesley remains hopeful that it will continue. He assures Knox that "it is certainly the design of Him that loves you to heal both body and soul; and possibly He delays the healing of the former that the cure of the latter may keep pace with it."[52] This linking of the illness with the state of the soul is not intended to say that it is the state of his soul that is the cause of his illness. It is a circumstance that God uses to encourage Knox to develop his life with God, as in Wesley's opinion, he is still a "servant of God" but not yet "a son of God."[53] The delay in healing is obviously concerning to Knox and increases his sense of despair and the passivity that normally goes with depression. Wesley gives an assurance that God neither forgets nor despises him,[54] and he must wait patiently for God to complete the work. He must not give in to despair and he should force himself to make use of the remedies suggested because Wesley has "little doubt of seeing [him] an healthy as well as an happy man."[55] It is now becoming obvious that a major factor in Knox's condition is his mental state and how that impacts both his physical health and spiritual life.

It seems to Wesley that part of the problem lies in the focus of Knox's thoughts, which are increasingly negative, and this is hindering his healing. In 1778 Wesley tells him that both his physical and mental health would improve if he would just live for today and not fret about tomorrow.[56] In Wesley's opinion, many of Knox's problems are due to his inability to trust God with his situation and as a result his lengthy

---

50. J. Wesley, *Letters*, 6:269. This information is contained in a letter from the following year.

51. J. Wesley, *Letters*, 6:219–20.

52. J. Wesley, *Letters*, 6:259.

53. J. Wesley, *Letters*, 6:272–73. The difference in Wesley's understanding is between one who has been awakened to their spiritual condition but not yet enjoying a full evangelical salvation. See Felleman, "John Wesley and 'Servant of God'" for a full explanation of the distinction and its implications.

54. J. Wesley, *Letters*, 6:269.

55. J. Wesley, *Letters*, 6:273.

56. J. Wesley, *Letters*, 6:307–8.

bouts of depression continue.[57] Wesley urges him not to despise the "small" things God has done for him and to be thankful for the recent small improvements in his health. The implication is that Knox needs to express his thankfulness, whether he feels like it or not. He needs to break free from the constraints of his depression by stirring up the gift of God and being thankful for what God has already done. This underscores the importance of thankfulness in changing thought patterns and the small gains in positivity will help him move from his current despair and passivity. However, the young man continues to struggle to do this and reports how he is worried that even this small measure of healing will be taken away from him. Knox's picture of God is colored by his mental state and leaves him doubting God's love and benevolence towards him. Wesley affirms that while he has no right to expect his improved health to continue,[58] our relationship with God is not based on our performance. Wesley agrees that he

> cannot claim it from God's justice; you do not merit it at His hands. But is this the measure whereby He deals with His poor creatures? Does He give us no more blessings than we deserve? Does he treat us in all things according to His justice? Not so; but mercy rejoices over judgement! Therefore expect from Him, not what you deserve, but what you want—health of soul and health of body: ask, and you shall receive; seek, and you shall find; not for your worthiness, but because "worthy is the Lamb."[59]

This emphasizes that God's mercy and grace are the heart of the Gospel and the source of everything we receive in life. We never arrive at a place where we can earn those blessings by anything we say or do. It is this theological misunderstanding that lies at the heart of Knox's lack of trust in God's love and goodness towards him. If he continues to see God as one who is harsh or who takes delight in making his life difficult, then it is no wonder that Knox lives in fear that anything God gives he will capriciously take away. Wesley has often pointed out (on the basis of Scripture) that God is love, and his love in our hearts casts out the fear he will act in an arbitrary manner towards us. Knox's anxieties reaffirm that he is still a "servant" rather than a "son" and does not yet know the fullness of God's love. There is no suggestion in any of this that improving

---

57. J. Wesley, *Letters*, 6:309, 314, 315.
58. J. Wesley, *Letters*, 6:317.
59. J. Wesley, *Letters*, 6:318.

his spiritual life will cure the illness itself, but it will absolutely impact his mental health in a positive manner. This, in turn, will enable him to flourish, even within the confines of the epileptic seizures continuing.

Soon after this letter the fits and the accompanying despondency return. Wesley once more encourages the young man to intentionally focus on God's mercies, but he should also continue to ride as often as he can.[60] Wesley is confident that his bodily disorder affects his mind and believes this is more a matter of diet and exercise than medicine for a cure.[61] Once more, he affirms that Knox's depression must not be taken as an infallible sign of his spiritual state:

> It is undeniable (1) That you have a bodily complaint. Your nerves are greatly disordered; and although it is only now and then that this rises so high as to occasion a fit, yet it has a constant influence upon you so as to cause a dejection of spirits. This dejection is no more imputed to you as a sin than the flowing of the blood in your veins.[62]

Wesley does affirm that illnesses arising from biological causes will impact our temperament and emotional life. Despair and dejection are not sin, and their expression cannot be sin as long since there is no willful concurrence with them. Sorting out the difference between actively choosing to dwell in misery and the natural outcome of physical illness and depression is not easy. In Wesley's opinion the main cause of his despondency are the temptations of Satan, who injects thoughts into his mind and then accuses him for them. This makes it all the more important for Knox to not lose faith and to keep trusting God for both spiritual and mental health: "You want to have the love of God fully shed abroad in your heart: you have only now and then a little touch of thankfulness, a small spark of that divine fire; and hence anger, or at least fretfulness and peevishness, more or less, will naturally arise."[63] It makes it all the more important for Knox to focus his thoughts on the fact that God is for him and not against him. He is urged to remember that God does care for him, and actively supports him each day, graciously helping him with his illness, all in preparation for receiving the blessing he seeks.[64]

60. J. Wesley, *Letters*, 6:320.
61. J. Wesley, *Letters*, 6:327–28.
62. J. Wesley, *Letters*, 6:364.
63. J. Wesley, *Letters*, 6:364.
64. J. Wesley, *Letters*, 6:364.

It is apparent at the start of 1780 that the mental problems are so deep seated because of the fits that lead Knox to withdraw from involvement in the church and community. This lack of social engagement and support means that any real change will not come easily or quickly. Once more Wesley notes that he has not made use of the remedies that he recommended and he urges him to now try the mineral water as it is very likely God will make it a means of lessening, if not removing, his bodily disorder. Wesley stresses again that it is very important that he not simply give into the depression and remain passive, but to act and be out in the fresh air and exercising, even when he does not feel like it. He reminds Knox that these are God's provision for our healing and "you have no reason to expect the spirit of an healthful mind unless you use the means that God has ordained."[65] In other words, to wait passively for immediate divine healing is to act in defiance of God's clear provision through the range of remedies available. It is apparent that Knox has not just withdrawn from going outdoors for his health but is no longer attending the chapel. This seems to be caused by his fear of having a fit in public, so it has now become a vicious circle: the more fits he has the less inclination to attend chapel, which then seems to increase the number of fits and their accompanying depression. This withdrawal from community worship has only negative consequences and so Wesley strongly urges him to trust God with the outing as he is not likely to be more uncomfortable there than he is at home.[66] Pragmatically, if it does not work as planned, then having two fits is less evil than losing fifty precious opportunities of attending chapel to hear the preacher, participate in worship and enjoy the fellowship. He urges him to break through the fear, which is a mere snare of the devil, because God is ready to save.[67]

This advice is apparently not well received but Wesley reaffirms his friendship and care for the young man. That means he cannot remain silent where the health of his young friend is concerned. He repeats his conviction that it is Knox's body that presses down his soul, and if God heals the body the mind will certainly be far easier. Even though it has been a long illness, Wesley does not despair of seeing him a happy man and full of peace and joy in believing.[68] It has become apparent that Knox

---

65. J. Wesley, *Letters*, 6:377.
66. J. Wesley, *Letters*, 6:377.
67. J. Wesley, *Letters*, 6:378.
68. J. Wesley, *Letters*, 7:39–40.

is very good at finding arguments against himself and the proposed remedies (both for inward and outward healing), and if he puts his mind to it he will never run out of them. This is a problem that Wesley has faced many times when people place reason above faith. In such a state, he will not find the place of victory that God longs to grant. Wesley agrees with him that God will not give faith to the double-minded, but he can take away the double-mindedness first and then give faith, and he can do that "today." It will take a "miracle," but why should he not expect one, for God always upholds his word? God knows him in his faults but will always respond to his cry for help.[69]

In the final year of their correspondence (1785) Wesley shares his mature thoughts on his situation. He notes that Knox still does not go to church or preaching house in case he has a fit and falls down, disturbing everyone.[70] Wesley repeats what he said earlier about the benefits of public worship and fellowship outweighing the embarrassment of having a fit in public. He cannot be sure that he will have a fit and having a fit once every month is less of an evil than shutting himself up in the house, with very limited social contact. He is only harming his health the more by not getting out and having exercise in the fresh air. "And you hurt your soul by neglecting the ordinances of God, which you have no authority to do unless you were sick in bed." He is to go out today and trust God for the outcome. In an insightful comment he adds: "if your mother hinders you, she will kill you with kindness."[71] The inference here is that he was not receiving much encouragement and support from his mother to be out and about. This was simply compounding the problem. We do get a glimpse that his advice was finally being acted upon. In the last letter we have, Wesley gladly notes that Knox is getting out and about a bit each day and soon he can return to public worship, for without this he will continue to forego God's blessing and hope of both inward and outward healing.[72]

---

69. J. Wesley, *Letters*, 7:44.
70. J. Wesley, *Letters*, 7:272.
71. J. Wesley, *Letters*, 7:273.
72. J. Wesley, *Letters*, 7:279–80.

Conclusion

John Wesley was deeply concerned with the health and welfare of both his own church members and the wider community. He understood health within a broad framework, covering the physical (outward health), as well as the mental and spiritual life (inward health) of the person. While he was formally a Cartesian in his description of the human person, with a physical body and a soul, in practice he stressed their interdependence. This makes it certain that outward health (physical) and inward health (mental/spiritual) are intimately connected. What impacted the one, impacted the other, and authentic human flourishing was not possible without the health of both. He acknowledged that both physical and mental illness impact spiritual life but did not believe that sin was necessarily the cause of either; only if the person had been complicit in acquiring their illness would he directly link the two. Nor did Wesley see sickness as God's inevitable punishment for sin, though God could use the illness as a means of grace if the person submitted to the work of the Spirit. Severe illness that produces high levels of pain, disorientation or physical limitation was not ever in itself a blessing. Wesley acknowledged that it was not the sickness itself that promoted spiritual vitality, but our response to God during the sickness. Even in these cases, Wesley did not advocate a passive acceptance of illness, since it was not something that God intended humanity to experience.

In terms of inward health, particularly depression ("lowness of spirits"), Wesley was equally clear that this was neither an inevitable sign of sin nor of God's punishment, though mild cases may be caused by the convicting work of the Holy Spirit. God was as willing to heal depression as he was any other illness and, as before, the person was not to passively accept it as a divine judgement. Wesley believed that many cases of depression had their origin in either a physical illness or an unhealthy lifestyle choice. The remedy was often to cure the illness and amend the lifestyle. Depression that had no obvious cause was also to be tackled with the wise use of a range of remedies focused on lifestyle choices. This required careful evaluation by the minister, as well as by doctors. Because severe depression resulted in despair and passivity, Wesley stressed the importance of family, friends, and church community in offering support and encouragement to the patient. Without this, they were liable to simply resign themselves to the despair, sometimes with fatal consequences. In all cases, prayer and the ministry of the worshipping community were essential. Prayer was always a choice means of grace, but so were lifestyle changes and formal treatments. Therefore, they ought always to go together, and prayer was especially beneficial in helping to calm the person through the ministry of the Holy Spirit. While eighteenth-century medicine offered very little in the way of effective treatments in comparison to ours, it is interesting to see how many of Wesley's lifestyle remedies are still strongly supported today: limiting the intake of alcohol and caffeine; eating a healthy diet and avoiding over-indulgence; having adequate daily exercise (particularly in the open air); cultivating regular sleep patterns (and avoiding excessive sleep); focusing on positive emotions and cultivating calm by meditative practices.

In his correspondence with Alexander Knox, Wesley demonstrates all the critical elements mentioned above as he sought to bring about physical, mental, and spiritual health. The approach taken with Knox throughout the correspondence ties inward and outward health together, and the remedy for one will have an impact on the other. Wesley offers Knox a range of remedies that are drawn from his work on "Nervous Disorders" and believes that Knox's continuing ill-health lies chiefly in his failure to make use of them. This is exacerbated by the lack of support from his mother, who seems to think that making an effort to overcome his depression would be pointless, believing that her son needed to improve his health first and then he could venture outside. Likewise, the lack of social contact made it very difficult for him to experience any encouragement and made it much easier for his mind to keep focused on the negatives and to remain passive. The failure to attend chapel also cut him off from a rich means of grace that would greatly help him cope with the despair. Pastorally, he regularly advised Knox to focus on God's grace, love, and mercy, rather than his own mental, emotional or spiritual state. He recognized that to focus on negative thoughts and feelings was always debilitating but there was a healing power in focusing on the positive elements of God's gracious provision for us. His continual advice on medicines, sleep, diet and exercise are part of his conviction that being healed by means is as much an answer to prayer as if the cure came by direct divine intervention. Thus he counsels Alexander to give himself totally to the Great Physician for the healing of body, mind and spirit, making use of all the means of grace that God had ordained, if he was ever to know both inward and outward health.

Bibliography

Better Health Channel. "Depression—Treatment and Management." https://www.betterhealth.vic.gov.au/health/conditionsandtreatments/depression-treatment-and-management. Accessed August 12, 2019.

Felleman, Laura Bartels. "John Wesley and the 'Servant of God.'" *Wesleyan Theological Journal* 41.2 (2006) 72–86.

Hughes, Melanie Dobson. "The Holistic Way: John Wesley's Practical Piety as a Resource for Integrated Healthcare." *Journal of Religion and Health* 47 (2008) 237–52.

Madden, Deborah. *'A Cheap, Safe and Natural Medicine': Religion, Medicine and Culture in John Wesley's Primitive Physic*. Leiden: Brill, 2007.

———. "Contemporary Reaction to John Wesley's *Primitive Physic*: Or, the Case of Dr William Hawes Examined." *Social History of Medicine* 17.3 (2004) 365–78.

———. "The Limitation of Human Knowledge: Faith and the Empirical Method in John Wesley's Medical Holism." *History of European Ideas* 32 (2006) 162–72.

———. "Medicine and Moral Reform: The Place of Practical Piety in John Wesley's Art of Physic." *Church History* 73.4 (2004) 741–58.

Maddox, Randy L. "John Wesley on Holistic Health and Healing." *Methodist History* 46.1 (2007) 4–33.

McEwan, David B. *The Life of God in the Soul: The Integration of Love, Holiness and Happiness in the Thought of John Wesley*. Milton Keynes: Paternoster, 2015.

Ott, Philip W. "John Wesley on Mind and Body: Toward an Understanding of Health as Wholeness." *Methodist History* 27.2 (1989) 61–72.

Rogal, Samuel J. "Pills for the Poor: John Wesley's *Primitive Physick*." *Yale Journal of Biology and Medicine* (1978) 81–90.

Wesley, John. *The Letters of the Rev. John Wesley*. 8 vols. Edited by John Telford. London: Epworth, 1931.

———. *The Works of John Wesley: Volume 2: Sermons II, 34–70*. Edited by Albert C. Outler. Nashville: Abingdon, 1985.

———. *The Works of John Wesley: Volume 3: Sermons III, 71–114*. Edited by Albert C. Outler. Nashville: Abingdon, 1986.

———. *The Works of John Wesley: Volume 4: Sermons IV, 115–151*. Edited by Albert C. Outler. Nashville: Abingdon, 1987.

———. *The Works of John Wesley: Volume 32: Medical and Health Writings*. Edited by James G. Donat and Randy L. Maddox. Nashville: Abingdon, 2018.

3

Divine Joy and Human Gladness in Life in Christ

John Mark Capper

CHARLES AND JOHN WESLEY grew up in a "spiritual" family. There was connection to the tradition of Christian faith as well as to the sense of the immediacy of the spirit of God. Whilst there have been explorations of the question of whether the childhood home of the Wesley brothers, the Epworth Rectory, was haunted,[1] it is sufficient to note that it was assumed to be a place of refuge in the presence of God and of family, a place of prayer and of spiritual nurture. As a home, place of refuge and nursery of faith, the Rectory was important in their spiritual and personal nurture.

Within the Christian tradition there are various typologies of spirituality. Some look to a future consummation as the source of human flourishing through a beatific vision or cosmic transportation. Others look to a robust experience here and now of life in all its fullness, if not in its completeness. The theology of the Wesleys embraced both without trying to harmonize or order the two. Their two points of reference seem to have been joy in reconciliation, experienced in this life, and happiness in life drawn to God. The two (points of reference, and brothers) are, of course, inseparable. The two brothers need to be understood against the ritual moralism of the Church of England in the eighteenth century and

---

1. See J. Wesley, "An Account of the Disturbances," 656. For a recent discussion, see Yates, "Jeffrey the Jacobite Poltergeist," 68–79.

the rigid legalism of the Puritans. The Wesleys typified a middle way—something of a way of the heart. Yet in many respects it was a deeply flawed way. This was due to their background and context and to their different approaches to key ideas, especially the nature and purpose of relationships, suffering and hope. One brother, Charles, lived a long and loving life in married relationship; the other, John, seems to have lived in reserved and constrained personal circumstances.

The relational inclusion of human beings who are "in Christ" into the eternity of God is a key theme in St. Paul.[2] As threefold persons and one God, always in relationship, the divine life is both locus and destination for Christian spirituality. Interdependence, trust, mutual suffering, shared responsibility, and joy characterize Christian life in the light of the divine life. Social trinitarianism has become a ubiquitous assumption in late twentieth and early twenty-first Christian thought. Its strengths include the recognition of an eternal dimension to human identity, an affirmation of relational truth and trust, a statement of eternal hope and an icon of divine inclusion. It has some downsides. It can lead to a lack of focus on the here and now, an avoidance of responsibility, its own inverted snobbery of my inclusion becoming your exclusion, and an acquiescence to the contemporary denial of death through the institutionalization of dying.

This chapter looks at a perichoretic human anthropology of flourishing as gladness, after Karl Barth, and considers the concept of flourishing and constraint developed by UK psychiatrist Pauline Watson in her book *'Two Scrubby Travellers': A Psychoanalytic View of Flourishing and Constraint in Religion through the Lives of John and Charles Wesley*. Beginning with the idea of flourishing as divine participation, the chapter will proceed to explore both Trinitarian expressions and human participation in the life of the divine through the writings of Karl Barth, sermons of John Wesley, and the hymnody of Charles Wesley. With particular reference to the Wesleys, the chapter then examines the concept of flourishing as restraint in the forms of self-denial, eschatology, and, finally, self-giving.

Flourishing as Divine Participation

A mid-twentieth century expression of perichoretic divine joy, found in and expressed from the life of the Trinity, can be found in Karl Barth:

---

2. For an exploration, see Parsons, "'In Christ' in Paul," 25–44.

> As and before God seeks and creates fellowship with us, He wills and completes this fellowship in Himself. . . . He is Father, Son and Holy Spirit and therefore alive in His unique being with and for and in another. . . . He does not exist in solitude but in fellowship. . . . That He is God—the Godhead of God—consists in the fact that He loves, and it is in the expression of his loving that He seeks and creates fellowship with us.[3]

Whilst Barth does not explicitly embrace the eastern Christian concept of *theosis*, he sets apart a space in which relational expressions of faith can flourish.

Parallels can be drawn with the Wesleys and their engagement with historical Christian practices. Most particularly comparisons may be witnessed in the Wesleys' piety as it is relational and flourishes in divine encounter and participation. As John Wesley says in his sermon, "What is Man?" (1788), humanity flourishes in a life joined to the divine:

> Remember! You were born for nothing else. You live for nothing else. Your life is continued to you upon earth, for no other purpose than this, that you may know, love, and serve God on earth, and enjoy him to all eternity."[4]

For John, it is enjoyment of God in relationship that is our reason for being. It is this fuller sense of human joy that we are drawn towards through this full and eternal reality of divine fellowship.

Participative Flourishing

All that is and can be lived by Christians is because they are in Christ, or as Barth describes it, in encounter. According to Barth, being in encounter: "is (1) a being in which one . . . looks the other in the eye,"[5] and they "discover one another";[6] and it "consists (2) in the fact that there is mutual speech and hearing,"[7] in which "the expression and address between I and Thou are reciprocal";[8] and it "consists (3) in the fact that

---

3. Barth, *CD* 2/1:275 (Where the German original of Barth's *Church Dogmatics* is cited, the abbreviation *KD* [for *Kirchliche Dogmatik*] is used.).

4. J. Wesley, *Works*, 4:26.

5. Barth, *CD* 3/2:250.

6. Barth, *CD* 3/2:251–52.

7. Barth, *CD* 3/2:252.

8. Barth, *CD* 3/2:259.

we render mutual assistance in the act of being."⁹ In this context, Barth says, "We now climb a step higher"¹⁰ into a healthy "altruism."¹¹ Having set the three parameters we have noted for being in encounter, Barth adds a fourth which "is the secret of the whole, and therefore of the three preceding stages."¹² This fourth aspect is that "the basic form of humanity stands under the sign that it is done on both sides with gladness."¹³

> I think that this unpretentious word "gladly," while it does not penetrate the secret [or perhaps mystery, that is of human joy and flourishing] before which we stand, does at least indicate it correctly as the *conditio sine qua non* of humanity.¹⁴

Understandings of participative flourishing are also found in the sermons of John Wesley. In "What is Man?" (1788), he notes the capacity of humankind for "love, hatred, joy, sorrow, desire, fear, hope . . . and a whole train of other inward emotions."¹⁵ They appear explicitly as well. There is glad "enjoyment" in his depiction of humanity. Here he refers to the "'created man in [God's] own image, after his own likeness.' And [he asks] what was the end of his creation? It was one, and no other: that he might know, and love, and enjoy, and serve his great Creator to all eternity."¹⁶ The only purpose of the creation of his listener is this: "you were created . . . for no other purpose—by seeking and finding happiness in God on earth to secure the glory of God in heaven."¹⁷

Watson notes that "in his sermon 'The New Creation' (1785), John Wesley describes the goal of life in Trinitarian terms."¹⁸ She notes this passage:

9. Barth, *CD* 3/2:260.
10. Barth, *CD* 3/2:260.
11. Barth, *CD* 3/2:261. Barth uses the image of a fish needing water as an illustration of this mutual concern, which he opposes to "unhealthy altruism." *CD* 3/2:261.
12. Barth, *CD* 3/2:265.
13. Barth, *CD* 3/2:265. ("Das Sein in der Begegnung besteht aber 4. darin, daß das ganze Geschehen, das wir bisher als die Grundform der Humanität beschreiben haben, unter dem Zeichen steht, daß es hinüber und herüber *gerne* geschieht." *KD* 3/2:318.)
14. Barth, *CD* 3/2:266. ("Ich denke, daß dieses anspruchlose Wort «gerne» das Geheimnis, vor dem wir nun stehen, zwar nicht auflöst, aber als die *conditio sine qua non* der Humanität wenigstens richtig bezeichnet." *KD* 3/2:319.)
15. J. Wesley, *Works*, 4:22.
16. J. Wesley, *Works*, 4:25–26.
17. J. Wesley, *Works*, 4:26.
18. Watson, *Scrubby Travellers*, 175.

> And to crown all, there will be a deep, an intimate, an uninterrupted union with God; a constant communion with the Father and his Son Jesus Christ, through the Spirit; a continual enjoyment of the Three-One God, and of all the creatures in him![19]

Alluding to his own life experience of grace, Wesley says:

> it is also matter of daily experience that "by grace we are thus saved through faith." It is by faith that the eye of the mind is opened to see the light of the glorious love of God. And as long as it is steadily fixed thereon, on God in Christ, reconciling the world unto himself, we are more and more filled with the love of God and man, with meekness, gentleness, long-suffering; with all the fruits of holiness, which are, through Christ Jesus, to the glory of God the Father.[20]

Wesley's sermon on "The Way to the Kingdom" describes faith as:

> a sure trust in the mercy of God through Christ Jesus. It is a confidence in a pardoning God. It is a divine evidence or conviction that "God was in Christ, reconciling the world to himself, not imputing to them their former trespasses"; and in particular that the son of God hath loved me and given himself for me; and that I, even I, am now reconciled to God by the blood of the cross.[21]

For Wesley and for Methodists, faith was real, embodied, even visceral. His description of faith was also embodied. According to nineteenth-century biographer Robert Southey, John Wesley expressed joy in his daily life. He observes:

> His countenance as well as his conversation, expressed an habitual gayety of heart, which nothing but conscious virtue and innocence could have bestowed. He was, in truth, the most perfect specimen of moral happiness which I ever saw; and my acquaintance with him has done more to teach me what a heaven upon earth is implied in the maturity of Christian piety, than all I have elsewhere seen, or heard, or read, except in the sacred volume.[22]

19. J. Wesley, *Works*, 2:510.

20. J. Wesley, *Works*, 1:614.

21. J. Wesley, *Works*, 1:230. See discussion in Chilcote, "John and Charles Wesley," 138.

22. Southey, *The Life of Wesley*, 344. Whilst written as a panegyric, the impact should probably be considered substantial, and significant in its time.

This "habitual gayety of heart" is the presence of the moral virtue, the spiritual fruit of joy. By its nature it is communal, relational and upbuilding. As God exudes joy, so the saints of God are saturated in divine delight.

Charles Wesley also writes of participative flourishing in his hymn "Father of Jesus Christ the Just":

> Thee without faith I cannot please:
> Faith without thee I cannot have:
> But thou hast sent the Prince of Peace
> To seek my wand'ring soul, and save:
> O Father! Glorify thy Son,
> And save me for his sake alone![23]

The response to redemption for the Wesleys is obedience and renewed commitment to God and to the good. The outcome of "being in Christ", the bearer of new identity, is a flourishing through obedience, new beginnings, and occasional healing. It is not merely a Christian life where joy occasionally happens. Joy is not the norm for fallen humankind: it is, however, the calling of the redeemed.

Flourishing in Joy, Gladness, and Human Gratitude

In the life, work, and teaching of John Wesley, gratitude (for what God has done) issues in benevolence. For Barth, gratitude issues in obedience. They both result in gladness, joy, and praise. The Wesleys exemplified this human flourishing. In his very last sermon, "On Faith," written in January, 1791, John Wesley asks the all-important and personally pressing question about the goal of the Christian life: "[H]ow will [the faithful] advance in holiness, in the whole image of God wherein they were created!"? He responds with reference to these dual foci of the Christian life: "In the love of God and man, gratitude to their Creator, and benevolence to all their fellow-creatures."[24] Happiness in and of God results in life lived in obedience to God and in joy.

23. C. Wesley, *Redemption Hymns* (1747), 19.

24. J. Wesley, *Works*, 4:196. Similarly, in his sermon "On Laying the Foundation of the New Chapel, Near the City-Road, London," Wesley asks his (mainly Church of England) audience, "Are you an happy partaker of this scriptural, this truly primitive, religion? Are you a witness of the religion of love? Are you a lover of God and all mankind? Does your heart glow with gratitude to the Giver of every good and perfect gift? The Father of the spirits of all flesh, who giveth you life, and breath, and all things?

Charles Wesley likewise finds that joy and gratitude are intrinsically related, and he responds with praise for the grace of the whole of creation:

> With singing we praise
> The original grace
> By our heavenly Father bestowed;
> Our being receive
> From his bounty, and live
> To the honour and glory of God.
>
> For thy glory we are,
> Created to share
> Both the nature and kingdom divine;
> Created again,
> That our souls may remain
> In time and eternity thine.[25]

In the presence of God, through being in Christ, one engages in the fulness of life, knowing its blessing even whilst taking up one's cross. John Wesley's well-known encouragement that Christians should "Sing lustily and with good courage"[26] follows the injunction "Let not a slight degree of weakness or weariness hinder you. If it is a cross to you, take it up and you will find a blessing." These all are shaped by the direction, "Above all sing spiritually." Perhaps "courage" and going beyond the limitations of the self, for Wesley, are the means of flourishing in joy and entering into divine fellowship.

Flourishing in Suffering and Denial

All of life is to be embraced and in all of life God is present and to be worshipped. In this both John and Charles Wesley echo the whole of life engagement of the Psalms. All of life is to be embraced, and in singing (or more particularly, in Divine Worship as the famous Appendix puts it) it is to be embraced spiritually, sometimes out of weakness, but always full of courage and with vibrant joy.

Who hath given you his Son, his only Son, that you 'might not perish, but have everlasting life?' Is your soul warm with benevolence to all mankind? Do you long to have all men virtuous and happy?" J. Wesley, *Works*, 3:592.

25. C. Wesley, *Family Hymns* (1767), 175.

26. J. Wesley, *Works*, 7:765. See also, Clarke, "John Wesley's 'Directions for Singing,'" 196.

Flourishing is found in suffering and in denial because in both suffering and denial gratitude links Christian believers to the joy of God whose life they share in Christ. For the Wesleys, giving up of self is not a denial in order that one might gain. It is a giving up *because* so much was given up for human reconciliation. "And can it be, that I should gain"?[27] Indeed. And the falling off of chains and the bold approach are undertaken in faith, yield to joy, and fill the redeemed heart with gratitude.

In Christ, all has been freely given. Those who are in Christ are also free to give of their bounty, be it large or small, and of the divine bounty. Both Wesleys are thoroughly Pauline in their embrace of the great expanse of Pauline metaphors of salvation. Their focus is not only on justification: it makes much of restoration and reconciliation. Being brought back into relationship is, for John Wesley, the heart of the Gospel. It is this which makes us right, not this being made right that allows us to come into relationship with the Almighty. John Wesley explains in his "Sermon on the Righteousness of Faith":

> Whosoever therefore thou art who desirest to be forgiven and reconciled to the favour of God, do not say in thy heart, "I must first do this: I must first conquer every sin, break off every evil word and work, and do all good to all men; or I must first go to Church, receive the Lord's Supper, hear more sermons, and say more prayers." Alas, my brother, thou art clean gone out of the way. Thou art still "ignorant of the righteousness of God", and art "seeking to establish thy own righteousness" as the ground of thy reconciliation. Knowest thou not that thou canst do nothing but sin till thou art reconciled to God? Wherefore then dost thou say, I must do this and this first, and then I shall believe? Nay, but first believe. Believe in the Lord Jesus Christ, the propitiation for thy sins. Let this good foundation first be laid, and then thou shalt do all things well.[28]

It is a commonplace to say that salvation gives birth to good works but is not born of good works. It needs to be repeated in every generation. Wesley was a key proponent of saying this and living this truth. Doing "all things well" meant a sober and moral life, but not a somber one; it meant a life of zealous service but not joyless servitude; and it meant facing challenges in the context of God's forgiveness and the sure foundation of faith. Flourishing is possible in difficulty because of what God in Christ

---

27. C. Wesley, *Hymns and Sacred Poems* (1739), 117.
28. J. Wesley, *Works*, 1:214.

has done. Denial of self is no denial of circumstances but is rather a way of living, of flourishing and joy. This was the practice of the Holy Club, that place where John Wesley learned to grown in theology of heart and mind together, where service, sacrifice and celebration were encouraged. The practice of self-denial was practiced in it so that Christian life might flourish. This was a critical step in Wesley's own journey from self-justification to finding reconciliation in Christ alone, apart from works.[29] This was the basis of his message. John Wesley saw himself as a "brand plucked from the fire" (Zech 3:2), offered new opportunity through being saved from the Rectory fire in 1709, when he was five years old.[30] His passion for those who were sick and dying, in prison and destitute was legendary. He considered the best way to help was in person, often supported with his voluminous correspondence.[31]

John Wesley's own life was colored with sadness and pain. His forebears were poor managers of money. His parents had lost eight children, including two boys called John, before he was born in 1703. It was a time of high infant mortality.[32] His parents may have expected that his life, too, might be short. According to Watson's psychoanalytic reading, John fits much of the profile of the "replacement child"; haunted by memories of his "ghost" namesakes in the rectory at Epworth, subjected to unrealistic expectations, and seeking perfection in others.[33] Watson concludes that both John and Charles "shared the intense fear and horror of inner badness, of 'the world, the flesh and the devil,' which had been a life-and-death struggle for their mother."[34] Both were rigorous in their ascetic self-denial. In their faith development, neither found peace in this path.[35] Their theology, in sermon and song, looks to the life of the world to come. To what extent the brothers' other-worldly focus was intensified by the presence of ghosts and the memories of deceased siblings is not clear. What is clear is the earnestness with which both preached the coming of judgement and the reality of life beyond the grave. This quickened

---

29. Watson, *Scrubby Travellers*, 100.
30. Watson, *Scrubby Travellers*, 101.
31. Watson, *Scrubby Travellers*, 101.
32. Watson, *Scrubby Travellers*, 124.
33. Watson, *Scrubby Travellers*, 125.
34. Watson, *Scrubby Travellers*, 136.
35. Watson, *Scrubby Travellers*, 136.

their drive for saving souls. In his old age, John said he dared not rest while he believed there was "another world."[36]

Eschatological Flourishing

The reality of another world was not a matter of fear. Rather it was an impetus to share good news and live well. To flourish in this world was possible in light of an eternal flourishing, the sure hope of glory and the trustworthy promise of the Savior. For the Wesley brothers the image of heaven and hell was a statement of reality. The promise of life in Christ was the basis for flourishing. Pauline Watson notes that "[f]or John, salvation was not merely an escape from hell or the achievement of heaven, which he considered a 'vulgar' idea, but a restoration to health and wholeness."[37] The making of "all things new" or "all things well" was not a deferred hope, a mere eschatological detail. It was a present call and the ground for ministry and mission, for care for the needy and for hope and joy. In describing John Wesley's eschatology, Angella Son observes:

> he denies a split between this world and the world to come, and he sees creation and salvation as one unifying historical activity. Wesley perceives eschatology as that which focuses on the fulfillment of God's promises, not just in another world to come, but in this very world.[38]

Wesley's eschatology is evident in his approach to physical health and the "great physician" too.

Both John and Charles spoke of the work of the "great physician": though normally used as a metaphor for redemption of sin in Christ, in their works it also alludes to making well.[39] John's interest in making well extended to the practical and his popular 1747 text, *Primitive Physic*, ran to twenty-three editions. Used widely, it was not merely a collection of folk remedies but was "based on wide reading of current medical literature."[40] Indeed, reflecting an eighteenth-century confidence in the rise of reason, John notes in the preface that religion and medicine have both developed

---

36. J. Wesley, *Letters*, 7:272.
37. Watson, *Scrubby Travellers*, 173.
38. Son, "John Wesley and Joy," 118.
39. Watson, *Scrubby Travellers*, 173.
40. Maddox, "John Wesley on Holistic Health," 4–6.

from the "chiefly traditional."[41] The preface's conclusion exhorts that the "love of God . . . is the sovereign remedy of all miseries" and that "by the unspeakable joy and perfect calm, serenity, and tranquility it gives the mind, it becomes the most powerful of all the means of health and long life."[42] Joy and wellness went together in the thinking of John Wesley, and he tended those in his care with a concern for their eternal welfare and their good health.

Randy Maddox, in his study of John Wesley's *Primitive Physic*, notes that Calvinists were less hopeful of healing in this life, considering its prime locus was the life hereafter. Wesley, however, sought to promote both bodily and spiritual healing in this present life.[43] Such a cohesive body-and-soul approach to well-being is evident in Methodism's practical implementation of education, health resources and so on. Cohesion or integration of the whole self in God is integral to the experience of joy. According to Angella Son's reading of Heinz Kohut, joy is both a "nutrient" and a "mark of the cohesive self."[44] Cohesion was miraculous, according to John Wesley, who notes in his description of the human as "a curious machine" that "the particles of which cohering, I know not how."[45]

A significant part of the struggles of the Wesley brothers involved the avoidance of the temptation of the corruption of true joy; that is, joy which seeks to find its basis in the things of this world—good though they may be. In 1734 John refused to return to Epworth to continue his ailing father's work, arguing that he was focused on making himself and others holy. On another occasion, John's nephew Samuel Wesley Jr. wrote accusingly: "I see your love to yourself but your love to your neighbour I do not see."[46] Of course it must be noted that this was early in John Wesley's ministry and shows the pressure his eldest brother had in continuing the ministerial work of their father. Whether then this points to John's selfishness or his single-mindedness can be debated. His later selflessness is expressed in his advocacy of spiritual matters despite great personal

---

41. J. Wesley, *Works*, 32:111.
42. J. Wesley, *Works*, 32:119.
43. Maddox, "John Wesley on Holistic Health," 7.
44. Son, "John Wesley and Joy," 115.
45. J. Wesley, *Works*, 4:20.
46. S. Wesley Jr., "Letter to John Wesley, December 1734," quoted in Moore, *The Life of John Wesley*, 178.

loss. Whilst tempted to appear pious, his desire is to be sensitive to others' profound spiritual and physical distress.

John's sisters were exasperated at his pastoral insensitivity when he wrote to Martha who lost nine of ten children, that "the death of your children is a great instance of the goodness of God towards you. You have often mentioned to me how much of your time they took up! Now that time is restored to you, and you have nothing to do but to serve our Lord."[47] Younger brother, Charles, enjoyed poorer health than John, often having pain and possibly depression. Watson notes that Charles' "mood swings from despondency to elation clearly continued after his conversion experience and, like John, his mood was lifted by activity."[48] Watson considers that these mood swings were not sufficient to suggest bipolar illness, but rather "resulted in his being able to be compassionate towards people in distress."[49] Compared with John, Charles was more pastoral and able to reach out beyond himself, even when things were not going well for him.[50] Charles and Sally lost their first child John, known as Jacky. He wrote a number of hymns about death and dying in children, including the following:

> Thankful I take the cup from thee,
> Prepar'd and mingled by thy skill:
> Tho' bitter to the taste it be,
> Pow'rful the wounded soul to heal.
>
> Be thou, O Rock of Ages, nigh:
> So shall each murm'ring thought be gone,
> And grief, and fear, and care shall fly,
> As clouds before the midday sun. . . .
>
> O death, where is thy sting? Where now
> Thy boasted victory, O grave?
> Who shall contend with God: or who
> Can hurt whom God delights to save?[51]

Human sadness is not obliterated in Christians. They grieve, and the Wesleys grieved. But that grief is not final or ultimately destructive. This is because Christians believe that Christ has conquered death. This

---

47. J. Wesley, *Letters*, 2:12. See also, Watson, *Scrubby Travellers*, 104.
48. Watson, *Scrubby Travellers*, 144.
49. Watson, *Scrubby Travellers*, 144.
50. Watson, *Scrubby Travellers*, 144–45.
51. C. Wesley, *Hymns and Sacred Poems* (1739), 144.

triumph is a regular theme in the hymns of Charles Wesley. Others may seek to use the pain of death to hurt the believer, but "who can hurt whom God delights to save?"[52] Flourishing may not be easily felt in the pain of grief. God's care, however, brings growth even in and through the tragedies of life. The life-giving Christian reality is found in his hymn of "Congratulation to a Friend, upon Believing in Christ," whose first line reads "What morn on thee with sweeter ray" and continues:

> Be blest the memorable day
> That gave thee Jesus Christ to find!
> Gave thee to taste his perfect grace,
> From death to life in him to pass! . . .
>
> Away let grief and sighing flee;
> Jesus has died for thee—for thee!
>
> And will he now forsake his own,
> Or lose the purchase of his blood?
> No! For he looks with pity down,
> He watches over thee for good;
> Gracious he eyes thee from above,
> And guards and feeds thee with his love.
>
> Since thou wast precious in his sight,
> How highly favour'd hast thou been!
> Upborn by faith to glory's height,
> The Saviour-God thine eyes have seen,
> Thy heart has felt its sins forgiv'n,
> And tastes anticipated heav'n.[53]

This assurance on first believing is the same assurance that allows death to be faced without fear of eternity and with certain hope of heaven. The life-giving hope transcends all circumstances, death and loss included. God watches over the believer "for good." God waits the forgiven sinner's arrival in glory. Death is conquered. In this hymn, death's undoing is considered in the abstract. It is set in the context of God's act of love and redemption. Death of a believer and observed in the death of a believer in the particular shapes Charles Wesley's hymn "Ah, Lovely appearance of Death!" (At the death of a friend, 1746). A hymn about death, though not of a child, this hymn has an emphasis on Jesus' self-giving. Mourning is real—it is the lot of those left "bound in a prison."

---

52. C. Wesley, *Hymns and Sacred Poems* (1739), 145.
53. C. Wesley, *Hymns and Sacred Poems* (1739), 203–4.

> To mourn and to suffer is mine,
> While bound in a prison I breathe,
> And still for deliverance pine,
> And press to the issues of death.
> What now with my tears I bedew
> O might I this moment become,
> My spirit created anew,
> My flesh be consigned to the tomb![54]

The eternal frame is emphasized by the lines where the hymnist observes the dead body, "longing to lie in his stead" (verse 2). It is a hymn confronting for Christians today. In Wesley's world of high child mortality, with death typically at home, it had immediacy. The mourning is real: so is the shared celebration of hope and of the new joy of the dead. The release from this life into glory is shown in the recognition of the blessing for the Christian who has died:

> How blest is our Brother, bereft
> Of all that could burden his Mind,
> How easy the Soul, that hath left
> This wearisome Body behind![55]

Both John and Charles desired to limit the grieving of the bereaved, in line with their eschatological views, but Charles alone of the two found a depth of empathy, even writing poems for "women in travail," in a number of poems speaking with the voice of a woman in labor.[56] This ability to empathize and enter into the suffering of another is a remarkable indicator of his ability to describe and then participate in the suffering of another. Consider these lines from an eighteenth-century male:

> Whisper to my list'ning soul,
> Wilt Thou not my strength renew,
> Nature's fears and pangs control,
> And bring Thy handmaid thro'.[57]

This sensitivity and participation are part of the flourishing as a human being which is proclaimed and lived by the brothers Wesley. Human flourishing is not only a personal or individual outcome of faith: Christian flourishing has its relational and corporate dimensions.

54. C. Wesley, *Funeral Hymns* (1746), 8.
55. C. Wesley, *Funeral Hymns* (1746), 7.
56. Watson, *Scrubby Travellers*, 145.
57. C. Wesley, *Family Hymns* (1767), 54.

Flourishing in Self-giving

John Wesley preached about life in Christ and the call to human flourishing. Charles Wesley refracted this in hymnody pointing to the fullness of life in eternity and calling believers to depend on God for strength and to live in compassion. So "Thankful I (whom God delights to save) take the cup from thee."[58] "Away let grief and sighing flee; Jesus has died for thee."[59] Addressed to others, these are taken inward: "My spirit created anew . . . hath left this wearisome body behind."[60] This is life in Christ, flourishing in pain and in the face of death. The self-giving sacrifice of Christ translates into the self-giving love of Christian flourishing. The healing is wrought by the "Great Physician" through the "salve or balm" through which Jesus, in his self-giving, makes us well.[61] Charles Wesley's hymn sings of balm that heals in self-giving relationship, through participative flourishing:

> He shares our pain, and grief, and fear,
> Wounded with every wounded soul,
> He bleeds the balm that makes us whole.[62]

It is in the incarnation of the eternal Son that victory is won, and healing is offered. Wellness and comfort are key foci for the Wesleys. They show God's glory here and now and for eternity. Karl Barth suggests that this salvation, the offer of eternity and healing, is offered through the coming of divine self-giving joy. He says, "We cannot overlook the fact that God is glorious in such a way that He radiates joy, so that He is all He is with and not without beauty. Otherwise His glory might well be joyless."[63] As Barth wrote, God gives his Holy Spirit "in order that His own relationship to His Father may be repeated in us."[64] Barth describes in trinitarian language what the Wesleys expressed in sermon and hymn: Self-giving relationship, founded on being "in Christ" is foundational for human identity and for a life of Christian flourishing.

---

58. C. Wesley, *Hymns and Sacred Poems* (1739), 144.

59. C. Wesley, *Hymns and Sacred Poems* (1739), 204.

60. C. Wesley, *Funeral Hymns* (1746), 7–8.

61. Watson, *Scrubby Travellers*, 173, explores this in the light of their mother Susanna's metaphor.

62. C. Wesley, *Scriptural Hymns* (1762), Vol. 2, 349.

63. Barth, *CD* 2/1:655.

64. Barth, *CD* 2/2:780.

For Barth, the calling of humans is to "live in [their] determination to be the reflection and echo of God and therefore the witness to the divine glory that reaches over to [them], rejoicing with the God who Himself has eternal joy and Himself is eternal joy."[65] Barth emphasizes God's joy in "elevating [humanity] above [themselves] . . . in . . . exuberance,"[66] and thus evoking a human response of gratitude, gladness, joy, and praise.[67] Hence "we must glorify [God] in joy and gratitude if we are not to sin wantonly against [God], if we are to let God be God."[68] The recognition of the otherness of God and the rightness of the humble response of gratitude provides a basis for exploring human obedience. It is thoroughly grace-based. It is, in many regards, the destiny that the Wesleys sought.

Within the Protestant tradition, the destiny of the elect can be conceived of as election to joy. In John Bunyan's *The Pilgrim's Progress from This World, to That Which is to Come* (1678), the journeys of Christian and Hopeful are to the Celestial City of *joy*. This view is not, however, based on a dualistic conception of escape from a world of pain to an eternity of joy. Rather, it is the inbreaking of joy into a world of pain. It is the inbreaking of joy which allows a life of joy and an escape which is *to joy* in its fullest.

The ongoing overflow of the joy of God, seen once in splendor in Jesus Christ, is continued in the Spirit's work. Writing from the viewpoint that God is known in relationship, Hardy and Ford have said that "the joy of God needs to be celebrated as the central and embracing reality of the universe, and everything else seen in the light of this."[69] The joy of the intra-triune relations as the basis for humanity in relationship underscores the human need for love and worship, for blessing and praise, for

---

65. Barth, *CD* 2/1:648-49.

66. Barth, *CD* 2/1:219.

67. Barth, *CD* 2/1:219, 223 (*KD* 251). See also *CD* 2/1:374-81, where Barth makes a case that "faith is joy and gratitude."

68. Barth, *CD* 2/1:375. Here Barth is exploring the perfections of mercy and righteousness. It is the substitution of Christ for us that is "the very essence of God's own being," which is to inspire this response of joy and gladness. Thus, it is that the entry of Jesus Christ into human existence can be a "great joy which shall be to all people." *CD* 2/1:374, alluding to Luke 2:10. (See also *CD* 3/2:60, where Barth discusses the joy which is for all in the birth of Christ.). The same dynamic, of human response grounded in the nature of God, is repeated under the rubric of love in *CD* 2/1:276-84, and of freedom in *CD* 2/1:321, for example.

69. Hardy and Ford, *Jubilate*, 13.

receptivity and expression[70]—because joyful freedom "is not merely the crown of humanity, but its root."[71]

Continuing and Concluding with a Flourish

For the Wesleys as for Barth, human flourishing is to be lived in continuing earthly life and embraced as part of life eternal. The joy which comprises the self-sufficient and yet self-giving life of God enables human life in generosity and joy. The spirituality, ministry, and lives of the Wesleys looked to eternity, not with a view to escaping this world and its pain, but as a means of embracing and transcending suffering and pain. Joy is founded in reconciliation and focused by the promise of glory and life in God. Karl Barth's thinking has added trinitarian depth to this and has linked glory and joy in God to gratitude and gladness in human life in Christ.

The incarnation of the Son of God, seen in the life of Jesus and preached and celebrated by John and Charles Wesley is the basis for human inclusion in Christ. It is the foundation for human flourishing, the overcoming of sin and for addressing life by living it to the full. For the Wesleys and Barth, human flourishing is possible through being in Christ. This gives us a view of human flourishing ignited by divine joy rather than by divine forgiveness alone and describes a fuller sense of human joy, drawn towards divine fellowship.

We have seen that in life and ministry, for the Wesleys, those "two scrubby travellers," divine joy and human gladness in life in Christ undergird a perichoretic human anthropology of flourishing as gladness. Pauline Watson's concept of flourishing and constraint have added insight to how the ascetic self-sacrifice of the Wesleys stood with rather than against their joyful flourishing. John Wesley's integrative eschatology affirmed this world and the world to come and healing as salvation found here and now and more fully in eternity.

The enjoyment of creation by the Creator, and reciprocal enjoyment of the Creator of the creation is brought to a finale in John Wesley's sermon "What is Man?" Far more than "a curious machine," for humankind "life is continued . . . upon earth . . . that you may know, love, and serve

---

70. Barth, *CD* 2/1:647–48.

71. Barth, *CD* 3/2:273. Thus: "Real man as God created him is not in the waste of isolation."

God on earth, and enjoy him to all eternity."[72] Perhaps it is summed up best by Charles Wesley:

> Bold I approach th' eternal throne,
> And claim the crown, through Christ, my own.[73]

Bibliography

Barth, Karl. *Church Dogmatics*. 13 vols. Translated by G. W. Bromiley. Edinburgh: T&T Clark, 1956–1975.
Bunyan, John. *The Pilgrim's Progress from This World, to That Which is to Come*. London: Ponder, 1968.
Chilcote, Paul Wesley. "John and Charles Wesley on 'God in Christ Reconciling.'" *Methodist History* 47.3 (2009) 132–45.
Clarke, Martin V. "John Wesley's 'Directions for Singing': Methodist Hymnody as an Expression of Methodist Beliefs in Thought and Practice." *Methodist History* 47.4 (2009) 196–209.
Hardy, Daniel W., and David F. Ford. *Jubilate: Theology in Praise*. London: Darton, Longmann and Todd, 1984.
Maddox, Randy. "John Wesley on Holistic Health and Healing." *Methodist History* 46.1 (2007) 4–33.
Moore, Henry. *The Life of the Rev. John Wesley, A.M.: In Which Are Included, The Life of His Brother, The Rev. Charles Wesley, A.M., and Memoirs of Their Family: Comprehending an Account of the Great Revival of Religion, in Which They Were the First and Chief Instruments*. Vol. 1. New York: Bangs and Emory, 1824.
Parsons, Michael. "'In Christ' in Paul." *Vox Evangelica* 18 (1988) 25–44.
Son, Angella. "John Wesley and Joy: The Implications of Wesley's Theology and Methodist Practices on the Development of Joy as Disposition Based on Heinz Kohut's Psychology of the Self." In *Wesleyan Theology and Social Science: The Dance of Practical Divinity and Discovery*, edited by Ronald W. Wright et al., 113–27. Newcastle: Cambridge Scholars, 2010.
Southey, Robert. *The Life of Wesley and the Rise and Progress of Methodism*. Vol. 2. 2nd American edition. Edited by C. C. Southey. New York: Harper, 1847.
Watson, Pauline. *'Two Scrubby Travellers': A Psychoanalytic View of Flourishing and Constraint in Religion through the Lives of John and Charles Wesley*. New York: Routledge, 2018.
Wesley, Charles. *Family Hymns* (1767). https://divinity.duke.edu/sites/divinity.duke.edu/files/documents/cswt/66_Family_Hymns_%281767%29_mod.pdf.
———. *Funeral Hymns* (1746). https://divinity.duke.edu/sites/divinity.duke.edu/files/documents/cswt/34_Funeral_Hymns_%281746%29_Mod.pdf.
———. *Hymns and Sacred Poems* (1739). https://divinity.duke.edu/sites/divinity.duke.edu/files/documents/cswt/01_Hymns_and_Sacred_Poems_%281739%29_CW_Verse_mod.pdf.

---

72. J. Wesley, *Works*, 4:20, 26.
73. C. Wesley, *Hymns and Sacred Poems* (1739), 119.

———. *Redemption Hymns* (1747). https://divinity.duke.edu/sites/divinity.duke.edu/files/documents/cswt/44_Redemption_Hymns_%281747%29_mod.pdf.

———. *Scripture Hymns* (1762), Vol. 2. https://divinity.duke.edu/sites/divinity.duke.edu/files/documents/cswt/64_Scripture_Hymns_%281762%29_Vol_2_mod.pdf.

Wesley, John. *The Letters of the Rev. John Wesley*. 8 vols. Edited by John Telford. London: Epworth, 1931.

———. *The Works of John Wesley: Volume 1: Sermons I, 1–33*. Edited by Albert C. Outler. Nashville: Abingdon, 1984.

———. *The Works of John Wesley: Volume 2: Sermons II, 34–70*. Edited by Albert C. Outler. Nashville: Abingdon, 1985.

———. *The Works of John Wesley: Volume 3: Sermons III, 71–114*. Edited by Albert C. Outler. Nashville: Abingdon, 1986.

———. *The Works of John Wesley: Volume 4: Sermons IV, 115–151*. Edited by Albert C. Outler. Nashville: Abingdon, 1987.

———. *The Works of John Wesley: Volume 7: A Collection of Hymns for the Use of the People Called Methodists*. Edited by Franz Hildebrandt and Oliver Beckerlegge. Nashville: Abingdon, 1983.

———. *The Works of John Wesley: Volume 32: Medical and Health Writings*. Edited by James G. Donat and Randy L. Maddox. Nashville: Abingdon, 2018.

Yates, Kelly Diehl. "Jeffrey the Jacobite Poltergeist: The Politics of the Ghost that Haunted the Epworth Rectory in 1716–17." *Wesleyan Theological Journal* 50.2 (2015) 68–79.

4

John Wesley on the State of the Nation and Its People

Glen O'Brien

Arnold Toynbee's influential *Lectures on the Industrial Revolution in England* (1884) demonstrated how agrarian enclosures, the invention of steam power, and the factory system, while increasing productivity, also contributed to class antagonism and lower living standards for the poor. Beginning in the 1920s with the work of Cambridge economic historian J. H. Clapham, Toynbee's interpretation has been subjected to considerable critique including the question of just how rapid and "revolutionary" were the changes brought about. It remains the general consensus however that the period we still refer to as the "Industrial Revolution" brought significant and lasting changes to the people of Britain, especially in relation to economics, manufacture, and trade. Population growth in a newly industrialized eighteenth-century England coupled with new modes of agriculture, including the enclosure system, put pressure on available food resources, especially in more remote counties and John Wesley was in a position to observe first-hand the impact of such shortages on the poor. Widespread starvation was rare, aided in part by the directing of grains from export markets to home consumption, especially after 1750. While there was nothing like the widespread famines experienced in France during the same period, there were periods of significant want, especially in the latter part of the century. These circumstances sometimes flared up into civic disturbances over inflated prices of bread and corn due to crop shortages and the period 1771–1773 was particularly marked by such disturbances.¹ In this chapter I will consider John Wesley's response to the adverse conditions experienced by the poor, arising from the economic conditions of the country, in his *Word to a Smuggler* (1767), *Thoughts on the Present Scarcity of Provisions* (1773), and *Serious Address to the People of England* (1778). These tracts demonstrate Wesley's concern for the well-being of the British population as a matter that called for government intervention and policymaking, designed to contribute to greater human flourishing.

Giving the King His Due

On the remote coastlands in the west of England, starvation and want could be staved off by circumventing customs and participating in the illegal smuggling of goods. In his 1767 tract, *A Word to a Smuggler*, Wesley took the high moral ground in opposing any participation in the illegal trade regardless of the pressing nature of one's personal circumstances.² Smuggling was endemic in the eighteenth century and proved impossible to stamp out. It was so widespread that in some communities it was considered almost a legitimate trade. It particularly flourished during times of war because the navy was too stretched to police the covert import and export of goods. The remote coastal areas of Devon and Cornwall were particularly suited to the trade. At Rye on 22 November 1773, Wesley remonstrated with the congregation to 'part with the accursed thing, smuggling' but to little effect.³ Twenty years earlier, in July 1753 he had met with the stewards of St. Ives, in the west of Cornwall and upon examining the society was stopped short at the realization that smuggling was widely accepted among them.

> I found an accursed thing among them – wellnigh one and all bought or sold uncustomed goods. I therefore delayed speaking to any more til I had met with them altogether. This I did in the evening and told them plain, either they must put this

---

1. George Rudé identifies riots over "the dearness of provisions" in rural areas in 1768, in 1772, and in 1773. Rudé, *Hanoverian London*, 202. Prest records other disturbances in the late 1740s, 1756–57, 1766 (the worst period), and 1782–84. Prest, *Albion Ascendant*, 164.

2. J. Wesley, *Word to a Smuggler*.

3. J. Wesley, *Works*, 22:393.

abomination away or they would see my face no more.... They severally promised so to do. So I trust this plague is stayed.[4]

In some poorer communities smuggling was considered an important part of the local economy and the goods smuggled found their way into the hands of people at every level of society. A parliamentary committee reported in 1745 that three million pounds of tea a year (three times the legal trade) was being smuggled into the country, including by gangs of Jacobite sympathizers operating in the south-east.[5]

Smuggling ran against the prevailing mercantile theory that a nation must produce a surplus in order to prosper with a corresponding privileging of exported over imported goods as a means of producing revenue. Imports were a drain on revenue and so were tolerated but discouraged. One problem for this model in the eighteenth century was that the many new products for which the English developed a taste, such as tea, tobacco, and French liquor, were imported goods which attracted taxation. This was an open door for the smuggling trade which, through circumventing the payment of duties, opened up a lucrative supply of such desirable goods. The global wars fought by Britain in the eighteenth century were funded at least in part by import duties, so the loss of this revenue was a concern for the king and the Parliament.

Wesley defined smuggling as "the importing, selling, or buying of run goods, that is, those which have not paid the duty appointed by law to be paid to the king."[6] He declared four types of people guilty of smuggling: (1) Those who ran smuggling vessels; (2) Ship's captains, officers, sailors, and passengers who avoid paying import duties on goods brought into the country; (3) Sellers of goods which have escaped import duty; and (4) Buyers of goods which have escaped import duty. Such goods included tea, liquor, linen, and handkerchiefs. The question may be asked what harm there was in this seemingly victimless crime. Wesley insisted

---

4. J. Wesley, *Works*, 20:469.

5. Prest, *Albion Ascendant*, 153.

6. J. Wesley, *Word to a Smuggler*, 3; J. Wesley, *Works* (Jackson), 11:174. I have provided here and throughout, both the reference to the primary sources, consulted in the Methodist Collection at the John Rylands Library, Manchester and also (for the convenience of the reader) to the Jackson edition of Wesley's *Works* where the political tracts appear. The social and political tracts have not yet been included in the critical edition of the *Works*, but *Volume 15: Domestic, Moral, Political and Economic Writings*, ed., David Hempton and Rebekah Miles is in preparation by Abingdon Press, through the Centre for Studies in the Wesleyan Tradition at Duke Divinity School, under the general editorship of Randy Maddox.

that smuggling was just as much stealing as highway robbery. In fact, it was worse since the highwayman steals from strangers, but the smuggler steals from his father, the king, since in England custom duties were owed to the king. From Wesley's point of view, to avoid paying such duties was tantamount to stealing. "King George is the father of all his subjects: And not only so, but he is a good father. He shows his love to [his subjects] on all occasions and is continually doing all that is in his power to make his subjects happy."[7] In Wesley's logic it would be shameful to rob such a father. There is a very personal element here, and in so many of Wesley's exhortations regarding the king, suggesting that for him the monarchy was more than an ideal or an institution (though it was both of those). He considered the king as a person, a Christian monarch, and a loving father to the nation. The importance of loyalty to such a person seemed self-evident to Wesley.

Wesley argues that since the Bible clearly states "Thou shalt not steal," Christians should never engage in smuggling and that buying or selling smuggled goods was stealing the king's property as much as if the king were to steal one's coat. He appealed to biblical precedents—Jesus taught his followers to "render unto Caesar the things that are Caesar's" (Matt 22:21) and Paul taught Christians to "render unto all their dues, custom to whom custom is due, tribute to whom tribute" (Rom 13:7). Robbing the king of his dues also defrauded every honest English subject because the loss of customs duties led to higher taxation, a burden which everyone would be called upon to bear. Buying smuggled goods also impoverished honest sellers who needed to lower their prices in order to compete with "run" goods. Some of these honest traders were themselves forced into stealing in order to feed their families so those who bought smuggled goods also had blood on their hands. Clearly smuggling was not, in Wesley's view, a victimless crime.

Wesley dealt with a number of the most commonly found excuses for smuggling, rejecting them one by one. Those who said they must deal in smuggled goods in order to stay in business would do better to find an honest way to make a living. The claim that the king benefited from the smuggling trade by regular seizures was rejected as frivolous. A hundred times the amount of goods were lost through smuggling than were seized. Some were claiming that the king could suppress the trade if he really wanted to do it but Wesley asked how he could so when custom

---

7. J. Wesley, *Word to a Smuggler*, 4; J. Wesley, *Works* (Jackson), 11:174.

house officials had themselves accepted payoffs and those who tried to be honest were threatened by loss of livelihood and even of life. The king did not have enough soldiers to watch every port and creek in Britain and in any case soldiers were as much open to corruption as customs officers. Admittedly, "great men and courtiers" were also involved in the trade, but this only proved them to be greater highway robbers and increased their guilt. Even if it could have been proven that the king somehow benefited from smuggling this would not excuse stealing.[8] For Wesley, those who say they engaged in smuggling with a clear conscience had deadened consciences and needed God to awaken them again. God may have overlooked for a time those who had engaged in smuggling while still feeling "happy in the love of God." However now that they have received light on the subject and know better, they must cease such activity or the light they have received will be removed from them.[9]

Those who said that they only bought a little brandy or tea now and then for their own personal use were simply admitting that they only stole a little. To those who said they did not receive smuggled goods themselves but only sent their child or servant to collect them, Wesley replied, "the Receiver is as bad as the Thief." Those who claimed they had been forced to receive smuggled goods by their husband, or father or master "will be hanged nevertheless." This might lessen but did not remove the fault. After all, it was better to suffer than to sin. No one could plead ignorance about the nature of the goods they received because the low price made its origin clear. Wesley advised those who could not source tea or wine legally to drink water, "for it is better to die than to live by thieving." He would not even allow for the wife who says that she must have what her husband provided, even if it is smuggled, or have nothing. Undoubtedly to have none is a less evil, than to be a partaker with a thief.[10]

The 1767 Conference asked, "how may we put a stop to smuggling?"

(1) Speak tenderly and frequently of it in every society near the coasts.

(2) Carefully dispense the *Word to a Smuggler*.

(3) Expel all who will not leave it off.

(4) Silence every local preacher who defends it.[11]

8. J. Wesley, *Word to a Smuggler*, 6–7; J. Wesley, *Works* (Jackson), 11:175–77.
9. J. Wesley, *Word to a Smuggler*, 7; J. Wesley, *Works* (Jackson), 11:177.
10. J. Wesley, *Word to a Smuggler*, 8; J. Wesley, *Works* (Jackson), 11:177–78.
11. J. Wesley, *Works*, 10:351. Also see, Rack, *Reasonable Enthusiast*, 445.

Wesley closed his *Word to a Smuggler* by exhorting his readers to keep close to the Word of God even if all around them departed from it. God may reward those who are faithful in this regard with temporal blessings, but if not they will at least be rewarded with "the testimony of a good conscience toward God" (1 Pet 3:21), joy in the Holy Spirit (Rom 14:17), "hope full of immortality" (Wis 4:1), and "the love of God shed abroad" in their hearts (Rom 5:5). The peace of God which passes all understanding shall then keep their hearts and minds in Christ Jesus (Phil 4:7).[12] It is a common feature of Wesley's tracts to finish them with such pious flourishes, always the preacher, taking the opportunity to drive home to the reader a close application.

Wesley was informed in 1776 that "the scandal of Cornwall, the plundering of wrecked vessels" still subsisted but that Methodists had sworn off it. His solution was that Cornish gentry stamp it out, making an example of the next plunderers by a firm execution of the law. He also offered the "milder way" of employers sacking all those known to have plundered a wreck and then refusing to re-hire them.[13]

Responding to the Conditions of the Poor

Wesley rode into Norwich on Monday 26 October 1772 and noted widespread unemployment. His response was at first a pious one, preaching from the text, "Seek ye first the kingdom of God, and his righteousness, and all these things shall be added unto you." Noting the unusual size of the congregations he wondered whether these thousands of people "who when they had fullness of bread never considered whether they had any souls or not, now they are in want begin to think of God."[14] Ward and Heitzenrater describe Wesley's "response to the economic difficulties of this autumn [as] a curious mixture of indignation, practical assistance, and pietism. Here the pietistic note is dominant."[15] *Thoughts on the Present Scarcity of Provisions*, written a few months later in January 1773, offered a more extended practical response.[16] It began as a letter to *Lloyd's Evening Post* and other newspapers in which Wesley laid out his

---

12. J. Wesley, *A Word to a Smuggler*, 8; J. Wesley, *Works* (Jackson), 11:178.
13. J. Wesley, *Works*, 23:28–29.
14. J. Wesley, *Works*, 22:350.
15. J. Wesley, *Works*. 22:350, 350n46.
16. J. Wesley, *Thoughts on the Present Scarcity*; J. Wesley, *Works* (Jackson), 11:53–59.

observations on the destitute unemployed in order to raise a charitable response and considers the impact on the poor of a downturn in economic conditions.[17]

A shortage of corn and oats had left many without sufficient food. Corn was used in distilleries and oats for feeding the horses that were raised for the pulling of the coaches and chaises of the wealthy. Monopolizing of farms has led to a rise in the prices of pork, poultry, and eggs. Land prices had increased to meet the demand of rising taxes. Wesley claims that thousands were perishing for lack of food through these three causes alone—distilling, taxes, and luxury. His solution to the shortage was to shut down the distilleries, raise fewer horses, reduce the size of farm leases, cut down on luxuries, and reduce taxes, though he doubted that any of this would be done given the nation's lack of the fear of God.

Wesley commended the "[m]any excellent things" that had been published on the present scarcity of provisions, with "men of experience and reflection" identifying many of the causes. What had been lacking however was a complete list of all the causes and an explanation of "how each particular cause affects the price of each particular sort of provision."[18] Wesley set out, rather ambitiously, to meet this need. First he noted the thousands of people who were "starving . . . in every part of the nation."[19] As perhaps the most widely travelled person in England, Wesley was well qualified to comment on the circumstances people were facing. His itinerant ministry took him constantly out among the people and he took a deep interest in the political, economic, and social circumstances that had a direct impact upon their lives.[20] He notes here that he had himself observed people feeding their children "stinking sprats" from a dunghill and making soup from bones taken out of the mouths of dogs. How could this be in a land of such abundance? People had no food because they had no work; and they had no work because those who used to employ them could no longer afford to do so because of the inflated

---

17. J. Wesley, *Letters*, 5:349–54.

18. J. Wesley, *Thoughts on the Present Scarcity*, 3–4; J. Wesley, *Works* (Jackson), 11:53.

19. J. Wesley, *Thoughts on the Present Scarcity*, 4; J. Wesley, *Works* (Jackson), 11:53.

20. Outler cites a number of similar contemporary accounts of the conditions of England's poor: William Cobbett, *Rural Rides* (1830), William Marshall, *A General Survey of the Rural Economy of England* (1787–98), F. M. Eden, *The State of the Poor* (1797), T. R. Malthus, *Essay on the Principle of Population* (1798). J. Wesley, *Works*, 3:569.

price of food. Prices were so expensive that sellers could not move their goods in order to make sufficient money to hire help.[21]

One of the factors often discussed in considering changes to eighteenth-century agrarian practices is the impact of the enclosure system. After 1750, enclosure spread rapidly aided by numerous enclosure acts and this process contributed to the creation of a hungry population. The enclosure system replaced the older open-field model of agriculture in which waste lands and the surrounding fields of a village were a vital source of sustenance to poorer people. Under enclosure, landowners appropriated waste lands and either bought neighboring strips of land or evicted tenants so as to acquire larger continuous pasture lands which were then enclosed by fences. Lands enclosed between 1700 and 1760 equaled about 312,000 acres, but by 1840 this had increased to over 5,500,000 acres.[22] Since land ownership was the key to both political office and the right to vote, enclosure was often driven by social ambition. The gathering of large tracts of land into the hands of the upwardly mobile was resented by small scale agricultural workers who saw the centuries-old right to cultivate the open fields surrounding the village being destroyed by monopoly. Even though enclosure provided the means of experimenting with the improvement of yields for the large-scale production of food needed to feed burgeoning populations in urban centers, the disastrous social effects of enclosure should not be lost on us.

> Scores of thousands of peasants suffered complete ruin. The small farmer, the cottager, the squatter, were driven off the soil, and their cottages were often pulled down. The land they had worked was enclosed, and became part of the park or ploughland of a large estate. Thus the English peasant village was destroyed.[23]

Permission to enclose was set in train by a single signature which led to a bill being read twice in the House of Commons. The committee to approve was usually made up of those who sponsored the bill so there was often a clear conflict of interest which supported wealthy landowners

21. J. Wesley, *Thoughts on the Present Scarcity*, 4–6; J. Wesley, *Works* (Jackson), 11:53.

22. Gregg, *Social and Economic History*, 23, citing J. L. Hammond and B. Hammond, *The Village Labourer*, 17.

23. Gregg, *Social and Economic History*, 27. For definitive treatments of the enclosure system see Turner, *English Parliamentary Enclosure*; Mingay, *Parliamentary Enclosure in England*; Mingay, *Social History of the English Countryside*.

and worked against the interest of small farmers. Cottagers and squatters were even worse off having lost their right to forage in the waste lands as well as the ancient right of gleaning. Their cottages were demolished and along with others whose lives had depended on the older village model they became homeless and indigent. As land was concentrated in the hands of the wealthy a landless proletariat was created.[24] Plumb pointed to the "large, fat, rubicund, pugnacious figure of John Bull, which graced the patriotic prints and cartoons" as always being depicted as a farmer,[25] yet the newfound prosperity bought on by new methods of agriculture was concentrated in the hands of a relative few while most of the poor found themselves in a new kind of feudalism, dependent upon wealthy landowners for their subsistence.

Wesley did not comment directly on the enclosure system though he must have observed its impact and he was concerned about the monopolizing of farmlands. He focused much of his attention on the impact of commercial ventures on the pricing of produce and thus on the livelihoods of workers. He attributed the rising cost of corn to the immense amounts of the crop needed to feed distilleries.[26] Wesley claimed that a little less than half of all the wheat produced in England was being converted into the deadly poison of gin that destroyed lives.[27] It was impossible to be accurate about how much grain went into distilling by the duty that was paid because distillers routinely failed to pay the duty. One distiller admitted that for every gallon on which he paid duty he made six gallons upon which no duty was paid.[28]

Wesley attributed the cause of the rise in the price of oats to the increased trade in coaches and chaises, estimating that there were four times as many horses to feed for the pulling of coaches and chaises as there had been a few years ago. If there were four times as many horses to feed and only twice as many oats produced, the price would by necessity be made exorbitant. The dearness of one kind of grain always raises the

---

24. For a less negative view of the impact of enclosure see, Marshall, *English People in the Eighteenth Century*, 231–82.

25. Plumb, *England in the Eighteenth Century*, 152.

26. In Britain in this period the term "corn" referred to wheat and other grains, not to the "maize corn" we normally associate with the Americas.

27. J. Wesley, *Thoughts on the Present Scarcity*, 6–7; J. Wesley, *Works* (Jackson), 11:53–54.

28. J. Wesley, *Thoughts on the Present Scarcity*, 8–9; J. Wesley, *Works* (Jackson), 11:55.

cost of other types so a high price on wheat and oats means a high price on barley as well.[29] Beef and mutton had also become more expensive because so many farmers had given up raising cattle, as well as sheep and oxen, in order to raise horses instead for which there was a more lucrative market, not only domestically, but to service the thousands of French exports yearly.[30] The price of pork, poultry, and eggs had increased because of the monopolizing of farmlands. Where once twenty farmers had run small properties, now one farmer would oversee one great farm. Where previously small-scale farmers had always sold their bacon, pork, chickens, and eggs at the market, now large monopolies could not be bothered with such trade, unless to raise a few pigs or poultry for their own use. So, the price of such items had doubled and even tripled.[31]

For Wesley the most terrible and destructive cause of inflated prices was luxury. "Only look into the kitchins [sic] of the great, the nobility and gentry, almost without exception . . . And when you have observed the amazing waste which is made there, you will no longer wonder at the scarcity, and consequently dearness, of the things which they use so much art to destroy."[32] The need to maintain such a luxurious standard of living had led to the raising of rents. If the farmer must pay a higher price for the land he works, he must necessarily raise the price of his produce. This in turn raises the price of the land setting up a vicious cycle.[33]

In addition to all these causes there were rising taxes to deal with including new taxes "which are laid on almost everything that can be named." There are taxes on earth and fire and water, even on light itself.[34] "Yet one element remains: And surely some man of honour will find a way to tax this also. For how long shall the saucy air strike a gentleman on the face, nay a Lord, without paying for it?"[35] Wesley attributed the

---

29. J. Wesley, *Thoughts on the Present Scarcity*, 9–10; J. Wesley, *Works* (Jackson), 11:55.

30. J. Wesley, *Thoughts on the Present Scarcity*, 10–11; J. Wesley, *Works* (Jackson), 11:54–55.

31. J. Wesley, *Thoughts on the Present Scarcity*, 11–13; J. Wesley, *Works* (Jackson), 11:56.

32. J. Wesley, *Thoughts on the Present Scarcity*, 13–14; J. Wesley, *Works* (Jackson), 11:56–57.

33. J. Wesley, *Thoughts on the Present Scarcity*, 14; J. Wesley, *Works* (Jackson), 11:57.

34. This may be a reference to the estimation of tax owing on the amount of window glass in one's home.

35. J. Wesley, *Thoughts on the Present Scarcity*; J. Wesley, *Works* (Jackson), 11:57.

proliferation of taxes to the need to service the growing national debt, estimating that where seventy years ago the national expense had been three million pounds a year; now four million pounds a year was being paid on interest alone.[36]

Wesley then laid out a whole series of practical suggestions designed to address the present scarcity of provisions. At least in his mind they were practical; whether they would have worked is another matter. Wesley was no economist and he often spoke from outside of his expertise, but he did at least attempt solutions.[37] He was convinced that work needed to be found for starving people and that in order for employers to provide work without ruining themselves the price of provisions needed to be reduced.[38] In the case of wheat and barley this could be achieved by prohibiting all distilling, by using rice as an alternative crop for the production of starch, and by importing rice and other grains. The price of oats could be reduced by lessening the demand for horses. This could be achieved by levying an export tax of ten pounds for every horse sold to France and by laying an additional tax on gentlemen's carriages. Beef and mutton prices could be reduced by increasing the breed of sheep and cattle, thus diversifying the market. Pork and poultry prices could be reduced if a ceiling of a hundred pounds a year were set on farm leases. Luxury must also be suppressed either by law, by example, or both. "I had almost said," he offers, "by the grace of God. But to mention this, has been long out of fashion."[39] The restraining of luxury would also bring down land prices since it would lessen the expense of housekeeping. The discharge of the national debt would reduce taxes but "all useless pensions" should also be abolished, "as fast as those who now enjoy them die. Especially those ridiculous ones, given to some hundreds of idle men, as governors of forts or castles: which forts have answered no end for above these three hundred years, unless to shelter jackdaws and crows."[40]

Wesley closed with his characteristic sarcasm, expressing doubt whether any of this would ever be done, for the nation had no fear of God

36. J. Wesley, *Thoughts on the Present Scarcity*, 14–16; J. Wesley, *Works* (Jackson), 11:57.

37. Haywood, "Was John Wesley A Political Economist?"

38. J. Wesley, *Thoughts on the Present Scarcity*, 17; J. Wesley, *Works* (Jackson), 11:57.

39. J. Wesley, *Thoughts on the Present Scarcity*, 17–20, quotation on p. 20; J. Wesley, *Works* (Jackson), 11:58.

40. J. Wesley, *Thoughts on the Present Scarcity*, 20–21; J. Wesley, *Works* (Jackson), 11:58–59.

and "there is such a deep, avowed, thorough contempt of all religion, as I never saw, never heard or read of, in any other nation, whether Christian, Mahometan or Pagan." All that is left is to hope that when God arises to judge, the people will fall into the hands of divine not human hands.[41]

Eleven years later Wesley wrote to William Pitt the Younger who had become Prime Minister in December 1783 at the age of 24. Writing from Bath on 6 September 1784, he offered the Prime Minister advice on taxes. After pointing out the fraudulent tax evasion he had encountered in town and country, he asserted that in Cornwall alone, the king was defrauded half a million pounds a year in customs duties suggesting that the national figure was more than five million. Distillers pay less than a fortieth of what they should and furthermore their vile trade takes twenty-thousand lives in a year. "You are a man. You have not lost human feelings. You do not love to drink human blood. You are a son of Lord Chatham. Nay, if I mistake not, you are a Christian. Dare you, then, sustain a sinking nation?"[42] Not stopping at recommending that distilling of spirits be made a felony, he went on to suggest a rather heartless measure to prevent suicide—an Act of Parliament ordering that the body of every "self-murderer" be hanged in chains in the streets as a preventative measure for others. According to Wesley, such measures would make Pitt's name "precious to all true Englishmen as long as England continued a nation."[43]

Wesley lived at a time when economic theory was undergoing a massive theoretical shift. Adam Smith's *Wealth of Nations* would be published in 1776 and set out a new theory that laid the groundwork for modern concepts of free market economics.[44] Smith spoke of the "invisible hand," which provided social benefit from self-interest. When the shopkeeper or artisan works hard for his own economic interest the labor and the produce that result benefit the wider society. This concept has become one of the platforms of *laissez-faire* economic models which argue for minimal if any restrictions on trade and industry, based on the conviction that this will generate prosperity and produce a greater benefit for the greatest number of people. Today's "trickle-down" economic theories, however, overlook distinctive features of Smith's ideas. As a moral philosopher

41. J. Wesley, *Thoughts on the Present Scarcity*, 21–22; J. Wesley, *Works* (Jackson), 11:59.
42. J. Wesley, *Letters*, 7:235.
43. J. Wesley, *Letters*, 7:236.
44. Smith, *Nature and Causes of the Wealth of Nations*.

he was concerned with the relationship between individuals and social groups and his ideas about the social utility of self-interest were based less on commercial and financial concerns than on the flourishing of communities. He warned against the dehumanizing effects of monopolies and the over-specialization of labor, both of which have become features of modern industrial economies.[45] Rioting crowds who demanded just food prices were experiencing a shift in the moral economy of the eighteenth century as the paternalistic role of the state toward the poor was being replaced by an open labor market with less sense of responsibility toward the needy. The relationship of "master to servant" was one that entailed personal responsibility and mutual obligation. This came to be replaced by a commodification of labor so that the boss-worker relationship formed a "cash nexus" in a developing new economy. In time, pre-industrial values such as traditional wisdom, shared experience and communal morality, no longer guided the new capitalist economy.[46] Notwithstanding his Christian moral concern to protect people against want, it is clear that Wesley was not simply a backward-looking traditionalist expecting earlier economic models to meet the needs of changing economic and industrial realities. He was aware of the changing landscape of economic theory and did his best to apply it to the needs of the poor.

The Cult of Commerce

Statistical analysis of trade was important in eighteenth-century Britain because it was seen as a marker of the growing strength of the Empire. Indeed, as Linda Colley claims, a "cult of commerce" emerged as a shaper of British identity.[47] In its chapter on trade, the 1718 annual directory *The Present State of Great Britain* claimed that "next to the purity of our religion we are the most considerable nation in the world for the vastness and extensiveness of our trade."[48] After the Seven Years War (1754–1763), Britain's foreign possessions were so vastly increased that it was difficult to service its commercial, administrative, and military needs. The opportunity for the accumulation of wealth by trade with overseas possessions

---

45. I am indebted to the Rev. Brendan Byrne of Mountview Uniting Church, Melbourne for these insights.
46. Hobsbawm, *Industry and Empire*, 66–70.
47. Colley, *Britons*, 55–100.
48. Colley, *Britons*, 59.

was eagerly taken advantage of by talented Scots who were often willing to accept administrative posts in which the less adventurous Englishman showed little interest. This booming trade and the consequent growth in the British economy contributed significantly to enthusiasm for Empire.

In *A Serious Address to the People of England, With Regard to the State of the Nation* (1778), claims that England was facing financial ruin were countered in attempt to encourage the populace.[49] "Nine capital articles" are examined—population, agriculture, manufacture, land and fresh water carriage of goods, salt-water carriage of goods, fisheries at home and abroad, taxes, revenue, and debt. On Wesley's account, agriculture had increased since 1759. Instead of farmhouses, barns, enclosures, and fences tumbling down in ruins, new ones were being erected. Many hundreds of thousands more acres were being cultivated than had been the case twenty years before. Farmers were wealthier than before, and their livestock had increased. On Wesley's estimate, a few branches of manufacturing, such as weaving, had perhaps seen decreases and this was understandable with the fluctuations of fashion. But decreases in some areas had been adequately compensated by increases in others. Since 1759 there had been a considerable increase in warehouses, magazines, machines, and engines of every kind.[50] It is interesting that here, when Wesley was attempting to reassure the population, he stressed the strength of economy and trade, whereas earlier in *Thoughts on the Present Scarcity of Provisions* (1773) where he was concerned to show the dire circumstances of the poor, he stressed their material want. He seemed aware that the wealth of the nation was sufficient to feed the poor but there was a problem with the equality of distribution.

Wesley saw the increase in wagons, roads, barges, and canals as a clear indicator of an increase in trade in land and fresh-water carriage of goods. Indeed, 1760–1830 would prove to be "the great era of road-making" and canal construction in Britain.[51] By the early eighteenth-century England's navigable waterways had doubled in length through dredging,

49. J. Wesley, *Serious Address to the People of England*; J. Wesley, *Works* (Jackson) 11:140–49. Originally the word "People" in the title was "Inhabitants," but Wesley later changed it. J. Wesley, *Works*, 23:76. Wesley took a similar approach in *A Compassionate Address to the Inhabitants of Ireland* (also early 1778) addressing the fears and rumors of foreign invasion and the growing strength of Washington's army. J. Wesley, *Works* (Jackson), 11:149–54.

50. J. Wesley, *Serious Address to the People of England*, 12–13; J. Wesley, *Works* (Jackson), 11:143–44.

51. Gregg, *Social and Economic History*, 43.

straightening and the creation of locks, providing a much more efficient and cheap mode of transportation of goods. Wagons drawn by horses on iron rails from the 1760s provided an even cheaper mode of goods transport. Through such means, trade was able to flourish in every part of the country, an advantage previously had only in coastal areas and those traversed by major waterways. Such transport infrastructure not only made goods available for commercial purposes over a wider area, but they were also major feats of civil engineering which further stimulated the economy by employing the engineers and laborers needed to put them in place. Recent reassessment of Joseph Massie's widely used survey of 1759 has led to the view that Britain had even larger commercial and manufacturing concerns in 1700 than had previously been supposed. By 1759, 36.8 percent of Britain's population was engaged in industry, building, and commerce, considerably higher than the European average. Textiles (wool, linen, silk, cotton), coal, iron, and shipbuilding all saw increases. Coal production alone increased fivefold over the century and iron output had doubled by 1780. The "Potteries" around Burslem in the West Midlands were at the leading edge in the production of a highly valued consumer item.[52] By 1800 Cornish tin and copper mining alone employed ten-thousand people.[53] Agricultural life held its own alongside this growth in industry. In 1800 around 36 percent of the population was employed in agricultural pursuits, smaller in percentage than in 1700 (45 percent) but a larger raw number.[54]

Wesley was convinced that any candid observer would see that England was, in 1778, in a much better financial position than had been the case twenty years previously. He warned his hearers not to be deceived to the contrary by any smooth-tongued orators. Instead they should be grateful for the abundant liberty, peace, and plenty they enjoyed.[55] There was only one thing the people should fear—God's judgement on the nation for its widespread contempt of God who would soon be avenged

---

52. Rule, "Manufacturing and Commerce," in Dickinson, *Companion to Eighteenth-Century Britain*, 127.

53. Rule, "Manufacturing and Commerce," 136.

54. Mingay, "Agriculture and Rural Life," in Dickinson, *Companion to Eighteenth-Century Britain*, 141.

55. J. Wesley, *Serious Address to the People of England*, 20–21; J. Wesley, *Works* (Jackson), 11:147–48.

on such a nation as this. Just as with the inhabitants of Nineveh only repentance could avert such a visitation.[56]

Conclusion

Wesley's convictions about the strength of the British economy and its trade markets, matches historians' understanding of the strength of the empire in the Atlantic world during this period. For all his personal asceticism he participated to some extent in the "cult of commerce" that marked this period of British expansion. He gloried in the strength of England's trade and industry and saw in it a bulwark against foreign incursion. The stronger the economy and the healthier the trade the less people need be concerned about losing their Protestant liberties. Over time he moved from the older view of a "fixed price" on goods to the more modern view informed by Adam Smith and Charles Smith of a fluctuating price that moved on a sliding scale to match the larger economic circumstances. Like Adam Smith, his economic views had a profoundly social dimension and expressed concern about the dehumanizing effects of monopolies. He never lost sight of the needs of the poor and the impact of larger economic forces on their livelihoods. His economic theory, such as it was, never lost a humanitarian concern. As lucrative as the slave trade was, England was better off without it, and its loss would not put an end to the nations' prosperity.[57]

Though his love for the poor was genuine and his preference for their company was made clear in his itinerant lifestyle, at the same time there is in Wesley a moralism that can only be described as evincing a lack of sympathy for, and even victim blaming of, the troubled poor. Those who bought smuggled goods, even if order to survive, had better starve than to steal. Employers should refuse work to anyone convicted of smuggling. Some were rebuked who had no thought for God in good times and had now turned to repentance during their time of want. Others were asked whether their laziness might have had anything to do with their present poverty. The bodies of suicides should be hung in the streets as a public warning against others tempted to the sin of self-murder.

56. J. Wesley, *Serious Address to the People of England*, 21–23; J. Wesley, *Works* (Jackson), 11:148–49.

57. For the manner in which independent traders challenged the Charter granted to the Royal Africa Company in order to obtain their share in the prosperity made available through the slave trade see Pettigrew, *Freedom's Debt*.

These are jarring instances of a lack of compassion that stand out in all the more bold relief given Wesley's usual compassionate stance.

When it came to practical solutions, Wesley was not satisfied with individual responsibility alone. He saw a place for government intervention through taxation and trade policies that might alleviate food shortages, and he advised the Prime Minister on such matters. No economist, he at least offered economic solutions to social problems which even if deemed impractical were driven by a genuine concern for struggling people. Again, though practical systemic solutions were offered, Wesley deemed the chief causes of want to be the gluttony and luxury of the wealthy, so individual morality remained an important factor in addressing poverty. There was always a personal moral demand in all of Wesley's social and political writings. Many of the people remained in distressing hunger and poverty while at the same time the nation's economic and commercial strength had never been greater. He did not condemn commercial interests, but self-indulgent luxury came in for sharp criticism. To live simply and frugally was to make room for the production of a greater degree of wealth that would benefit the greater number of people. It was not socialism, but it was the kind of conviction that would inform the Methodist social conscience and contribute to so much human flourishing in the century that followed.

Bibliography

Colley, Linda *Britons: Forging the Nation, 1707–1837*. New Haven: Yale University Press, 2005.

Dickinson, H. T., ed. *A Companion to Eighteenth-Century Britain*. Oxford: Blackwell, 2002.

Gregg, Pauline. *A Social and Economic History of Britain, 1760–1972*. London: Harrap, 1973.

Hammond, J. L., and Barbara Hammond. *The Village Labourer, 1760–1832: A Study in the Government of England before the Reform Bill*. London: Longmans, Green and Co., 1920.

Haywood, C. R. "Was John Wesley A Political Economist?" *Church History* 33.3 (1964) 314–21.

Hobsbawm, Eric J. *Industry and Empire: The Economic History of Britain since 1750*. London: Weidenfeld and Nicolson, 1968.

Marshall, Dorothy. *English People in the Eighteenth Century*. London, Longmans, Green and Co., 1956.

Mingay, G. E. *Parliamentary Enclosure in England*. London: Longman, 1997.

———. *A Social History of the English Countryside*. London: Routledge, 1990.

Pettigrew, William A. *Freedom's Debt: The Royal African Company and the Politics of the Atlantic Slave Trade, 1672–1752*. Chapel Hill: University of North Carolina Press, 2013.

Plumb, John. *England in the Eighteenth Century*. Harmondsworth: Penguin, 1963.

Prest, Wilfrid. *Albion Ascendant: English History, 1560–1815*. Oxford: Oxford University Press, 1998.

Rack, Henry D. *Reasonable Enthusiast: John Wesley and the Rise of Methodism*. Nashville: Abingdon, 1993.

Rudé, George. *Hanoverian London, 1714–1808*. Berkeley: University of California Press, 1971.

Smith, Adam. *An Inquiry into the Nature and Causes of the Wealth of Nations*. London, 1776.

Toynbee, Arnold. *Lectures on the Industrial Revolution in England: Popular Addresses, Notes and Other Fragments*. Cambridge: Cambridge University Press, 2011.

Turner, Michael. *English Parliamentary Enclosure: Its Historical Geography and Economic History*. Folkestone, CT: Dawson, 1980.

Wesley, John. *A Compassionate Address to the Inhabitants of Ireland*. Belfast, 1778.

———. *The Letters of the Rev John Wesley: Volume 5*. Edited by John Telford. London: Epworth, 1931.

———. *The Letters of the Rev John Wesley: Volume 7*. Edited by John Telford. London: Epworth, 1931.

———. *A Serious Address to the People of England, with Regard to the State of the Nation*. London, 1778.

———. *Thoughts on the Present Scarcity of Provisions*. London, 1773.

———. *A Word to a Smuggler*. London, 1775.

———. *The Works of John Wesley: Volume 3: Sermons III, 71–114*. Edited by Albert C. Outler. Nashville: Abingdon, 1986.

———. *The Works of John Wesley: Volume 10: The Methodist Societies: The Minutes of the Conference*. Edited by Henry D. Rack. Nashville: Abingdon, 2011.

———. *The Works of John Wesley: Volume 11*. Edited by Thomas Jackson. London: Wesleyan Methodist Bookroom, 1872.

———. *The Works of John Wesley: Volume 20: Journals and Diaries III, 1743–1754*. Edited by W. Reginald Ward and Richard P. Heitzenrater. Nashville: Abingdon, 1991.

———. *The Works of John Wesley: Volume 22: Journals and Diaries V, 1765–1775*. Edited by W. Reginald Ward and Richard P. Heitzenrater. Nashville: Abingdon, 1993.

———. *The Works of John Wesley: Volume 23: Journals and Diaries VI, 1776–1786*. Edited by W. Reginald Ward and Richard P. Heitzenrater. Nashville: Abingdon, 1995.

5

Care of Souls in the Classic Tradition

Revisiting Thomas Oden

KATE BRADFORD

The classic pastoral tradition held consensual answers to virtually all the relevant questions of contemporary soul care. Caring for another's soul means to seek the health of the inner life of the person, which involves mending and nurturing of that personal center of the self, viewing God as the primordial giver of care. Pastoral counsel is soul care in the sense that it seeks to address the inner wellspring of personal decisions with wisdom, prudence and love. To care for souls means to be accountable for shepherding the inner life of persons through the crises of emotional conflict and growth in responsiveness to God.

Soul is what distinguishes a living being from rocks. That the human soul has the unique capacity among all creatures to behold and reflect the mystery of God is the subject of pastoral care. Tragically, soul is capable of stumbling and falling, of abusing freedom, and of being led into captivity. Psyche (soul) is the seat of emotive and religious life, and the person relationship to God.

—Thomas Oden[1]

---

1. Oden, *Change of Heart*, 200, italics mine.

Introduction

Across a year-long period over 1979–1980, Dr. Thomas C. Oden set out to alert as many pastoral theologians and pastoral care and counselling organizations and associations of a set of dangers that he had identified. His concern was that the academic discipline of pastoral care had veered away from classic Christianity, the ancient course set by Scripture and the early Church Fathers. Oden, a much-published American theologian who had previously written from a liberal/progressive perspective, launched a searing and unexpected challenge to the dominant psychological models of clinical pastoral care; a discipline that purported to be grounded in theological principles. Oden sought to deliver his message to a cluster of organizations and publishers that were associated with clinical pastoral training models. The most widely known of these being the hospital-based training method, Clinical Pastoral Education (CPE). The associations with connections to this method of training were the Association of Clinical Pastoral Education (ACPE), the American Association of Pastoral Counselors (AAPC), and the Society of Pastoral Theology (SPT). This paper reviews Oden's passionate appeal to return to a care of souls as described in Scripture and some classic texts of Christianity and seeks to evaluate the outcome of his addresses and writings at this time.

In 1979 Oden published his book, *Agenda in Theology: Recovering Christian Roots*, which sought to reframe the concept of "agenda," a much-used term in pastoral theology. The burden of this work was Oden's concern to affirm the priority of God's agenda rather than that of the pastoral carer or the client. In the same year he addressed the St. Louis Convention of the AAPC[2] and the International Congress of Pastoral Care and Counselling in Edinburgh.[3]

The Edinburgh conference occupies a critical place in the twentieth-century history of pastoral care; it was the first Christian international conference of its kind, and the American model of CPE was still in its

---

2. The date of the address is recorded in the archives at Drew University as follows: "Recovering Lost Identity." Plenary Session Annual Conference, American Association of Pastoral Counselors, April 21, 1979; found here: https://uknow.drew.edu/confluence/display/Library/Thomas+Oden+Publications%2C+1960-2000--+Finding+Aid. This was published in 1980 in Oden, "Recovering Lost Identity," and later reprinted as the first chapter of his book *Care of Souls*, which is an expansion of his addresses in St. Louis and Edinburgh.

3. See Lyall, "Pastoral Care."

infancy in Europe.⁴ Oden used his platform to warn the European conference against errors that he believed were prevalent in American models of pastoral care:

> [T]his very non-theological, pragmatic, non-classical (even anti-classical) tradition of American pastoral care that is now blithely being exported around the world, with Dietrich Stollberg in Germany and several figures in England leading the way problematically toward the Americanization of pastoral care in Europe.⁵

Oden was deeply concerned by the likelihood that the European church would adopt an American version of pastoral care and clinical training and therapeutic skills. He was concerned that they would import a system that integrated only "very superficially" with Christian ministry and "at worst, pastoral counselling has learned that it can get along quite well without Christ and the Apostles, scriptures and the church fathers and with minimal pastoral reference."⁶

Oden contended that CPE and similar training organizations had extensively reconfigured the ministry of pastoral care in a manner that left it detached from its theological moorings and traditional Christian heritage.⁷ Despite this loss of critical convictions, the influence of CPE eventually reached beyond progressive churches into churches that were noted for their theological conservatism. By the 1960s every major seminary, regardless of theological stripe, had incorporated courses in the psychology of religion, counselling, and programs of CPE into the curriculum.⁸ In counter to this tide, Oden advocated that caring for others

---

4. ECPCC, "History."
5. Oden, "Recovering," 10.
6. Oden, "Recovering," 17.
7. Oden, *Care of Souls*, 32.
8. Within conservative evangelical denominations there emerged those such as Jay Adams and James Dobson who advocated "Christian counseling," hoping to avoid the secular humanism that dominated the social sciences. Nevertheless, they, like their liberal counterparts, cast the gospel in the mold of the therapeutic. While conservative doctrinal assertions are given ascent and traditional moral values are upheld, theology takes second place to psychology. Whether liberal or conservative, the minister is now given a place among the helping professions with all the rights and privileges that such an exalted station obtains. For more on this see, Pless, "Your Pastor is Not."

as Christ has cared for us had always been an intrinsic part of the church's ministry.[9]

The modern academic discipline of Pastoral Theology was an innovation that arose after WWII. The focus of this new discipline was the education of ministers as practitioners, and the training incorporated a variety of psychological insights.[10] The method drew heavily on the psychology of Carl Rogers mediated through the theologian Paul Tillich's method of correlation, which sought to correlate theology with human experience. Oden himself had championed Tillich's method in several books until his faith and beliefs underwent a radical transformation during the 1960s and early in 1970. It was this unique vantage point that gave Oden critical insight into the modern pastoral care movement. Oden being, as one reviewer said, both the product and one of the producers of the plight of modern theology.[11]

Oden's new insight probed the underlying assumptions of modern pastoral care (MPC) and asked: How was the ministry of pastoral care or soul care understood by the early theologians of the church? What is a stable definition of pastoral care? What is the relationship between theology and psychology? What happens to the role of a pastoral office when a pastor provides pastoral counselling but has no congregation? What are the differences between pastoral care offered by clergy and laity? What changes in a pastoral ministry when pastoral care is paid for by the government? How does client-centered therapy differ from pastoral guidance; are both forms of pastoral care? What is the relationship between pastoral care and pastoral counselling? Oden came to believe that the lack of clarity in MPC stemmed not from a lack of definitions, but instead was due to a deliberate disruption and break with past traditions.

---

9. Oden, "Pastoral Care," 39. Boisen's program in 1925 began the continuous sequence of clinical pastoral training experiences later institutionalized and renamed Clinical Pastoral Education. Hunter, "Pastoral Theology," 82. The first program in clinical training for theological students was developed in 1923 in Cincinnati, by William S. Keller, a physician and layman. Keller developed a type of summer internship for theological students where they were attached to a local program, for example, a mental hospital or a social welfare agency. The group then met at the weekend to discuss the relevance of this work to the work of a parish minister. Thornton, *Professional Education for Ministry*, 41–46.

10. Hiltner articulated the most prominent early example of this theological perspective in his *Preface to Pastoral Theology*.

11. Berzonsky, Review of *Agendas in Theology*, 270–71.

Who Was Thomas Oden?

Thomas Oden's theological journey was firmly enmeshed within the places, events, and times through which he lived. Specific events and experiences coincided with his formative years, including the Great Depression, the Dust Bowl (and the related dust storms), and dislocation due to his father's war service. His university years coincided with postwar optimism, fear of nuclear holocaust, and the potency of the Methodist Student Movement (MSM). Through the MSM, he was drawn to the radical edge of politics and theology and the new psychotherapeutic treatments. As a theological student, Oden found himself near the center of a progressive liberal agenda to use the church as a vehicle to bring about social change. To understand Oden and his theological journey, it is necessary to locate him contextually.

Thomas Oden (1931–2016) was born into a close-knit and loving extended family in Altus, a small prairie town in Oklahoma. He was the middle child of an attorney and music teacher, with an older brother and younger sister. The family were devout members of a pietist Methodist congregation and community.[12]

Yet, in contrast to his stable and settled home, the 1930s and 40s were unsettled times for the Oden family, who moved to Oklahoma City for three years during Oden's early teens. This move was necessitated by the appointment of his father to a wartime post as a prosecutor against black-market offenders 1942–1946.[13] The family returned to Altus when the posting was concluded. But in 1949 Oden was back in Oklahoma City to attend university. During his time at university, he met Edrita Pokorny and married her on August 10, 1952. They had three children: Clark (1956), Edward (1961), and Laura (1963).[14]

During Oden's seminary training, he confidently negotiated and embraced the features of modern theologies: Bultmann's modern man; the notion of *Kairos*; the dynamics of the present moment; and the symbolic Christ-event as the central event in history. Alongside Bultmann, Oden embraced Tillich's theology of "culture" and "being" where "culture" was the term given to all activities that gave expression to human thought and concern.[15]

---

12. Oden, *Change of Heart*, 22–23.
13. Oden, *Change of Heart*, 25–26.
14. Oden, *Change of Heart*, 76.
15. O'Neill, *Tillich*, 21.

Tillich proposed that within culture what concerned humanity ultimately was "being" itself, understood by humanity as "ultimate concern" or "God." Religion, for Tillich, was that part of culture that articulated the meaning with which it was concerned.[16] The relationship between humans and ultimate-reality-in-itself was mediated by finite religious symbols through culture. "The main function of the symbol—namely, the opening up of levels of reality which otherwise are hidden and cannot be grasped in any other way."[17] Tillich proposed a *method of correlation*, explaining that "by making an analysis of the human situation out of which existential questions arise, the theology uses symbols used in the Christian message which are the answers to these questions."[18] Despite Oden's exposure to the thought of Karl Barth during his PhD studies at Yale Graduate School, under the direction of H. Richard Niebuhr, he continued to favor Bultmann's demythologizing of the New Testament so as to accommodate a modernist world view. Oden preferred Tillich's method of correlation rather than Karl Barth's starker rejection of any synthesis between Christianity and culture.

In addition to the weighty modern theological content of Bultmann and Tillich, Oden's pastoral theology was being informed by the contemporary zeitgeist and various movements. As Oden recounted, an addictive accommodation was taking place, baptizing fads as if they were identical with Christianity:[19] civil rights, women's rights, abortion, Vietnam, demythologizing, client-centered therapy, Transactional Analysis, Gestalt therapy, humanistic psychology, paranormal phenomena, biorhythm charts, pyramids, tarot cards, and astrology. Yet in his seminary teaching, he appeared to be relatively orthodox—if by that one means using an orthodox vocabulary.[20]

"Going away from Home as Far as I could Go"

It was during his time at university, that his attitude around faith and his experience of religion changed. Oden recollected, "I lost the capacity for heartfelt, extemporized prayer. I would have considered it a gauge to pray

16. O'Neill, *Tillich*, 21.
17. Tillich, "Religious Symbols," 191.
18. Tillich, *Systematic Theology*, 70.
19. Oden, *Agenda for Theology*, 22.
20. Oden, *Change of Heart*, 81.

aloud with other college sophomores. I also left behind my love for the church's Scriptures, prayers and especially its hymns, but I always knew they would be there if I went back to find them."[21]

At university, Oden was exposed to the full range of modern thought that would equip him later to make so thorough an assessment of the modern clinical pastoral care movement. He availed himself of the entire intellectual and social smorgasbord on offer at university. He became familiar with the work of Nietzsche, Freud, and Marx.[22] He joined the post-World War II pacifist movement and became enamored with every aspect of the 1950s ecumenical Student Christian Movement. During this time, Oden encountered the revolutionary counter-cultural Social Gospel Movement, first at Oklahoma University, and then at Southern Methodist University's Perkins School of Theology. Being enamored with modernity, he sought out existential intersections between psychology and Christian theology. It was not university alone that had guided Oden to the left. This process had begun with exposure to teaching at church youth summer camps that prioritized a "vision of social justice" ahead of "personal religious experience."[23]

As stated above, in this progressive environment, Oden entered the intellectual world of what Paul Ricoeur referred to as the three "Masters of Suspicion."[24] Marx sought to expose religion's role as an "opiate of the masses." Freud sought to demystify religion's illusory role of "wish fulfilment" and Nietzsche unmasked religion's "slave morality" or "refuge of the weak." Oden aligned with these masters and came to believe that truth in religion "would be finally reducible to economics (with Marx), or psycho-sexual factors (with Freud), or power dynamics (with Nietzsche)." He confessed, "I did not recognize modernity's captivity to secular humanistic assumptions." Oden had allowed these thinkers to set the agenda and reframe his encounter with Scripture. He endeavored to read the New Testament entirely without the premises of incarnation and resurrection. Yet, as he entered his post-critical phase of ministry and returned to the early Church Fathers, he was able to assess the fragmentary truths and insights that psychology and sociology afforded.

---

21. Oden, *Change of Heart*, 54.
22. Oden, *Change of Heart*, 43.
23. Oden, *Change of Heart*, 47.
24. Ricoeur, *Freud and Philosophy*.

It may seem strange that Oden saw his future in theology and seminary, but as he explained, seminary was a logical step if one viewed ministry through a modernist framework, believing as he did that the church could be an effective instrument of social change. He earnestly believed that he *was* in step with his church and the leftward turns that he took early in his theological career were evidence of him trying to be faithful to his church, and the leadership—especially the national youth leadership of Methodist student movement at that time. Oden depicted the youth movement as being "a world of its own, with extensive organizational and strong political convictions. It was designed for propaganda that promoted social change according to the Social Gospel vision pouring out of the theological schools" drawn from socialist and pacifist ideals.[25] Oden had been radicalized through the ecumenical Student Christian Movement, and with this revolutionary mindset, Oden entered the church seeking to effect political change.[26]

Looking back on this time, Oden confessed, "I could still speak of God, sin and salvation but always only in demythologized, secularized and worldly-wise terms. God became the liberator; sin became oppression and salvation became human effort. The trick was to learn to sound Christian while undermining traditional Christianity."[27]

A Crisis of Faith and Theology

In the late 1960s several events created a profound dissonance for Oden that had the effect of disquieting him. The cumulative effect was to shatter Oden's enchantment with modernity. The first of these events happened while Oden had been in Europe during 1966 and had attended a World Council of Churches conference in Geneva. During a protest march at the Geneva Conference, Oden describes scales falling from his eyes when he heard speeches endorsing political utopias moderated by liberation movements while at the same time ignoring "totalitarian regimes."[28] Oden saw the fruitlessness of all he'd worked for up to that point, "the call to repentance, faith and discipleship was reduced to political action, the WCC's special vocation had become to change all societies fundamentally

---

25. Oden, *Change of Heart*, 47.
26. Oden, *Change of Heart*, 50.
27. Oden, *Change of Heart*, 81.
28. Oden, *Change of Heart*, 113.

through politic and wealth transfer."[29] Oden had previously been heavily involved in many of the radical left's movements and had shared in their attempt to produce ecumenicity via those counter-cultural protests.

Three years later in Houston, Oden had a similar experience of revulsion at a rally:

> I sat on a park bench near the amphitheater to a read a handout copy of "Socialist World"—a propaganda piece of which I hadn't seen a copy in several years, but its themes were all too familiar to me. The paper was saturated with labor-left messianic rhetoric. I thought back two decades to . . . when I actually was a socialist. I felt overcome with relief and embarrassment that I had come so close to being trapped in that world. As the tumultuous decade was coming to a close, life on the cutting edge was draining me. I was experiencing a revulsion against self-preoccupation, narcissism and anarchy.
>
> For some reason I had in my pocket that day my India paper edition of the 1662 Book of Common Prayer, which I had purchased at Blackwell's Bookstore in Oxford. I turned to the collect for the day. Under the shade of the majestic gnarled tree I read out loud: "Almighty Father, who has given thine only Son to die for our sins, and to rise again for our justification; Grant us to put away the leaven of malice and wickedness, that we may always serve thee in pureness of living and truth; through the merits of the same thy Son Jesus Christ our Lord. Amen." My eyes filled with tears as I asked myself what I had been missing in all of my frenzied subculture of experimental living.[30]

The third event that Oden described in detail happened early the next year. In December 1969 the family relocated to New York for Oden to take up a teaching position at Drew University. At Drew, he met conservative Jewish scholar, Will Herberg (1901–1977), who became his friend and mentor, and challenged Oden's modernist theology.

Oden had given Herberg a copy of his most recent book *Beyond Revolution: A Response to the Underground Church* (1970). In a discussion about the book when Oden was defending himself against Herberg's assertion that his errors were more profound than he realized, he recollected that, "My irascible, enduring Jewish friend leaned into my face and told me that I was densely ignorant of Christianity and he could not permit me to throw my life away. You will remain theologically uneducated

---

29. Oden, *Change of Heart*, 113.
30. Oden, *Change of Heart*, 126.

until you study carefully Athanasius, Augustine and Aquinas. . . . If you are going to be credible theologian . . . you had best restart your life on firmer ground."[31]

This began Oden's study of the early church theologians, or, as he termed it, classic Christianity. Oden described going to a quiet place and to the great minds of ancient Christianity and in the course of his study discovered who he was.[32] "I had been enamored with novelty. Candidly, I had been in love with heresy. Now I was waking up from this enthrallment to meet a two-thousand-year stable memory."[33]

Although Oden's *realization* came suddenly, it is apparent from his writing throughout the 1960s and his personal account in his autobiography, that the transition had begun during the early 1960s when he started to notice examples of hidden orthodox memory, which he later termed a period of transition. It is to these traces that we will now turn.

Beginning to Recover a "Hidden Orthodox Memory"

Oden's writings of the 1960s reveal someone who is wrestling with major existential and faith questions. In 1960, Oden mounted a spirited defense of Tom Driver's oratorio, *The Invisible Fire*. This work, based upon Wesley's life, spoke of an invisible fire that burnt through the pious pretensions of the religious. He wrote, "The Holy Spirit hounds man to quest for authentic meaning. It drives him to repentance, sets him out on a pilgrimage which can end only with one's being discovered by the divine love for which one seeks. The prevenient grace of God creates thirst for life, and graciously parches the land of the routine."[34] He affirmed that man cannot find God but rather God seeks out man, and that pious works will not satisfy a holy God, but leaves the earnestly pious man in despair. Oden concluded that the offense caused by the drama was "best understood [as] the real cutting edge of the drama,"[35] functioning as a mirror before those criticizing the work and reflecting back their own self-righteousness. In another reflection, a meditation on a T. S. Elliott

---

31. Oden, *Change of Heart*, 136–37.
32. Oden, *Change of Heart*, 138.
33. Oden, *Change of Heart*, 140.
34. Oden, "*Is* the Fire Invisible," 872.
35. Oden, "*Is* the Fire Invisible," 874.

poem, Oden seems to be irresistibly drawn to the cross of Christ as a sign of the "still point of the turning world."[36]

Oden described his credo during this time as, "a new birth without bodily resurrection, and forgiveness without atonement," a psychological gospel of freedom from anxiety, guilt, and boredom, rather than an event of divine salvation.[37] He "drifted towards a Christ without a cross and a conversion without repentance."[38] However, his liberal position was being increasingly undermined by the intrusion of a "hidden orthodox memory." Reading H. Richard Niebuhr's essay, "God and the gods," challenged him to think about where meaning came from[39] and to think about the distinctions between the world and the Word. The results of these reflections were published as *The Crisis of the World and the Word of God* (1962). Oden came to realize that even in his waywardness he had a trust in God and that he belonged to a community of those who confessed the One known as the Father.[40] Understanding God as Father was an incremental step towards biblical theism and away from Tillich's pluralist *Ultimate Concern*, the "power of being-itself understood by humanity as God."[41]

Becoming a Pastoral Theologian

Oden's primary theological model was Tillich's method of correlation, which provided the operating system for his pastoral theology. The method "attempts to correlate the various analyses of the human predicament produced in modern culture with the 'answers' provided by 'the symbols of the Christian message.'"[42] In addition to the method of correlation, Oden followed Tillich's concept of acceptance. According to Oden, within Tillich's schema, "Christian faith hinged primarily on our willingness to 'accept our acceptance.'" "Tillich believed we were accepted by the 'ground of being,'" a conceptual understanding which was premised upon

---

36. Oden, "The Christology of T. S. Eliot," 95.
37. Oden, *Change of Heart*, 86.
38. Oden, *Change of Heart*, 89.
39. Oden, *Change of Heart*, 84.
40. Oden *A Change of Heart*, 85.
41. O'Neill, *Tillich*, 21.
42. Hammond, "An Examination of Tillich's Method," 248–51.

an idea rather than an event in history.⁴³ In Tillich's schema there was no cross or resurrection, only a "dehistorized Christ, who was a useful moral example of absolute acceptance."⁴⁴

Oden deepened his research into Freud and Jung, but if Tillich had been Oden's primary theological resource, his corresponding psychological resource was Carl Rogers. Oden grasped the essence of Roger's client-centered therapy during 1958 while teaching a course in pastoral care at Perkins. As he applied Rogers' methods, Oden recognized the value of personal congruence, empathy, and unconditional positive regard. He saw how they could facilitate "positive constructive psychological change."⁴⁵ Oden repeatedly returned to pastoral issues and from the late 1950s he sought a way to integrate "a therapy of personal self-disclosure with a theology of divine self-disclosure with special reference to the polarities . . . between Carl Rogers and Karl Barth."⁴⁶

In 1960, Oden asked a question which proved to be programmatic for much of his later enquiries: "What is the Christian understanding of the self, if there is such, and what would follow from this as to the content of self-acceptance, self-affirmation, and self-realization as it is understood by the Christian community?"⁴⁷

Throughout the early 1960s, Oden endeavored to search for "deep and hidden correlations between two presumably separate worlds: theology and psychotherapy."⁴⁸ Oden's pastoral writing during this time documented a diminishing of the relative weight afforded to psychology and an elevation of theological principles. There was also a gradual shift away from Bultmann and Tillich toward Barthian concepts of revelation. This change represents the beginning of significant departure from the trajectory of the mainstream American modern pastoral care movement and its theological dependence upon Bultmann and Tillich.

Oden was invited to share his explorations in correlations between the thought of Carl Rogers and that of Karl Barth at a European symposium entitled "Insight and Revelation."⁴⁹ Oden was endeavoring to find a

43. Oden, *Change of Heart*, 90.
44. Oden, *Change of Heart*, 90.
45. Oden, *Change of Heart*, 72.
46. Oden, *Change of Heart*, 69.
47. Oden, "What is Mental Health," 202.
48. Oden, *Change of Heart*, 88.
49. "Insight and Revelation" was later published as *Kerygma and Counseling*.

way to describe the relationship and connections between theology and psychology. Theologically, he attempted to follow Barth, where revelation was something beyond the self, the external revelation of God—the divine disclosure of himself. By way of contrast, psychology worked with insight—the human capacity to see within. Insight is something that one grasps, "whereas one is grasped *by* revelation."[50] Here Oden differed sharply from the pastoral education in the tradition of William James that was prevalent at the time, by explaining that, "Theology differs from psychology of religion, which is concerned with observing and studying as its object the religious affections and religious experience. Theology seeks rather to understand and clarify the view which faith has of its object, namely the particular idea of God which is peculiar to Christian faith—the idea of God as revealed in Jesus Christ."[51] Oden appealed to Outler's conservative Wesleyan criteria for theology, "scriptural truth experienced in life and illuminated by reason and tradition."[52]

In attempting to provide a nexus between theology and psychology, Oden proposed three analogies between therapy and theology: "first, the analogy of the divine incarnation and empathy; second, the analogy of divine forgiveness and human self-acceptance; third, the analogy of divine grace and permissiveness."[53] Along similar lines, Oden drew parallels between Rogers' more general attitude of unconditional love and God's forgiveness. In linking Rogers' approach of unconditional love with God's forgiveness, Oden believed (and came to regret) that he had unwittingly aided the leap of a specific psychotherapeutic phrase which was uncritically assumed as common theological currency. The term, "unconditional love" was to be widely and indiscriminately mapped over the theological concepts of the covenantal love of God the Father.

Encountering the European Interlude

Oden's recovery of his "hidden orthodox memory" and the consequent change in theological direction was aided by a study year in Heidelberg, Germany in 1965–66. There he encountered European existential pastoral care writers who were ministering and writing during 1930–60s in

---

50. Oden, "Revelation and Psychotherapy," 240.
51. Oden, "Revelation and Psychotherapy," 241–42.
52. Oden, "Revelation and Psychotherapy," 243.
53. Oden, "Revelation and Psychotherapy," 254.

traditions that were entirely independent from the modern American pastoral care movement. These pastoral practitioners, whose works were not published in English until the decade from the mid-1950s, have been termed the *European Interlude* by Donald Capps.[54] These writers were mediating between theology and psychotherapy, without collapsing one into the other.

Furthermore, the Europeans did not make use of Tillich's "method of correlation." Oden's time in Germany also allowed him to meet many of his theological interlocutors and to explore in-depth ideas related to existentialism and pastoral theology. He met the theologians Karl Barth, Rudolph Bultmann, Wolfhart Pannenberg, and Austrian psychiatrist and Holocaust survivor, Viktor Frankl. During this time, he also attended the Ecumenical Bossey Institute in Switzerland, established by Paul Tournier for the study of theology and psychology, and met English Psychiatrist, Frank Lake, in Nottingham.

Exposure to Reformed Protestant thought in post-second-world-war Europe clarified for Oden that the moralistic pietism and liberalism in which he had been schooled shared an essentially "optimistic view of man and progressive views of history" so as to make serious confession of sin unnecessary.[55] In such a view, the modern American man was no "miserable sinner, but . . . a protector and defender of God and a sturdy builder of his kingdom on Earth."[56] The European tradition, on the other hand, was not optimistic about humanity or history and was more concerned with renovation of individual hearts than whole societies. In the Reformed European tradition, Scripture held a preeminent role, and Oden noted that the rich Lutheran tradition of pastoral care had a deep maturity. He commented on the difference between American and Continental pastoral care traditions: "We continue to witness the regrettable estrangement of American clinically oriented pastoral care from the exegetically oriented Continental tradition."[57] This continental tradition was evident in the work of pastoral theologians such as Eduard Thurneysen, Frank Lake, and Paul Tournier.

Oden's book *Kerygma and Counseling* (1966) was researched before his time in Germany and addressed themes of correlation. This book was

54. Oden, *Contemporary Theology and Psychotherapy*, 9. Oden notes that much of the pastoral writing had been undertaken by doctors.
55. Oden, "Priority of Pardon," 20.
56. Oden, "Priority of Pardon," 20.
57. Oden, *Contemporary Theology and Psychotherapy*, 54.

an attempt to explain parallels between Carl Roger's psychotherapy and the notion of self-revelation and Karl Barth's theology of divine revelation.[58] Oden advanced the theory that underlying psychotherapy is a "God that is for us" who remains hidden in psychotherapy but is revealed in the Gospel. Oden continued to explore these themes in *Theology and Psychotherapy* (1967).

In 1969, Oden addressed another Barthian theme prominent in Eduard Thurneysen's writing, the need for confession of sin. In "The Priority of Pardon to Penance," Oden asserted that "God's forgiveness is logically and psychologically before rather than, as usually conceived, after repentance."[59]

The same year he also developed new ideas in his book *The Structure of Awareness*. He sought to explain the phenomenological temporal framework in which humans live, which entails anxiety about the future, struggles with past guilt, and boredom in the present. Although this book dealt with phenomenology and nature of being, Oden was no longer trying to bridge the gap between psychotherapy and theology. Drawing on insights from Martin Heidegger and with parallels to Victor Frankl's work on meaning, Oden introduced a new paradigm. He suggested that there was an "implicit and hidden meaningfulness or trustworthiness to being itself, which is discernible because of God's self-disclosing participation in the world. What we are to imitate in Jesus, for example, is his unconditional trust of reality."[60]

By the end of the 1960s, Oden's further engagement with the Barthian thought of H. Richard Niebuhr and several European pastoral practitioners had resulted in a shift in his intellectual convictions. He was less enamored with the work of Tillich and Bultmann. His interests moved away from transformation of society to transformation of individuals. Oden resisted any hostile dualism between faith and psychological process (as he believed Thurneysen was guilty of) and held that psychology and theology explained different aspects of reality, theology is the study of divine revelation and psychology the study of human insight.

Despite this theological shift throughout the 1960s, Oden's loyalties remained divided. He continued to be "exhilarated" by the New Age

---

58. For an excellent discussion on Oden's method of correlation in *Kerygma and Counseling*, See Hunsinger, *Theology and Pastoral Counseling*, 35–45.

59. Oden, "Priority of Pardon," 19.

60. Anderson, Review of *Structure of Awareness*, 113.

movement and he closely followed the work of "the most experimentally orientated psychotherapists."[61]

Recovering the Care of Souls in the Classic Tradition

The decisive turn in Oden's theological convictions occurred after Will Herberg's challenge to carefully study Athanasius, Augustine, and Aquinas.[62] "Herberg's rebuke sent Oden back to the sources, specifically the patristic sources. His attention was first caught by patristic theology's ability to answer humble questions of pastoral counselling. Its unexpected practicality drew him deeper into the theological riches of the patristic writings."[63] With this shift in thinking, Oden did not desire to wipe his memory and experience clean. He explained that he had not changed his mind but rather had experienced a change of heart and sought to put both his mind and heart in service of Christ.[64]

As Oden's ongoing interest was pastoral theology, this field bore the first fruits of his study of the Scriptures and the patristic writings. A decade of studying classic Christian texts led Oden to the conclusion that liberal protestant theology was going in the wrong direction and needed to return to its Classic Christian roots. This he outlined in his 1979 book, *Agenda for Theology*. Due to the influence of liberal theology upon pastoral theology, his mission was to awaken the entire pastoral care movement from its slumber and return it to its Christian roots.

Oden had not only undergone a 180-degree turnaround in his understanding of where authority in matters of life and faith resided, but he overturned the prevailing paradigms around pastoral theology and pastoral care so as to render them almost unrecognizable to the modern mind. Oden released pastoral care from its clinical captivity, returning it to its status as a ministry within the church. He rediscovered timeless pastoral theological truths that had been developed over centuries and lamented that pastoral theology in the twentieth century had been left in the hands of modern pastoral theologians, who depended so heavily on modern psychotherapy and social theory, such as he himself had done.[65]

---

61. Oden, *Change of Heart*, 122.
62. Oden, *Change of Heart*, 136.
63. Trueman, Review of *Change of Heart*.
64. Oden, *Change of Heart*, 137.
65. Oden documented the complete disconnect between twentieth-century

Resolving to Make No New Contribution to Theology

Oden located *true* or *classic* pastoral care as that branch of Christian theology that deals with the care of persons by pastors. It is pastoral because it pertains to the offices, tasks, and duties of the pastor. It is care because it has charge of, and is deliberately attentive to, the spiritual growth and destiny of persons. Pastoral care is analogous to a physician's care of the body. Oden resolved to make no new contribution to theology. Thus, his pastoral theology was shaped by Scripture and patristic writers. However, the pastoral insights and enquiries that he brought to the texts were enriched by his broad understanding of psychology and the social sciences, as can be seen in his use of psychological concepts and language.[66] Oden also deemed it appropriate to use the term "care of souls." "Since that sphere over which one exercises [pastoral] care is the psyche . . . pastoral care is also appropriately called the care of the souls."[67]

As noted, Oden's earlier career had been dedicated to the "interdisciplinary area of the interface between psychology, ethics and religious experience."[68] The later Oden abandoned notions of such an interface. He reinterpreted the relationship between theology and psychology. A Christian psychological approach should be shaped by the theological anthropology found in Scripture and the Patristic writings. Oden sought to chart a course between the integration of Christianity and psychology found in writers such as Paul Tournier, on one hand, and the dualism he perceived in the pastoral theology of Eduard Thurneysen, on the other hand. Oden discerned therapeutic writings in St. Paul's epistles and the church fathers looked for the long-tern transformation of souls and his ministry direction was toward systematic theology and equipping the church.

Oden drew attention to the unqualified use of Christian terms in the modern pastoral care movement, many of which contravened the

---

pastoral theology and historical pastoral theology. He saw a complete abandonment of scripture and the pastoral wisdom of previous centuries and cited key pastoral theologians in his research. See "Recovering Lost Identity" for chart summaries of the research he presented.

66. This is a theme that he returns to repeatedly through the period of the 1960s to 80s culminating in his four volume Classical Pastoral Care Series: *Crisis Ministries* (1986); *Becoming a Minister* (1987); *Pastoral Counsel* (1989); and *Ministry through Word and Sacrament* (1989).

67. Oden, *Becoming a Minister*, 5.

68. Oden, "The New Pietism," 41.

use of the same terms in Scripture. He differentiated Christian faith from psychology and the social sciences because the Christian faith rested on the revelation of God through Jesus Christ, whereas knowledge in the humanities was dependent upon human investigation.

By 1979, Oden identified that modern pastoral care (MPC) had reached a crisis and a point of bifurcation. If MPC was to honor the theological descriptor, *pastoral*, in its name, it needed to return to classic Christian theology, which was identified with the living Christ (the one who lived, died, and rose) as the single, unifying center or core of the Christian tradition. If MPC was to reject this heritage, it would become a post-modern secular discipline that would be *pastoral* in name only.

Oden's Vision for Classical Soul-Care

Oden's framework for pastoral ministry and soul-care was ecclesial with the aim of building the church. His focus was on equipping ordained clergy for their pastoral office within the church. While his books include practical sections, he does not include case studies or *verbatim* transcripts of pastoral encounters. Included in the responsibilities of those in pastoral office are: the equipping of lay people for works of service, visitation of the sick and imprisoned, feeding the hungry, and caring for those in need.[69] Oden considered soul care, or cure of souls, as *the* spiritual task of those set apart for ministry authorized by the church and qualified to speak in matters of the spirit and to "provide a straightforward biblically grounded clarification"[70] on matters of a spiritual nature.

Oden sought to follow Scripture by reserving the words "pastoral care" and "soul care" for the ministry of pastors. He preferred to refer to lay ministries with terms such as Christian care, hospitality, charity, benevolence, and visitation. He endorsed a biblical pattern of ministry which "extends outwardly to members of the Christian community, to other communities, to non-Christians (Gal 6:9–10), and to the whole world (1 John 4)."[71]

Oden also noted a principle that a Christian has a greater responsibility to people who are proximally closer to them.[72] He explained, "The

69. Oden, *Essentials*, 190, 250.
70. Oden, *Essentials*, 190.
71. Oden, *Pastoral Theology*, 281.
72. Oden, *Pastoral Theology*, 278.

mercy of God is to be shared with all, and without discrimination on the basis of race, sex, clan or nationality. Charity is not just for 'people like us.' Nonetheless, the specific place where the claim of charity is addressed is always a particular locale. There the universality of God's love penetrates the highly specific vector of local need."[73] For Oden, this was an aspect of God's providential care.[74]

In relation to pastoral counselling and chaplaincy in public institutions, Oden expressed concerns around issues of vocation and conflict of interest. He also voiced a two-fold reservation around ministries of formal pastoral counselling. Firstly, an ordained pastor's priority is soul-care, which may or may not lead to attending to the counselling needs of the other person. Secondly, he was concerned by the anomalous situation of a pastor receiving payment for a service rendered, or in the case of a full-time pastoral counsellor, is this person still a pastor if not having oversight of a parish? Oden sought to separate the pastoral office from counselling ministries and resisted any form of payment for service.

Oden's mature work followed the hierarchical and organizational order of the early church: the pastor has a hierarchical relationship over the flock, the church takes priority over the public space, and theology interprets psychology and shapes practice. Oden may have contributed to the secularizing of pastoral care, but his own repentance following twenty years chasing progressive modern ideas led him to dedicate his remaining life to reform and revitalization within the church.

Conclusion

Oden shaped his view of pastoral ministry from a plain reading of the shepherding passages in Scripture and his interpretation of the patristic writers. He believed pastoral ministry was a ministry of the clergy rather than the laity, took place within the sacred space of the church rather than the public space, and is a ministry where the pastor takes responsibility for the spiritual practice of soul-care that gives priority to the revelation of Scripture rather than insights from psychology and the social sciences.

Oden understood well the pitfalls of innovative correlations between psychotherapy and modern theology and the modern pastoral care movement's lack of dependence upon Scripture and the extent to

---

73. Oden, *Pastoral Theology*, 281.
74. Oden, *Classic Christianity*, 742.

which pastoral theology had become loosed from its classical moorings.[75] He broke the unchallenged monopoly that Boisen, Hiltner, and others of modern pastoral care movement had over pastoral care and created a space to return again to the atoning death and resurrection of Christ, the forgiveness of sins found in him, and to the writings of the early church to establish the central point of Christian pastoral care.

In the final analysis, soul care was a sacred Christian ministry, "caring for another's soul means seeking the life for the health of the inner life of the person, which involves mending and nurturing of that personal center of the self, viewing God as the primordial giver of care. . . . Psyche (soul) is the seat of emotive and religious life, and the person's relationship to God."[76]

Bibliography

Anderson, Herbert. Review of *The Structure of Awareness*, by Thomas C. Oden. *Princeton Seminary Bulletin* 62.3 (1969) 112–13.

Berzonsky, Vladimir. Review of *Agenda's in Theology: Recovering Christian Roots*, by Thomas C. Oden. *St. Vladimir's Theological Quarterly* 24.4 (1980) 270–71.

Chartier, Myron Raymond. "Pastoral Theology: Essentials of Ministry." *Journal of Psychology & Theology* 12.2 (1984) 158.

Driver, Tom. *The Invisible Fire: An Oratorio Expressing John Wesley's Experience of Conversion and Recalling the Beginnings of Methodism*. Music by Cecil Effinger and libretto by Tom Driver. Commissioned by the National Methodist Student Movement and the National Council of Churches in 1957. Nashville: Cokesbury, 1960.

European Council for Pastoral Care and Counselling. "History: European Pastoral Care and Counselling Movement." http://ecpcc.info/history.

Hammond, Guyton B. "An Examination of Tillich's Method of Correlation." *Journal of the American Academy of Religion.* 22.3 (1964) 248–51.

Hiltner, Seward. *Preface to Pastoral Theology*. Nashville: Abingdon, 1958.

Hunsinger, Deborah van Deusen. *Theology and Pastoral Counseling: A New Interdisciplinary Approach*. Grand Rapids: Eerdmans, 1995.

75. Pattison and Lynch draw attention to Oden as an exception, who works both with a classic theological point of view *and* gives weight to the human experience and insights from the social sciences; because as they note, pastoral theology privileges liberal or radical models of theology as human experience is key in shaping the theology, which is more challenging if a theologian is working with a traditional or conservative theology. "This is one reason why relatively few conservative Evangelical theologians have had a significant impact on the field. . . . [T]hey prefer to give primacy to the theological tradition and its application rather than present experience." Patttison and Lynch, "Practical and Pastoral Theology," 412.

76. Oden, *Change of Heart*, 200.

Hunter, Rodney J. "Pastoral Theology: Historical Perspectives and Future Agendas." *Journal of Pastoral Theology* 16.1 (2006) 7–30.

Lyall, David. "Pastoral Care in Scotland since 1950." *Theology in Scotland* 20.2 (2013) 33–43.

Oden, Thomas C. *Agenda for Theology: Recovering Christian Roots.* San Francisco: Harper and Row, 1979.

———. *Becoming a Minister.* Vol. 2 of *Classical Pastoral Care.* New York: Crossroad, 1987.

———. *Care of Souls in the Classic Tradition.* Philadelphia: Fortress, 1984.

———. *A Change of Heart: A Personal and Theological Memoir.* Downers Grove: InterVarsity, 2014.

———. "The Christology of T. S. Eliot: A Study of the Kerygma in 'Burnt Norton.'" *Encounter* 9 (1960) 93–101.

———. *Classic Christianity: A Systematic Theology.* San Francisco: Harper, 2009.

———. *Contemporary Theology and Psychotherapy.* Philadelphia: Westminster, 1967.

———. *The Crisis of the World and the Word of God.* Nashville: Methodist Student Movement, 1962.

———. *Crisis Ministry.* Vol. 1 of *Classical Pastoral Care..* New York: Crossroad, 1986.

———. "Is the Fire Invisible?" *The Christian Century* (July 27, 1960) 872–74.

———. *Kerygma and Counseling: Toward a Covenant Ontology for Secular Psychotherapy.* Philadelphia: Westminster, 1966.

———. *Ministry through Word and Sacrament.* Vol. 4 of *Classical Pastoral Care..* New York: Crossroad, 1989.

———. "The New Pietism." *Journal of Humanistic Psychology* 12.1 (1972) 24–41.

———. *Parables of Kierkegaard.* Princeton: Princeton University Press, 1978.

———. "Pastoral Care and the Unity of Theological Education." *Theology Today* 42.1 (1985) 34–42.

———. *Pastoral Counsel.* Vol. 3 of *Classical Pastoral Care..* New York: Crossroad, 1989.

———. *Pastoral Theology: Essentials of Ministry.* San Francisco: Harper and Row, 1983.

———. "The Priority of Pardon to Penitence." *Pastoral Psychology* 20 (1969) 19–24.

———. *Radical Obedience of Rudolph Bultmann, with a Response by Rudolph Bultmann.* Philadelphia: Westminster, 1964.

———. "Recovering Lost Identity" *The Journal of Pastoral Care* 34.1 (1980) 4–23.

———. "Revelation and Psychotherapy." *Continuum* 2.2 (1964) 239–64.

———. *The Structure of Awareness.* Nashville: Abingdon, 1969.

———. "What is Mental Health?" *Journal of Pastoral Care* 14.4 (1960) 193–202.

O'Neill, Andrew. *Tillich: A Guide for the Perplexed.* London: T&T Clark, 2008.

Patttison, Stephen, and Gordon Lynch. "Practical and Pastoral Theology." In *The Modern Theologians: An Introduction to Christian Theology Since 1918*, edited by David F. Ford, 408–26. 3rd ed. Oxford: Blackwell, 2005.

Pless, John T. "Your Pastor is Not Your Therapist: Private Confession—The Ministry of Repentance and Faith." *Logia* 10.2 (2001) 115–20.

Ricoeur, Paul. *Freud and Philosophy: An Essay on Interpretation.* Translated by Denis Savage. New Haven: Yale University Press, 1970.

Thornton, Edward. *Professional Education for Ministry.* Nashville: Abingdon, 1970.

Tillich, Paul. "Religious Symbols and Our Knowledge of God." *The Christian Scholar* 38.3 (1955) 189–97.

———. *Systematic Theology.* Vol. 1. London: Nisbet & Company, 1953.

Trueman, Carl. Review of *A Change of Heart: A Personal and Theological Memoir*, by Thomas C. Oden. *First Things* (February 2015) https://www.firstthings.com/article/2015/02/paleo-orthodoxy.

6

Human Technological Enhancement and Christian Perfection

Victoria Lorrimar

Visions of humans enhanced through genetic engineering, artificial intelligence, and nanotechnology are gaining momentum in academic and commercial arenas. Transhumanism is a movement advocating for the enhancement of the human condition through the deployment of these advancing technologies, and the futures envisioned by prominent transhumanists are extending beyond the academy to capture popular imagination.[1] For many, these narratives of "technocultures" and human enhancement are reminiscent of science fiction, and often dismissed for this reason, but they receive enough traction in the public sphere that they are worth taking seriously.

A few examples of the kinds of human enhancements that are proposed will set us up for reflection. Radical life extension is a growing area of research (and funding).[2] Transhumanist Aubrey de Grey and colleagues envision what they term "engineered negligible senescence," proposing to prevent ageing by targeting the various biomolecular processes

---

1. Bostrom and Depaul, "Transhumanist Values," 3.

2. For one example of serious engagement with anti-ageing research, see Google's company Calico: https://www.calicolabs.com/.

associated with progressive loss of vitality on an individual basis.[3] For example, they suggest that a combination of gene therapy, exercise, and growth factor supplementation can counter various kinds of age-related cell loss, while genetically engineered muscle might negate a decline in hormone secretion.[4] The logic of the philosophical Ship of Theseus is applied (as the ship voyaged, each plank was replaced one at a time so that the ship was perpetually replenished) to biological cells.[5] Life extension in an enhancement context is not merely a lengthened life (which could include prolonged senescence), but a slowing down or reversal of the ageing process that also effects an increase in health and quality of life.[6]

Another dimension of human enhancement to consider is the notion of "hedonic recalibration." David Pearce describes this in conjunction with his "abolitionist project"—the annihilation of sentient suffering according to the "hedonistic imperative." Pearce argues that pain and suffering can be removed from our experience entirely through pharmaceutical and genetic intervention, and thus promotes the eradication of pain in all sentient life (beginning with humans).[7] Well-being is genetically programmed in this vision of enhanced humanity.[8]

In a similar proposal, Julian Savulescu and Ingmar Persson call for the use of biomedical means of moral enhancement, focusing especially on the development and application of psychopharmaceuticals to this end.[9] As traditional approaches to moral education have had only limited success, they contend, global environmental catastrophe can only be avoided through biomedical means of moral enhancement.[10] Essentially, they argue that the human psychology and morality that has developed through evolutionary pressures is no longer fit for purpose in the advanced technological and populous societies most people inhabit today.[11] Moral enhancement is not merely desirable, in this view, but imperative to keep up with the likely effects of cognitive enhancement.[12] Through drug

---

3. For a summary of de Grey and colleagues' proposal for "engineering negligible senescence" see Grey et al., "Time to Talk SENS."
4. Grey et al., "Time to Talk SENS," 456.
5. Temkin, "Is Living Longer," 352.
6. Barazzetti and Reichlin, "Life Extension and Personal Identity," 398.
7. Pearce, "The Abolitionist Project."
8. Bostrom, "The Transhumanist FAQ," 44.
9. Persson and Savulescu, "Unfit for the Future," 498.
10. Persson and Savulescu, *Unfit for the Future*, 9–10.
11. Persson and Savulescu, "Unfit for the Future," 486.
12. Persson and Savulescu, "Perils of Cognitive Enhancement." Note that they

treatment and genetic engineering, we might speed up the "motivational internalisation of moral doctrines."[13] Increasing oxytocin levels, for example, may increase trust and other pro-social behaviors.[14] Similarly, increasing serotonin levels through the use of selective serotonin reuptake inhibitors (SSRIs) can reduce aggression and increase cooperation.[15] More generally, moral enhancement should target dispositions related to altruism and justice.[16]

At the more radical end of transhumanist proposals is the notion of "mind-uploading." Hans Moravec, former director of robotics at Carnegie-Mellon University and developer of advanced robots for both NASA and the military, was the first scientist to seriously propose the idea of living perpetually via a digital substrate. In his 1988 work *Mind Children*, he envisioned a procedure in which the entirety of the information encoded within the neurons of a human brain could be read, copied and uploaded to a computer.[17] Rather than a radical extension of biological life, this approach seeks immortality through software existence.

The transhumanist picture of humans determining their own future evolution has engendered various responses in the wider public, with objections offered from both secular and religious perspectives. The concept of human-driven technological "redemption" challenges traditional Christian positions on human creativity and salvation, and the cry of "playing God" is often levelled at the use of technology to alter human nature (though, of course, there are difficulties in defining what precisely human nature is, and what constitutes an alteration of it). Theologians who offer qualified endorsement to the possibility of human enhancement often draw on some form of co-creation theology, considering humans to be co-creators with God.

Transhumanist hopes for the human future construe human flourishing in terms of control—a person is the author of their own destiny, even their biological destiny. Bioethicist and transhumanist James Hughes posits that "we cannot imagine the grandeur of transhuman civilisation," likening this to the way in which the present civilization transcends that

---

interpret cognitive enhancement loosely to include the use of external aids such as supercomputers.

13. Persson and Savulescu, *Unfit for the Future*, 107.
14. Persson and Savulescu, *Unfit for the Future*, 119.
15. Persson and Savulescu, "Unfit for the Future," 499.
16. Persson and Savulescu, "Perils of Cognitive Enhancement," 169.
17. Moravec, *Mind Children*, 109.

of our Paleolithic ancestors.[18] Transhumanism is the epitome of Enlightenment aspiration, the means by which we might finally realize a "single tolerant democratic society."[19] For transhumanists, human enhancement is the route to a good life.

Secular humanism, on the other hand, presents a rather different vision of human flourishing. This vision is exemplified by Leon Kass, founding chair of the U.S. President's Council on Bioethics, who calls for a public bioethics that begins "by reflecting upon the highest human goods and understanding the latest technological advances in this light."[20] In addressing human enhancement questions particularly, Kass interrogates the ends, the means, and the overarching narrative of meaning behind the drive to master one's own nature.[21] He identifies a problem whereby the means to a particular end (e.g., a brightened mood) is rendered unintelligible (e.g., through biopharmaceutical intervention), cut off from the human significance that usually accompanies the natural means (e.g., a personal achievement or the arrival of a loved one) to such an end.[22]

Kass defines human flourishing as "a life-long *being-at-work* exercising one's *human* powers *well* and without great impediment."[23] This flourishing is disrupted, diluted, and distorted by the technological enhancement of human capacities.[24] For the best things in human life, Kass argues, are conditioned by finitude: "engagement, seriousness, a taste for beauty, the possibility of virtue, the ties born of procreation, the quest for meaning."[25] He further speculates that "genuine human flourishing is rooted in aspirations born of the kinds of deficiencies that come from having limited and imperfect bodies."[26] For secular humanists, flourishing is

---

18. Hughes, "The Big Questions," 71.

19. Hughes, "The Big Questions," 71. Gregory Stock makes a similar case that human flourishing occurs as a result of free market liberalism, and that technological enhancement of humans will also increase liberal democracy (Stock, *Redesigning Humans*, 59).

20. Kass, "Reflections on Public Bioethics," 246.

21. Kass, "Ageless Bodies, Happy Souls," 16.

22. Kass, "Ageless Bodies, Happy Souls," 22.

23. Kass, "Ageless Bodies, Happy Souls," 23, emphasis original.

24. Kass, "Ageless Bodies, Happy Souls," 24.

25. Kass, "Ageless Bodies, Happy Souls," 25; cf. Kass, "L'Chaim and its Limits."

26. Kass, "Ageless Bodies, Happy Souls," 27.

realized not through enhancement, but is already found in the contours and limits of a natural human life cycle.[27]

If we want to frame this in theological terms, though the positions already discussed would not affirm this kind of language, we might talk about creaturehood and deification as two aspects of human existence. Secular humanists align with the former, valuing the finite, while transhumanists are drawn to the deification pole in their radical vision of transformation.

In practice, theologians tend to emphasize one of these poles to the detriment or neglect of the other as well. On the deification side, Philip Hefner, for example, argues that humans are co-creators with God, and goes as far as to say that transhumanism "partners" with God in the "editing and revision" of human being (referring to our biological makeup).[28] Of course, the Christian Transhumanist Association are at the extreme end of such a trajectory, denying any value to our creatureliness in favor of radical transcendence.[29]

An emphasis on creaturehood tends to play a conserving function in the enhancement debate. We see this most clearly in the popular sphere in many of the "playing God" arguments, but also in theological work like Brent Waters', which focuses on human limitation as a marker of our creaturehood and prerequisite for flourishing.

In theological conversations around transhumanism and human enhancement, Wesleyan theology sometimes comes up as a natural dialogue partner. Wesley speaks of human perfection as something we can work toward this side of the *eschaton*—surely there is some purchase in that notion for some kind of technological assistance? There is the expectation that Wesleyans would align more with the deification emphasis than an affirmation of creaturely limitation.

This is to misconstrue what Wesley means by Christian perfection, however. He points out of "perfected Christians" that "They are not free from ignorance, no, nor from mistake. . . . They are not free from infirmities, such as weaknesses or slowness of understanding, irregular

---

27. Kass, "Ageless Bodies, Happy Souls," 26. While Kass has been offered as representative of the secular humanist position here, political scientist Francis Fukuyama and political philosopher Michael Sandel both take similar stances (Fukuyama, *Our Posthuman Future*; Sandel, *The Case Against Perfection*).

28. Hefner, "The Animal that Aspires," 161.

29. See https://www.christiantranshumanism.org/.

quickness or heaviness of imagination."[30] It is a very different picture from the transhumanist engineering our way to transcendence.

The notion of perfection as something to which we might work toward in the here and now, however, and the inference that this is somehow attainable, does offer more scope for technology to operate in our improvement, and to promote flourishing in various ways. Yet there is an ascetic dimension to Wesley's understanding of healing, connected with prayer and fasting, that runs counter to the excess and self-interest of transhumanist visions of the good life. Flourishing is not constituted by an absence of pain, or a consistent positive affect, but involves self-control and even abnegation.

Whereas the idea of Christian perfection will only take us so far in a Wesleyan engagement with human enhancement, his theology of grace may prove more fruitful. Randy Maddox sums up Wesley's overall picture of grace as "responsible grace"—"it empowers our response but does not coerce that response."[31] The fact that Wesley affords a role for "grace-empowered human co-operation in salvation" then shifts our attention to determining what precisely we understand by salvation.[32]

In his sermon "On Working Out Our Own Salvation," Wesley firmly precludes any kind of hubris or pride by reminding us that grace enables any "working out" that we might do.[33] On the one hand, human nature is entirely corrupt in its natural state, yet his understanding of prevenient grace comes close (at least in consequence) to the argument in other Christian traditions that nature is always already graced (there is no nature without grace). This goes a long way to dissolving the tension between creaturehood and deification. If we recognize dependence on God as a fundamental aspect of creaturehood, and therefore do not separate out an abstract concept of "nature" from its proper relation to and origin in God, then we can affirm deification through divine grace as a process that does not undermine our creatureliness.[34]

This is where Wesley's own picture of salvation is interesting. We might expect from his emphasis on co-operation, growth, and therapeutic concerns that he would sympathize with a more Eastern perspective

---

30. J. Wesley, *Works*, 13:146–47.
31. Maddox, *Responsible Grace*, 86.
32. Maddox, *Responsible Grace*, 91.
33. J. Wesley, *Works*, 3:202.
34. Burdett and Lorrimar, "Creatures Bound for Glory," 253.

on salvation—salvation as *theosis* perhaps. Maddox notes the surprising finding that Wesley construes salvation mainly within a Western formulation of forensic justification and atonement for sin.[35]

What if we broaden out this view of salvation? With respect to the role that technology might occupy in our co-operation, and our working out our own salvation, Ron Cole-Turner asks "Is this simply a case of Christians needing to update their repertoire of the modalities of grace?"[36] For, even in our own attempts to enhance ourselves, God remains the agent of transformation; these endeavors are only enabled by grace. For Christians, the only objective can be "to transform the person in the direction of the new creation in Jesus Christ."[37] While Cole-Turner is open to the use of human enhancement technologies as a part of this transformation, his enthusiasm is not unqualified. "A new self through prayer is not the same as a new self through technology."[38] Religious means of self-modification and technological means can complement each other,[39] however, technology must not be established as a rival god.[40]

Moving away from the topic of salvation, we might also look to Wesley's sermon "The Use of Money" for general guidance. With respect to wealth, Wesley summarizes the appropriate Christian attitude toward money by arguing that we should (1) gain all we can, (2) without causing harm to ourselves or our neighbors, in mind, body, or soul, (3) ensure we do not throw away what we have gained, and (4) use the wealth we gain to do good (i.e., we should not indulge our own wants while the needs of others remain unmet).[41] If this kind of logic were to be applied to human enhancement technologies (acknowledging that this is taking Wesley's thoughts on money far beyond their original context),[42] then there may

---

35. Maddox, *Responsible Grace*, 96.
36. Cole-Turner, "Introduction," 9.
37. Cole-Turner, "Introduction," 10.
38. Cole-Turner, "Biotechnology and the Religion-Science," 941.
39. Cole-Turner, "Biotechnology and the Religion-Science," 941.
40. Cole-Turner, "Biotechnology and the Religion-Science," 941; Cole-Turner, *The New Genesis*, 51.
41. J. Wesley, *Works*, 2:266–85.
42. Given Wesley's general interest in technology, and his fascination with the "curious machine" that is the human body (J. Wesley, *Works*, 4:20), however, it is perhaps not unreasonable to bring his thought to bear on contemporary human enhancement concerns.

be a place for such technologies, though in a very different vision of the human future than that advocated by transhumanists. One of the major criticisms of transhumanist ideology is the likelihood that it will only exacerbate existing inequality, as the elite few are better positioned to access new and expensive technologies.[43]

Indeed, the proper end of any kind of human activity, according to another of Wesley's sermons, "What is Man?" is "to know, love, and serve his great Creator."[44] Resonating with his notion of Christian perfection, and again at odds with most transhumanist impulses, is his injunction that "You were not created to please your senses, to gratify your imagination, to gain money, or the praise of men; to seek happiness in any created good, in anything under the sun."[45]

So, we certainly cannot use Wesleyan thought to advocate for human technological enhancement, but neither does it rule out our applying such technologies as circumstances may warrant. We are not playing God when we use technology to improve our human condition (even when our own capacities become the object of improvement), rather by grace we are allowed to co-operate in God's ongoing work of creation and redemption. It may be for us to "work out our own salvation," but we are to do it with "fear and trembling,"[46] not the triumphant no-holds-barred attitude of the transhumanist.

Wesley's emphasis on Christian perfection is freeing in some respects—unlike secular humanists (and some Christian conservatives), human limitations are not protected as the exclusive realm of human flourishing. But neither are we dependent on becoming something other than we are now in order to flourish. We are *creatures bound for glory*, and God's grace enables us to flourish at all points along that trajectory.[47] By assigning God and grace as the proper agent of the future glory we anticipate, we also shift the final responsibility of engineering such a future away from us, as transhumanists would have it. Biotechnological enhancements take their fitting place; they are neither categorically prohibited nor imperative. Like other applications of technology, they

---

43. Tom Shakespeare, in foreword to Eilers et al., *Human Enhancement Debate and Disability*.
44. J. Wesley, *Works*, 4:26.
45. J. Wesley, *Works*, 4:26.
46. J. Wesley, *Works*, 3:202.
47. Burdett and Lorrimar, "Creatures Bound for Glory," 253.

become the subject of ongoing ethical deliberation.[48] Whether technology might assist in cultivating the kind of holiness Wesley envisions is a separate question, but one that is open for exploration rather than answered at the outset.

This is not to say that Wesleyanism is the only Christian tradition with the resources to draw on in properly locating human technological enhancement. Certainly Wesley is an asset for Christians thinking through enhancement questions for another reason though—he exemplifies the "pastor theologian" approach, eschewing the heady inaccessibility that often characterizes academic work in favor of the more practical formats of liturgies, sermons, catechisms, etc.[49] Given that prospective enhancement technologies are provocative and confronting for lay Christians, we might learn from the pastoral approach to theology modeled by Wesley. At the very least, a Wesleyan account of flourishing encompasses both the secular humanist respect for creaturely finitude and the transhumanist drive to bring about transformation, and goes further than either a fearful Christian response to technological innovation or a wholehearted embrace of technological "redemption."[50]

Bibliography

Barazzetti, Gaia, and Massimo Reichlin. "Life Extension and Personal Identity." In *Enhancing Human Capacities*, edited by Julian Savulescu et al., 398–409. Chichester: Wiley-Blackwell, 2011.

Bostrom, Nick. "The Transhumanist FAQ: A General Introduction (Version 2.1)." World Transhumanist Association, 2003. http://www.nickbostrom.com/views/transhumanist.pdf.

Bostrom, Nick, and Michael Depaul. "Transhumanist Values." *Journal of Philosophical Research* 30 (2005) 3–14.

Burdett, Michael, and Victoria Lorrimar. "Creatures Bound for Glory: Biotechnological Enhancement and Visions of Human Flourishing." *Studies in Christian Ethics* 32.2 (2019) 241–53.

Cole-Turner, Ronald. "Biotechnology and the Religion-Science Discussion." In *The Oxford Handbook of Religion and Science*, edited by Philip Clayton, 929–44. Oxford: Oxford University Press, 2008.

———. "Introduction: The Transhumanist Challenge." In *Transhumanism and Transcendence: Christian Hope in an Age of Technological Enhancement*, edited by Ronald Cole-Turner, 1–18. Washington, DC: Georgetown University Press, 2011.

---

48. Lorrimar, "Human Flourishing," 561.

49. Maddox, *Responsible Grace*, 17.

50. The need for a more imaginative approach to apologetics is outlined in Davison, *Imaginative Apologetics*.

———. *The New Genesis: Theology and the Genetic Revolution*. Louisville: Westminster John Knox, 1993.

Davison, Andrew, ed. *Imaginative Apologetics: Theology, Philosophy and the Catholic Tradition*. London: SCM, 2011.

Eilers, Miriam, et al., eds. *The Human Enhancement Debate and Disability: New Bodies for a Better Life*. Basingstoke: Palgrave Macmillan, 2014.

Fukuyama, Francis. *Our Posthuman Future: Consequences of the Biotechnology Revolution*. New York: Farrar, Straus & Giroux, 2002.

Grey, Aubrey de, et al. "Time to Talk SENS: Critiquing the Immutability of Human Aging." *Annals of the New York Academy of Sciences* 959 (2002) 452–62.

Hefner, Philip. "The Animal That Aspires to Be an Angel: The Challenge of Transhumanism." *Dialog* 48.2 (2009) 158–67.

Hughes, James. "The Big Questions: What Comes After Homo Sapiens?" *New Scientist*, November 15, 2006. https://www.newscientist.com/article/mg19225780-076-the-big-questions-what-comes-after-homo-sapiens/.

Kass, Leon. "Ageless Bodies, Happy Souls: Biotechnology and the Pursuit of Perfection." *The New Atlantis* 1 (2003) 9–28.

———. "L'Chaim and its Limits: Why Not Immortality?" *First Things* 113 (2001) 17–24.

———. "Reflections on Public Bioethics: A View from the Trenches." *Kennedy Institute of Ethics Journal* 15.3 (2005) 221–50.

Lorrimar, Victoria. "Human Flourishing, Joy, and the Prospect of Radical Life Extension." *The Expository Times* 129.12 (2018) 554–61.

Maddox, Randy. *Responsible Grace: John Wesley's Practical Theology*. Nashville: Kingswood, 1994.

Moravec, Hans. *Mind Children: The Future of Robot and Human Intelligence*. Cambridge: Harvard University Press, 1988.

Pearce, David. "The Abolitionist Project." http://www.abolitionist.com/.

Persson, Ingmar, and Julian Savulescu. "The Perils of Cognitive Enhancement and the Urgent Imperative to Enhance the Moral Character of Humanity." *Journal of Applied Philosophy* 25.3 (2008) 162–77.

———. *Unfit for the Future: The Need for Moral Enhancement*. Oxford: Oxford University Press, 2012.

———. "Unfit for the Future? Human Nature, Scientific Progress, and the Need for Moral Enhancement." In *Enhancing Human Capacities*, edited by Julian Savulescu et al., 486–98. Chichester: Wiley-Blackwell, 2011.

Sandel, Michael. *The Case Against Perfection: Ethics in the Age of Genetic Engineering*. Cambridge: Belknap, 2007.

Stock, Gregory. *Redesigning Humans: Choosing Our Children's Genes*. London: Profile, 2002.

Temkin, Larry. "Is Living Longer Living Better?" In *Enhancing Human Capacities*, edited by Julian Savulescu et al., 350–67. Chichester: Wiley-Blackwell, 2011.

Wesley, John. *The Works of John Wesley: Volume 2: Sermons II, 34–70*. Edited by Albert C. Outler. Nashville: Abingdon, 1985.

———. *The Works of John Wesley: Volume 3: Sermons III, 71–114*. Edited by Albert C. Outler. Nashville: Abingdon, 1986.

———. *The Works of John Wesley: Volume 4: Sermons IV, 115–151*. Edited by Albert C. Outler. Nashville: Abingdon, 1987.

———. *The Works of John Wesley: Volume 13: Doctrinal and Controversial Treatises II*. Edited by Paul Wesley Chilcote and Kenneth J. Collins. Nashville: Abingdon, 2013.

7

Healing our Intellectual Ambivalence

The Salvation Army and the Challenge of Higher Education in the New Millennium

Dean G. Smith

Introduction

AT A TIME OF rapid and unprecedented social and cultural change, the Church needs to draw upon her full intellectual capital to tackle the significant challenges facing her. In negotiating the new millennium the Salvation Army faces considerable headwinds due to the fact that not only does the movement face the challenges of our time, but it also faces the even greater challenge of addressing its own ambivalence to the life of the mind in general and higher education in particular.[1] I say an even greater challenge here because without addressing the problem of ambivalence the movement cannot hope to adequately address the challenges

1. With the development and funding of research universities and other independent institutions and centers on a growth trajectory around the world, it is not difficult to make a case for the importance of research and higher learning to governments around the world. Yet the number of such institutions across the Salvation Army world is no more than one or two at best.

facing it. The problem is pressing given that our ambivalence has left us significantly weakened intellectually and vulnerable to redundant thinking—doing "today's job with yesterday's tools, with yesterday's concepts."[2]

In order for the Salvation Army to achieve its full potential in the twenty-first century, there is an urgent need to understand and overcome this ambivalence and to fully embrace a culture of higher learning.[3] The implications of such a shift in attitude and focus would then lead to a shift in practice.[4] The movement would finally follow through on William Booth's dream of a University of humanity with the establishment and further development of institutions of higher learning with capacity not only in teaching but also in higher research.[5]

What I will be arguing in this paper is that nothing less than a radical reorientation in the movement's theology and practice will bring us to a point where we will finally overcome our ambivalence and be in a position to use all the intellectual and theological resources at our disposal in addressing the challenges of our day. Our relevance and effectiveness depend on it. Here the emphasis on the importance of theology to the vitality of the movement cannot be overstated. And perhaps the fact that this is not more broadly recognized within our movement[6] reinforces the very point I am making.

My case for a theological reorientation leading to a shift in outlook and practice, as the appropriate response to the problem of ambivalence, will be set out in the following steps. I will begin by highlighting the importance of intellectual engagement by the Church and emphasizing the dangers attending any failure to draw upon her full intellectual capital to tackle the significant challenges facing her. I will then test my claim of ambivalence with specific reference to the Salvation Army by considering the conclusions coming out of the most recent writing of leaders and academics on the topic of higher education. I will then offer what I

---

2. McLuhan and Fiore, *The Medium is the Massage*, 8.

3. My argument is focused on higher education broadly understood. However, theological higher education must take some precedence given that it our theological "big ideas" that give shape to our values, our way of seeing the world. It is these values that should then frame all of our Intellectual and higher education endeavors.

4. This is more of a reorientation than a shift given the movement's Wesleyan heritage.

5. The Salvation Army is poorly placed in the area of higher research.

6. The fact that there are few if any Secretaries of Education on senior Salvation Army boards aids my point.

believe to be the best explanation for the Salvation Army's ambivalence to the life of the mind and higher education by addressing the problem at the conceptual level—by considering the big ideas that continue to shape the Salvation Army's corporate mindset. Next, I will outline some of the costs to our movement of our ambivalence. I will then go on to offer a response to the problem being addressed that is nothing less than a call for reorientation to our Wesleyan theological heritage. Finally, I will offer some practical suggestions that follow from my analysis and critique.

The Importance of Intellectual Engagement

Throughout its history the Church has proved more than capable of addressing the challenges of the day by drawing upon her intellectual capital. When the gospel needed to be proclaimed beyond the bounds of Judaism, it was a philosophically astute Paul who was able to help with the transplanting of the gospel into Greek soil. When Gnosticism and persecution proved serious threats to the early Church, theologians like Irenaeus and Justin Martyr found the best form of defense in intellectual attach. These early apologists met these challenges head on and used all the learning at their disposal to both understand and address the threats being posed. During the sixteenth century the reformers Martin Luther and John Calvin addressed the Church's parlous moral and educational state with all the intellectual tools at their disposal.

However, along with these more positive examples of the Church drawing upon her intellectual capital to address the challenges facing her, in more recent times there have been some more sobering results. The failure to seriously engage the challenges of Modernity has left the Church weakened as it has grappled to respond to a secular age.[7] And this is especially true of the Anglo-American Evangelical traditions. With the twentieth century ushering in a period of cultural and social change like no other, Anglo-American Evangelicals were in the position of having little influence upon social, political and cultural life except over a very narrow and shallow field of thinking.[8] During this time Evangelicals spent a great deal of time and energy fighting internal battles over questions to do with biblical authority and Salvationists engaged in often

---

7. For a comprehensive account on the history of the secularization of Western cultural and social orders see Taylor, *A Secular Age*.

8. Noll, *Scandal of the Evangelical Mind*, 4–5.

unhelpful debates over the doctrine of sanctification. All the while we were becoming increasingly disengaged from the pressing issues of the time. In light of these examples both positive and negative it is difficult to imagine how an attitude of ambivalence towards the life of the mind and to higher education could do anything other than severely limit the Salvation Army's ability to adequately address the challenges facing it and achieve its missional objectives. It is to this question of ambivalence that I now turn.

The Salvation Army and the Problem of Ambivalence

In reflecting on the significance of the new Millennium for The Salvation Army, Roger Green in the May 1999 edition of *Word and Deed* outlines a way forward for a Salvationist Theology. In that article, he begins by making a positive statement in relation to the movement's theological moment in history. To back up his claim he identifies six signs from that provide a way of facing our history and orienting the Salvation Army's theological development into the future.[9] He rejects the notion that our founders had little interest in theology maintaining that, "both William and Catherine Booth were people of profound theological insights and convictions."[10] However, he does acknowledge that in more recent times we have been negligent in our educational endeavors at local, national, and international levels. Then in a guest editorial to the May 2005 edition of *Word and Deed*, devoted in part to a discussion on The Salvation Army and higher education, the then General John Larsson opens the discussion by challenging the theory/practice binary. He makes the claim that "it is high time to discard forever the false presupposition that has dogged us as an Army that higher education and action are opposites."[11] He then goes on to highlight the founder's vision for a University of Humanity to back up his claim.

Donald Burke then challenges these largely positive sentiments about the Army's theological trajectory in the May 2005 edition of Word

9. The six signs are: (1) The Publication of Salvation Story; (2) The Publication of Word and Deed; (3) The establishment of the International Spiritual Life Commission; (4) The Publication of the Officer Magazine; (5) The establishment of Booth University College; and (6) The burgeoning work of Army and non-army scholars over recent times.
10. Green, "Facing History," 23–39.
11. Larsson, "Wanted," 5.

and Deed where he highlights the Salvation Army's ambivalence to the life of the mind by reappropriating Mark Noll's famous line declaring that, "[t]he scandal of the Salvationist mind is that there is not much of a Salvationist mind."[12] In that same edition Jonathan Raymond acknowledges that although the Salvation Army is active in providing primary, secondary and special or technical education globally, in respect of higher education, "the Salvation Army occupies a very humble place at the table of higher education." He also acknowledges that "to say "Salvation Army higher education" may sound to some like an oxymoron."[13]

Now while on the face of it these views seem contradictory, perhaps both are, to some degree at least, historically true. Green's claim that the Booth's positive attitude to matters theological seems relatively uncontroversial in light of the fact that the Wesley's desire to unite knowledge and vital piety flowed through to the Booths who were formed within the Wesleyan Methodist tradition. However, It also seems to be the case that somewhere along the line the Salvation Army diverted from this intentional approach to unite knowledge and vital piety and instead gave way to other overriding influences that would set the movement on a course that would disjoin the pair, and our movement would throughout much of the twentieth century embody a stance of ambivalence towards the life of the mind and higher education in particular.

An Attempt at the Best Explanation for Our Ambivalence

What I will do now is set out what I believe to be the best explanation for our ambivalence to the life of the mind and to higher education in particular. My approach is to tackle the problem of ambivalence at the conceptual level, the level of big ideas, both theological and philosophical, that continue to shape the Salvation Army's theological mindset. These, according to E. F. Schumacher,[14] are the ideas with which we think, "they are the very instruments through which we look at, interpret and experience the world."[15] They are the beliefs beyond testing and assumptions that ground a paradigm or worldview and shape particular habits of

---

12. Burke, "The Scandal of the Salvationist Mind," 41.
13. Raymond, "The Salvation Army and Higher Education," 11.
14. Schumacher, *Small is Beautiful*, 63–64.
15. Schumacher, *Small is Beautiful*, 63–64.

mind.¹⁶ And it is at this level that we need to go to uncover the reasons for our ambivalence. Without understanding and critiquing these big ideas, these assumptions, all we end up doing is attempt to solve the problems we have created with the same theologizing and church practices that have created them in the first place.[17]

In setting out my explanation, I will draw on the work of Richard Tarnas as outlined in his book *The Passion of the Western Mind* where he explores the development of ideas in the West. In this historical narrative Tarnas clearly acknowledges the significant influence that Christian ideas have had on the Western mindset. What is relevant to my argument relates to his claim that there were from the beginning, contraries, two significant aspects or outlooks within the Christian vision or worldview. One outlook was "rapturously optimistic and all-embracing" and "its complement was sternly judgmental, restrictive and prone to a dualistic pessimism."[18] He readily acknowledges that at first impression such is the difference in outlook that one might be tempted to conclude that these are in fact two entirely distinct world views coexisting and overlapping within Christianity.[19] According to Tarnas, however, "the two outlooks were inextricably united, two sides of the same coin, light and shadow."[20]

And we can see throughout Western Christian history that there have been significant attempts by theologians, with varying degrees of success, at holding together the exultant and dualistic outlooks. These theologians include Augustine, Aquinas, and what is significant for our own tradition, John Wesley. Yet even the Wesleyan synthesis, that sought to bridge the two outlooks and that framed the Salvation Army's early theology, would not be able to hold out against significant historical influences that would ultimately lead the Salvation Army to fully embrace the dualistic and pessimistic outlook with devastating consequences for the life of the mind and higher education.

If, as Tarnas argues, the two contraries within Christianity are in fact united, two sides of the same coin, light and shadow, then any disjoining

---

16. Worldview here, like the term paradigm, refers to a conceptual scheme or framework, an overarching set of beliefs that orient a particular culture. Mindsets or Habits of mind, on the other hand, are subsets of an overarching worldview or paradigm.

17. Calian, *Survival or Revival*, 132.

18. Tarnas, *Passion of the Western Mind*, 120.

19. Tarnas, *Passion of the Western Mind*, 120.

20. Tarnas, *Passion of the Western Mind*, 120.

of the pair can only result in an incomplete, one-sided view that is either exultant and optimistic or dualistic and pessimistic. Here is, I believe, the key to understanding the Salvation Army's ambivalence to the life of the mind and to higher education. During the twentieth century the Salvation Army would be influenced by a theological and cultural movement that would occasion the disjoining the two outlooks and fundamentally overturn the Wesleyan synthesis. The Salvation Army would embody the dualistic and pessimistic outlook in relation to the world and humanity and by implication, the life of the mind and higher education.

However, before exploring the influences upon, and implications of, the Salvation Army mindset during the twentieth century, I need to describe more fully the two outlooks or aspects referred to by Tarnas. The contraries as already indicated are exultant Christianity and dualistic Christianity. The exultant Christian vision is that which is most clearly discerned in the Christian contemplative and mystical tradition. According to Tarnas,

> The dominant insight expressed in this understanding was that in Christ the divine had entered the world, and that the redemption of humanity and nature was now already dawning. . . . The peculiar sense of cosmic joy and immense thanksgiving expressed in early Christianity seemed to derive from the belief that God, in a gratuitous overflow of love for his creation, had miraculously broken through the imprisonment of this world and poured forth his redeeming power into humanity. The divine essence had fully re-entered into materiality and history, initiating their radical transformation.

He then draws attention to the other outlook within the Christian vision,

> The other side of the Christian vision focused more emphatically on the present alienation of man and the world from God. It therefore stressed the futility and otherworldliness of redemption, the ontological finality of God's "otherness," the need for strict inhibition of worldly activities, a doctrinal orthodoxy defined by the institutional Church and a salvation narrowly limited to the small portion of mankind constituting the Church faithful. Underlying and consequent to these tenets was a pervasive negative judgement regarding the present status of the human soul and the created world, especially relative to the omnipotence and transcendent perfection of God.[21]

---

21. Tarnas, *Passion of the Western Mind*, 120–22.

It is this later dualistic outlook of the Christian vision that has prevailed in the West and in modern Anglo-American Evangelicalism in particular and has been a topic addressed quite comprehensively in recent times. In a paper published in 1990, Grace Jantzen argued that western theological discourse had for the most part been stuck supporting a destructive binary logic that sets God over against the world, the sacred over the secular, the soul over against the body, and the spiritual over against the material.[22] To emphasize the ubiquity of this dualistic way of thinking M. James Sawyer, in his book *A World Split Apart*, argues that "we in the twenty-first century are so immersed in [this] dualistic thinking that we do not even recognize its pervasive influence; it is 'just the way things are.'"[23]

But how did this dualistic tendency come about? In *The Passion of the Western Mind*, Tarnas comprehensively traces this outlook within Western Christianity. However, for my purposes a brief summary will suffice.

When Christianity moved away from its Hebraic roots and into the Greco-Roman world the holistic exultant vision was largely lost, and a dualistic metaphysic and cosmology became the norm. In respect of the human person the dualism can be discerned in the distinction between what belongs to the material world and what belongs to the world of spirit or the divine realm. In the West, dualism reasserted itself in a dominant interpretation of the work of Augustine.[24] "In his wake Western Christianity became one-sidedly oriented towards the spiritual, while the material order was viewed as temporary and secondary at best, if not outright evil."[25] This dualism, according to Sawyer, had severe consequences for both theology and piety. "It denied the importance of the created world and placed Christian hope in a spiritual heaven after death rather than a bodily resurrection."[26] In the high middle ages Thomas Aquinas developed a synthesis between Aristotelian philosophy and the revealed truths of Christianity and while his synthesis partially rescued the tradition

---

22. Jantzen, *Healing our Brokenness*, 131–41.

23. Sawyer, *A World Split Apart*, loc. 52.

24. I acknowledge that there is some contention about whether Augustine was to blame for this or those who followed in the tradition.

25. Sawyer, *A World Split Apart*, loc. 238.

26. Sawyer, *A World Split Apart*, loc. 252.

from Augustinian otherworldliness, his own view was characterized by another dualism—that between natural and supernatural knowledge.[27]

In looking to Augustine, the Reformers would reinforce the ontologically dualistic Judeo-Christian view.[28] In restoring a predominantly biblical theology against the Scholastic theology that was rejected by the reformers, the modern mind was purged of any exultant notion of nature being permeated with divine rationality.[29] The distinction between nature and grace, nature and the supernatural, matter and spirit, God and the world, would be drawn even more starkly than ever. The exultant view which acknowledged the ubiquity of Godly wisdom (see Prov 8:1–2) and grace would now become the minority view within Protestantism. This world was characterized not so much as the creation of a good God, as having fallen under the domination of Satan. Even the soul was contaminated to the point that it was not free to share in the divine life. There was now an unbridgeable gulf between the divine life and the created and human life that was now completely devoid of grace, goodness, and wisdom. It would only be by supernatural means that God and creation could be reconciled. For a significant number there would be no grace, no light to be had, because they were not included in the company of the redeemed. For those who belonged to the company of the redeemed the possibility of a spiritual life came only because the spirit of God deigned to breathe new life into a dead soul. For the reformers it was by faith and not by reason or any other faculty that a person could be saved. And the source of that saving faith was the Holy Scripture and the Spirit of God. It would be the words of Paul in 1 Corinthians 1:25 and 3:19, and not the words of Proverbs and Ecclesiastes, that would inform the pessimistic and dualistic Protestant Evangelical worldview.

In the post-Reformation period, the cosmological dualism of Newton and the epistemological dualism of Descartes and Kant would uphold the distinctions between God and the world and spirit and matter. In the case of modern science, reality would be reduced to the material side of the binary, while Anglo-American Evangelical Christianity, for the most part, reduced reality to the spiritual side of the binary. The end result would be a secular age and a disenchanted universe.[30]

---

27. Sawyer, *A World Split Apart*, loc. 301.
28. Tarnas, *Passion of the Western Mind*, 238.
29. Tarnas, *Passion of the Western Mind*, 241.
30. Taylor, *A Secular Age*.

Here in summary is a historical sketch of the dominance of the dualistic perspective in Western Christendom. But what about the specifics related to our own Salvation Army tradition? What influences have led to the disruption of the Wesleyan synthesis, to the disjoining of two outlooks in the twentieth century and the embodiment of the dualistic and pessimistic outlook? Further, how have these influences, how has this disruption to the Wesleyan synthesis, reinforced the attitude of ambivalence to the life of the mind and higher education?

Before proceeding further, however, I need to explain what I mean by the Wesleyan synthesis. We have considered the contraries within Christianity, the exultant and optimistic outlook, and the dualistic and pessimistic outlook. But how exactly does Wesley's approach differ from that taken by many in the Western Christian tradition who have embodied the dualistic and pessimistic outlook? What we see in the thought of John Wesley is an attempt to unite the contraries together in a synthesis. This synthesis attempted to bridge the gulf between grace and nature, spirit, and matter. The Reformer's emphasis on the doctrine of total depravity was moderated in Wesley by way of the doctrine of prevenient grace. While Wesley accepted the doctrine of total depravity it would remain for him and Wesleyans generally an abstract concept. Because of the universality of prevenient grace there was nobody who could be described as dead in their trespasses and sins. From the moment of our conception prevenient grace was active in restoring our spiritual faculties to the point where we could experience the lure of God. This "theological realism" both upholds the effects of sin and the universality of grace. And yet this outlook is most definitely slanted towards an optimistic view of the human person and the created order.

The conceptual worlds of spirit and matter were also bridged by upholding both the work of the Spirit and the sacramental implications of the Incarnation in the life of holiness. Now there have always been tendencies within Western Christianity to value more highly the spiritual over the material. Both Gnostic and Docetic tendencies have a long history within Christianity. But Wesley understood only too well that with the doctrine of the Incarnation as central to the Christian faith, material reality could be the means of grace. The importance he gave to the practice of the sacraments only confirms his desire to hold together the contraries within Christianity.

I need to return now to considering the influences that have led to the disruption of the Wesleyan synthesis and how these have set us on the path of ambivalence to the life of the mind and higher education. My approach here is to consider our own history as part of a broader movement. Indeed, our own history cannot be understood apart from that of modern Evangelicalism. But given the highly contested nature of the term "evangelical," careful attention needs to be given to the history and changing meaning of the concept.

In his book *The Remaking of Evangelical Theology*, Gary Dorrien identifies three Evangelical paradigms in Evangelical history.[31] The first derives from the confessional and dissenting movements of the sixteenth century. This is what Weber calls "classical" evangelicalism. The second paradigm, pietistic evangelicalism, derives from the eighteenth-century German and English Pietistic movements and in the United States, Revivalism and the Great Awakening. The third paradigm, fundamentalist evangelicalism, derives from the nineteenth and twentieth centuries. What is of interest here is that while the Salvation Army was the product of the second paradigm—pietistic and revivalist evangelicalism—in the early twentieth century the Salvation Army along with many other Evangelical groups such as the Free Methodist Church, the Church of the Nazarene, and the Wesleyan (Methodist) Church would became aligned with the third paradigm as a result of being drawn into the modernist-fundamentalist controversy.[32]

It is in fact the influences of pietism, revivalism and fundamentalism that characterize the type of evangelicalism that has shaped the Salvation Army in the twentieth century and that has led to our present hiatus in respect to the life of the mind and higher education. Clearly the pietistic influences cannot, by themselves, account for the Salvation Army's attitude of ambivalence. After all, John Wesley was thoroughly committed to learning and the revivalist preacher Jonathan Edwards is recognized as being a significant American philosopher. However, there were within pietism and revivalism the dualistic tendencies that when brought together with fundamentalist influences in the early twentieth century made for a perfect storm in relation to attitudes toward the life of the mind and higher education. It is to the influence of fundamentalism in the twentieth century that I will now turn.

According to Mark Noll, the three broad theological emphases that provided energy to the fundamentalist movement during the twentieth

---

31. Dorrien, *Remaking of Evangelical Theology*, 2.
32. Dorrien, *Remaking of Evangelical Theology*, 164.

century were Holiness (or "higher life" or "Keswick") spirituality, Pentecostalism, and premillennial dispensationalism.[33] Now while Noll acknowledges that these movements were never entirely aligned, "together these movements shared a stress on the dangers of the world, the comforts of separated piety the centrality of evangelism, and an expectation of the end."[34] What is not in doubt, and what is particularly relevant to my case, is that, according to Noll, "the fundamentalist era remains critical for evangelical thinking, since it so thoroughly established habits of mind for looking (or not looking) at the world."[35]

But how did the influence of fundamentalism contribute to the disjoining of the two outlooks within Christianity and ultimately to the reinforcement of the attitude of ambivalence to the life of mind and higher education? One answer to this question is to point out the general pessimism of the dualistic strand within the Christian outlook and Anglo-American Evangelicalism in particular. While the optimistic and exultant strand focuses on the goodness of creation, the universality of grace and the already begun transformation of the cosmos, the pessimistic strand emphasizes the fall and the ultimate difference between nature and grace, the world of light and the world of darkness, the world of spirit and the world of matter, Godly wisdom and the wisdom of this world.

This pessimistic dualism gives little credence to the human capacity for the intellectual penetration of the world's meaning or ability of the material world to mediate truth. Instead the "spiritual" among us must rely totally on supernatural and unmediated means to knowledge, namely Word and Spirit. According to David Gushee, "if evangelicals are best identified as essentially a massively successful rebranding effort of old-school fundamentalism, the starting point from which the modern evangelical community emerged was obscurantist and provincial, routinely anti-intellectual, antiscience, and antimodern."[36]

The Cost of Our Ambivalence

One of the significant costs of our ambivalence has been our inability to engage meaningfully with the broader culture. We have neither had the

---

33. Noll, *Scandal of the Evangelical Mind*, 115.
34. Noll, *Scandal of the Evangelical Mind*, 120.
35. Noll, *Scandal of the Evangelical Mind*, 122.
36. Gushee, *Following Jesus Out*, 119.

inclination or the tools to do so. In a paper that I delivered at the Nazarene Theological College in Brisbane entitled *Revisiting Christ and Culture*, I identified the Christ against culture position as the one that Evangelicals have tended to hold throughout the twentieth century, and the one most familiar to me as a young person growing up in the Salvation Army in the 1970s. Now there are dangers in making normative claims based on one's experience, and I recognize that my risk is heightened by the fact that I write from my very specific Australian context for an international audience. However, I believe there is sufficient evidence that many Salvationists growing up in the Western world during this time period would relate to my experience.

The best way to sum up my experience looking back is that I lived in a cultural bubble. I had the sense that I lived in two worlds and that one of those worlds was in some significant respects not real. I picked up early that as Christians we were in a battle for our souls, that the world was not our home, and that the role of the Church was to win back the world for Jesus in readiness for our leaving this world for our real home in heaven. I remember clearly singing the chorus of a song with the words, "O I'm climbing up the golden stairs to glory."[37]

At the time that I was growing up, I did not have anything like the perspective that an adult develops over time. But now, as I look back, I can see that significant historical events were shaping the twentieth century and our country along with other Western nations. The Vietnam war impacted our country, we had entered an atomic age, a cultural revolution was well under way with rock and roll music defiantly seeking to usher in a new world. Traditional sexual morays were being challenged, gender equality was being raised as an issue, and the environmental movement was becoming politically active. And yet what is my memory of these monumental changes? At the time I had no sense of the significance of these cultural movements and the significance of the cultural shift that was taking place. I cannot remember a sermon grappling with the ethics of war or the implications of the Cultural Revolution with counter-cultural children challenging the traditional materialistic values of their parents. Any reference to the young protestors of the time, "hippies" as they came to be known, was normally derogatory.

What I do remember are the many sermons that focused on the life of the soul. Getting saved, keeping saved, and getting others saved

---

37. Booth, "Climbing up the Golden Stair."

was the focus. This evangelical call to be saved was often done within a warm and pastoral setting with people genuinely wanting the best for us. On the other hand, I also remember attending a youth group event and watching the film "The Late Great Planet Earth," which I can only think was designed to literally scare the hell out of us as we considered our eternal destiny. I remember that there was a lot of talk about living the Holy life and that if I really wanted it, I could know the experience of entire sanctification. To my teenage mind such an experience would ultimately bring a peace to the war that was going on within me. A war that I now realize had as much to do with the physical and psychological changes happening in a developing teenager's body as with the state of my soul. I attended youth camps and experienced many "mountain top experiences" only to come screaming down to earth on the first or second day back of school. I also remember moving forward many times as I sought the blessing of a clean heart, again only to be disappointed soon after. The emphasis was on keeping ourselves pure and undefiled from the sin and corruption of the world.

My experience was of course not unique, but it is illustrative of a general tendency within some strands of Evangelicalism. In his biography, the Australian writer Tim Winton, interestingly born in the same year as me, expresses many of the same sentiments as he reflects on his own years of growing up in the 1970s, even though he was brought up in the Baptist Church and on the opposite side of the continent. He makes this telling comment about his Church's inability to meet the intellectual challenges of the day.

> Our pietist theology sprang from a simpler, more static world. Our thinking was cautious and faithful but hopelessly flatfooted. Confronted with the upheavals of the time it was quickly exposed as insufficient.[38]

Another significant cost to the Salvation Army is related to the important matter of maturity in the faith. If we take Fowler's stages of faith as a theoretical framework for understanding faith development, I would hesitantly suggest that our movement is in danger of being stuck in theological adolescence. According Fowler, as we grow in our faith we pass through various stages of development. One of the crucial stages happens when we move from stage 3 (Synthetic-Conventional faith) to stage 4

---

38. Winton, *The Boy Behind the Curtain*, 111.

(Individuative-Reflective faith). And so, it is to Fowler's own description of these stages and the events that precipitate them that I now turn.

Stage 3 typically has it rise and ascendency in adolescence, but for many adults it becomes a permanent place of equilibrium.[39]

> During this stage youths develop attachments to beliefs, values, and elements of personal style that link them in conforming relations with the most significant others among their peers, family and other adults. Identity, beliefs and values are strongly felt, even when they contain contradictory elements. However, they tend to be espoused in tacit rather than explicit formulations. At this stage, one's ideology or worldview is lived and asserted; it is not yet a matter of critical and reflective articulation.[40]

Stage 4 most appropriately takes form in young adulthood but for a significant group it emerges only in the mid-thirties or forties.[41] According to Fowler,

> for this stage to emerge, two important movements must occur, together or in sequence. First, the previous stage's tacit system of beliefs, values and commitments must be critically examined. . . . Evocative symbols and stories by which lives have been oriented will now be critically weighed and interpreted. Second, the self, previously constituted and sustained by its roles and relationships, must struggle with the question of identity and worth apart from its previously defining connections. This means that persons must take into themselves much of the authority they previously invested in others for determining and sanctioning their goals and values.[42]

To summarize, in the transition from stage 3 to stage 4, individuals begin to look with critical awareness at their system of beliefs and values tacitly held. They begin to separate themselves out from the group that has up to this time provided a sense of identity and belonging. This is often a time of alienation and disembodying. If the conditions are not optimal, a person's faith development can be arrested.

Now there is no reason to suppose that the same conditions leading to arrested development in an individual might not also apply to a

---

39. Fowler, *Stages of Faith*, 172.
40. Fowler, *Faithful Change*, 61.
41. Fowler, *Stages of Faith*, 182.
42. Fowler, *Faithful Change*, 62.

corporate entity. The key to understanding the important transition from stage 3 to stage 4 is the role of critically examining one's beliefs during a time of dis-embedding in the context of a safe environment with appropriate mentors. I am not sure that critical examination of one's beliefs has ever been a normal expectation for Salvationists. One observer suggests, "that in the evangelical church we have a reaping-centred Christianity, but we don't know what to do with people as they mature in their Christian faith."[43]

Fowler's view of faith development certainly clashes with the traditional view of progress with holiness traditions like our own. Implicit in our movement's view of progress is the idea that once a person is sanctified, further growth and development should be in an ever upward and unbroken trajectory. Any major disruption to one's faith development of the sort identified by Fowler has often been interpreted as backsliding within our movement.

In Fowler's scheme the sometimes-monumental disruption to faith development that occurs between stage 3 and 4 is to be interpreted in a positive light rather than a negative one. The disruption that occurs is a sign of ongoing faith development and not dissolution of faith. What has often been read as backsliding is a person beginning to take responsibility for his or her own faith journey. It is sobering to consider how many faith seekers have left our ranks because of our failure to adequately engage with them as they have entered the critical stage of their faith journey. We have neither had the intellectual tools or the inclination to do so.

A Wesleyan Response

So far in this paper I have sought to make the connection between The Salvation Army's ambivalence towards the life of the mind in general and higher education in particular, and the failure of the Western Church in general to hold together the contraries within the Christian worldview. The resultant dualistic and pessimistic outlook has emphasized the ontological difference between God and the world, the divine over the human in Christ, revelation over reason, the sacred over the secular, the city of God over the city of man, and (unmediated) grace over (fallen) nature. The failure to uphold the contraries and balance this dualistic way of thinking with an exultant and optimistic emphasis has led Evangelicals

---

43. Jamieson, *A Churchless Faith*, 103.

generally and Salvationists in particular to emphasize revelation at the expense of reason, and with a deep ambivalence towards material and bodied life has taught a more direct, and simple way to God—the word and work of God given through the power of the spirit directly to our spirit with little intellectual effort required. In fact, we are encouraged to "let go and let God."[44]

What I believe is crucial to our movement overcoming its ambivalence to the life of the mind and to higher education is a radical theological reorientation to the Wesleyan worldview. The movement's dualistic and pessimistic focus has for too long now kept us from the resources that would heal the destructive dualisms that have dogged our theology, our cosmology and our anthropology and by implication, our praxis. Balancing the contraries and giving due emphasis to an exultant, optimistic, grace-enabled approach to life is much more possible in a Wesleyan framework and offers resources for overcoming our ambivalence to the life of the mind and in turn for us to more ably engage meaningfully and missionally with the challenges of a new Millennium.

In this section I will single out two important Wesleyan foci that have the potential to correct and transform our worldview and to heal our divided conceptual reality. These are the doctrines of Incarnation and the Human Person. I have found it particularly helpful to view these through the correcting prism of the Eastern Christian framework, a move not foreign to Wesley himself.[45]

First let me say something about the Eastern approach to anthropology—an approach that Wesley sought to integrate into his own theological understanding. The Eastern Church both in its exegesis and theology makes a distinction between the image and likeness of God as indicated in the Genesis account of the creation of humans. The West has tended not to make such a distinction. Eastern theologians acknowledge that the primary effect of sin was sickness and death entering the created order and impacting our likeness to God. What remains in spite of sin is the image of God in humans.

---

44. Interestingly, Martin Lloyd-Jones offers a critique of the Holiness movement's intellectual failures. Consider the following quote taken from Murray, *D. Martyn Lloyd-Jones*, 74: "You asked me to *diagnose* the reasons for the present weakness and I am doing it. . . . If you teach that sanctification consists of 'letting go' and letting the Holy Spirit *do all the work,* then don't blame me if you have no scholars!"

45. See Maddox, *Responsible Grace*.

The doctrine of total depravity, which is so much a part of our western theological understanding, is something rejected by the East. Nature is not something that can be depraved and the image of God in the human person can never be lost. Now as we have seen Wesley in his doctrine of prevenient grace sought to bridge the two traditions. While there is an acknowledgement of the damaging effects of sin there is also the recognition that God's prevenient grace becomes active in our lives from our conception so that at a very basic level the effects of sin are overcome and from that point frees our will so that we are no longer dead in our sins and cut off from God. By the grace of God our spiritual faculties are sufficiently restored so that we are able to respond to the gentle lure or wooing of God throughout our lives. The implications of this along with an emphasis on a deep view of the Incarnation are significant for any understanding of the role of reason and higher education.

The Eastern view of the Incarnation is also significant for a more holistic view of human life in general and the life of the mind in particular. Western Evangelical Christianity has tended to focus on the death and resurrection of Christ in its soteriology. The Eastern Church, on the other hand, has always maintained that the entire Christ-event is itself salvific. That is, the Incarnation is itself redemptive. And this is not only true for humans but for the entire creation. Paul reflects this more cosmic understanding of the Incarnation. Romans 8:22–23 says, "We know that the whole creation has been groaning in labor pains until now; and not only the creation, but we ourselves, who have the first fruits of the Spirit, groan inwardly while we wait for adoption, the redemption of our bodies." This same narrative of cosmic redemption brought to effect by the Incarnation follows on from the deep view of the creation where the Logos not only brings everything into being but also holds all things together. Colossians 1:15–16 says, "[The Son] is the image of the invisible God, the firstborn of all creation; for in him all things in heaven and on earth were created, things visible and invisible, whether thrones or dominions or rulers or powers—all things have been created through him and for him." This cosmic redemption that is even now under way includes all created reality including our intellect.

Within a Wesleyan framework, we can see that we are not incapable of reason but rather we participate in the reason, the Logos of God. Our embodied reason itself becomes a means of grace and rather than leading us astray can, with appropriate discernment, be trusted to inform a coherent and trustworthy view of things. Indeed, it is important that we give attention to the faculty of reason to meet the challenges of our time. This reason is not sectarian and limited to a particular privileged perspective but rather is embodied by all created reality bearing the image of God. Indeed, we would do well to attend to Proverbs 1:20–21, "Wisdom cries out in the street; in the squares she raises her voice. At the busiest corner she cries out; at the entrance of the city gates she speaks."

Some Practical Suggestions that Follow from My Analysis

In this final section I will offer some practical suggestions that follow from my above analysis. Firstly, given my claim that the Salvation Army's ambivalence to the life of the mind and higher education can be traced to the disruption of the Wesleyan synthesis and the failure to keep in balance the contraries within Christianity, it would seem reasonable to suggest that as a movement, we need a radical and constructive reorientation in our theology and practice to the Wesleyan worldview. We need to rediscover our theological roots and in particular the exultant and optimistic strand within our tradition. Dare I suggest that we need to develop a reoriented catechism that sets out clearly the Wesleyan distinctives for an international audience?

In terms of our theology this will mean a rebalancing of our approach to holiness to include a more profoundly Christological focus. I see this rebalancing as a both/and approach rather than an either/or one. We have an excellent study by David Rightmire on the pneumatological foundations of our holiness tradition,[46] and this has been a valuable contribution to our theological self-understanding. What is needed now is an accompanying study on the Christological/Incarnational foundations of our holiness tradition.[47] I have every reason to believe that this rebalancing would have particular implications for the way we view the life of the mind and higher education.

Finally, we will know that our theology and practice are in alignment and the problem of ambivalence to the life of the mind and to higher education is being seriously addressed when we see Secretaries for Education on our most senior Army boards, when more of our Colleges of Higher Education are engaged in original higher research as well as teaching. And we will know that the problem of ambivalence is being overcome

---

46. Rightmire, *A Study of Holiness Foundations*.
47. Smith, "The Sacramental Life," 189.

when more Officers, Soldiers, and Friends of the Salvation Army find a place to pursue their calling to be teachers and researchers in Army institutions of higher learning to the glory of God. Dare we imagine the day when William Booth's idea of a university of Humanity will be finally realized.

Conclusion

What can we conclude then about the Salvation Army and the challenge of higher education for a new millennium? We have seen that our ambivalence to theological higher education is an attitude that continues to plague our movement and is fundamentally a problem at the most basic theological and philosophical level. Our failure to uphold the Wesleyan synthesis has seen our movement, in concert with others, disjoin the contraries within Christianity, the result being the embodying of the dualistic and pessimistic outlook that gives little credence to human potential for achieving real knowledge of God and the world outside that received by way of special revelation. The unhelpful dualisms that have plagued Western Christianity have uniquely impacted Salvationists, and the emphasizing of pneumatology over Incarnation, revelation over reason, has led us to devalue the life of the mind and limited our ability to engage meaningfully and missionally with the broader culture.

Realignment with the Salvation Army's Wesleyan heritage offers a way to heal the destructive dualisms informing our worldview and our ambivalence to the life of the mind and higher education. After all, Wesleyans do not live in a world divided between light and darkness, the sacred and secular, spiritual and material. Just as we can never accept the idea that anyone is cut off from God because God's prevenient grace is universally active and effective, neither can we be ambivalent about the life of the mind and higher education in particular. If it is not just our souls being redeemed but our entire lived reality including our bodies, our minds and indeed the entire rational cosmos, then we better have a good reason for rejecting that which God calls good.

Bibliography

Booth, Emma. "Climbing up the Golden Stair." In *The Song Book of the Salvation Army*. London: Salvation Army, 1986. https://hymnary.org/text/o_my_heart_is_full_of_music_and_o_tucker#instances.

Burke, Donald E. "The Scandal of the Salvationist Mind." *Word and Deed* 7.2 (2005) 41–60.
Calian, Carnegie S. *Survival or Revival: Ten Keys to Church Vitality*. Louisville: Westminster John Knox, 1998.
Dorrien, Gary. *The Remaking of Evangelical Theology*. Louisville: Westminster John Knox, 1998.
Fowler, James W. *Faithful Change: The Personal and Public Challenges of Postmodern Life*. Nashville: Abingdon, 1996.
———. *Stages of Faith*. New York: HarperOne, 1981.
Green, Roger, J. "Facing History: Our Way Ahead for a Salvationist Theology." *Word and Deed* 1.2 (1999) 23–40.
Gushee, David, P. *Following Jesus Out of American Evangelicalism*. Louisville: Westminster John Knox, 2017.
Jamieson, Alan. *A Churchless Faith: Faith Journeys Beyond the Churches*. New Zealand: Garside, 2002.
Jantzen, Grace. "Healing Our Brokenness: The Spirit and Creation." *Ecumenical Review* 42 (1990) 131–41.
Larsson, John. "Wanted: Informed Men and Women of Action." *Word and Deed* 7.2 (2005) 5–7.
McLuhan, Marshall, and Quentin Fiore. *The Medium Is the Message: An Inventory of Effects*. London: Penguin, 1967.
Murray, Iain H. *D. Martyn Lloyd-Jones: The Fight of Faith, 1939–1981*. Edinburgh: Banner of Truth, 1990.
Noll, Mark, A. *The Scandal of the Evangelical Mind*. Grand Rapids: Eerdmans, 1995.
Raymond, Jonathan, S. "Salvation Army and Higher Education: The 2004 Andrew S. Miller Lecture." *Word and Deed* 7.2 (2005) 9–39.
Rightmire, R. David. *A Study of Holiness Foundations*. Alexandria, VA: Crest, 2016.
Sawyer, James, M. *A World Split Apart: Dualism in Western Culture and Theology*. Leandro, CA: Sacred Saga, 2014, Kindle Edition.
Schumacher, E. F. *Small is Beautiful*, London: Vintage, 2011.
Smith, Dean. "The Sacramental Life: Toward an Integrated Christian Vision." *Wesleyan Theological Journal* 50.2 (2015) 186–201.
Tarnas, Richard. *The Passion of the Western Mind*. New York: Ballantine, 1991.
Taylor, Charles. *A Secular Age*. Cambridge: Belknap, 2007.
Winton, Tim. *The Boy Behind the Curtain*. Australia: Penguin Random House, 2016.

8

Human Flourishing until Death

Living Well until the Very End

Kirsty Beilharz

Introduction

This chapter looks at the ways in which mindful processing of death's stages, ceremonies or faith-based rituals that facilitate interaction with friends and relatives, communion with God, and acknowledgement of the individual, is a community responsibility, which has been eroded in contemporary Western culture. This discussion also considers the science of dying (thanatology) and ways that meaning, dignity, and growth can be nurtured in the final hours and days of life in order to maintain the process of spiritual transformation until the very end.

What Does It Mean to Die Well?

This is a question often examined in the Palliative Care literature and it is a question that will be answered differently for different individuals, influenced by their personal wishes and the customs and assumptions of one's worldview, ethnic traditions, religious views, and other factors. Common end-of-life desires include the reconciliation of significant relationships, both with the transcendent and with significant family or others. People often want family or particular friends present, and not to die alone. People frequently cite "dignity" and lack of pain, which suggests the absence of physical and emotional suffering or embarrassing corporeal deterioration, a sense of acceptability and coherent memories implanted in bystanders, and again, dying without the loss of control. For some, the idea of legacy, of how they will be remembered, and giving and leaving something important behind for their loved ones is important, perhaps related to the concept of "living on" in the shape of memories, gifts, enabling, or worth beyond the somatic self, the dread of being forgotten, and the desire to remain present.

Associated with concerns about pain and suffering, some will say they wish to die quickly, not messily or protractedly, and furthermore may specify the environment in which they would like to die, whether it is a beautiful and significant setting, nostalgic place, or simply in a location considered comfortable and safe (which may translate to good medical care rather than home). Nonetheless, most Australians do say they would like to die at home, even when this can restrict adequate medical care or create a burden for family. Most of us would like to die at peace: a spiritual dimension of acceptance, satiety, *eudemonia* or fulfilment. Satisfaction can come from the reassurance of transcendent union or from having lived well (to the best of one's ability; and fully) making the most of opportunities, fulfilling the various facets of life that are important, of feeling that one's life was meaningful and purposeful. The antitheses of life lived well are feelings of futility and wasted opportunity. Faith, meaning, and peace are universally accepted descriptors of *spirituality*.

The Spirituality of the End of Life

According to Julie Lunn, "Charles Wesley understood sanctification as growth into maturity as a human being and resignation to God based on deep trust in God"[1]—and this ultimate surrender and giving over to God reaches its climax as a person approaches death. To take this away from someone then, through euthanasia (voluntary assisted dying) or sedation is to take away the final rite of passage. Wesley's theory was particular and slightly unorthodox in the belief that there is a stage of

---

1. Lunn, "Becoming Truly Human," 1. This section is reliant upon Lunn's evaluation and follows its basic order.

sanctification reserved for final conscious dying. His view has something in common with the Tibetan Book of Dying, the *Bardo Thödol*, insofar as lucidity and conscious dying are preferable for the smooth unagitated passing in the Tibetan Buddhist tradition, when it is believed that the soul experiences reincarnation, and that the manner of death can affect reincarnation.

Erik Erikson, on psychosocial development, articulates stages of life and alternate responses: at the stage of old age, a person may respond with integrity or despair. Erikson describes integrity as "a sense of *coherence* and *wholeness*" and the strength of wisdom.[2]

James Fowler, on *stages of faith* (which are closely modeled on Erikson) suggests that the final years are concerned with "transformation of present reality in the direction of a transcendent actuality."[3] Like Wesley, Fowler describes a phase of acquiescence and reconciliation. Whereas the earlier stages describe individuation: a person affirming identity independent from their inherited beliefs and behaviors; followed by questing and affirming or rejection of "birth," faith by their own investigation rather than untested familial beliefs; the final stage of faith starts to move away from the insular individual towards the transcendent and spiritual priority. Whilst Fowler's description of individuation and moving away from communal inherited beliefs and conformity of communal decision-making has been criticized for its ties to the generally Western worldview and assertion of autocracy, it still makes sense in view of the Christian redemption narrative aiming towards reconciliation and ultimate Eucharistic unity.

Elizabeth MacKinlay cites Cummings, who also describes ageing in terms of Eucharistic and kenotic emptying.[4] This emptying may consist of material divestment, withdrawal from social and family roles and responsibilities, coexistent with devotion, simplicity, and greater attention to spiritual life and preparation for the next stage. Possessions and authority diminish in importance to make way for God.

Writing of maturity and death, Westmoreland says that for the Wesleys, "Of the behaviours that seemed to denote spiritual maturity, one seemed very significant: the decision to submit to, trust in, rely on, or be

---

2. Erikson, *The Life Cycle Completed*, 65, emphasis original.
3. Fowler, *Stages of Faith*, 200.
4. MacKinlay, *The Spiritual Dimension of Ageing*, 21.

obedient to God."[5] Charles Wesley did not deny that sanctification was possible in this life, but wanting to obfuscate spiritual pride, became convinced that sanctification was a gift given by God a few moments before death. John Wesley maintained that sanctification could be *both* a process of gradual growth *and* instantaneous. According to Lunn, Charles Wesley experienced life-long sanctification, i.e., continuous transformation towards Christlikeness, through the filter of his own embodied suffering and illness, and his own pursuit of holiness. Lunn suggests, therefore, that suffering is requisite of Christian maturity in Charles' thinking.[6]

> Nature's high-mindedness
> How shall I lay aside?
> I cannot, Lord, myself abase,
> Myself divest of pride:
> But if thou speak the word,
> The word imparts the fear,
> And poor, and vile, and self-abhor'd
> I at thy feet appear.[7]

> This, this is all my heart's desire,
> When mercy doth my soul require,
> By Jesus found mature in grace,
> In full conformity divine
> My spotless spirit to resign,
> And see my Saviour face to face.[8]

Lunn notes that "in Wesley's day the verb 'to resign' or 'resignation' could convey the meanings it has today," seeing the definitions of "resigning the will, and resigning the whole being to God" as especially pertinent for Wesley.[9]

For centuries, the *ars moriendi* tradition held a prominent place in the life of believers. The *ars moriendi* (or "art of dying") was a body of literature that helped Christians prepare for death. Although practice of the *ars moriendi* was beginning to fade during Wesley's era, he discovered the riches of the tradition by reading Jeremy Taylor's book, *The Rule and*

---

5. Westmoreland, *Can Spiritual Maturity*, 202.

6. Lunn, "Becoming Truly Human." The importance of suffering for Charles Wesley's faith and theology has also been thoroughly documented by Cruickshank, *Pain, Passion, and Faith*.

7. C. Wesley, *Scripture Hymns* (1762) Vol. 2, 284.

8. C. Wesley, *Preparation for Death* (1772), 46.

9. Lunn, "Becoming Truly Human," 9.

Exercises of Holy Dying. Wesley's mediation of the art of dying was so successful that the early Methodists were known for their "good deaths." A physician who treated several Methodists made the claim to Charles Wesley, "Most people die for fear of dying: but I never met with such people as yours. They are none of them afraid of death; but calm, and patient, and resigned to the last."[10]

In death, material and physical securities are stripped away: "for Charles the resignation of things, people in death, the will, were means through which an attitude of resignation towards God of his whole being was formed."[11] For Charles Wesley, "[In] the end-experience of death . . . [it] may be that the greatest spiritual growth occurs as one struggles with physical losses and dying."[12] "The spiritual experience of resignation to God in death, which was so significant for the Wesleys, not only for those dying but also through their deathbed testimonies to faith for those left behind, is also one we have largely lost. In our culture death is *clinical*; the dying are frequently sedated against pain, but also at the cost of any significant spiritual experience at the point of death."[13]

By the bedside, approaching death is a time of prayerfulness, reconciliation, acquiescence, acceptance, peace, reflection, meditation, and forgiveness. It is a time of few or no words, of being, of presence. The experience will create a lasting memory for those present.

Confronting Death Constructively in a Culture of Denial

Despite the spiritual importance of death, we live in a culture of denial, death aversion. At first, given the seeming ubiquity of death themes in popular media, this may seem surprising. However, normalization and desensitization of criminal violence and death in pop culture such as TV, movies, novels, graphic novels, and video games come at the cost of genuine familiarity, empathy, and sacredness. Our generation has witnessed improvements of medical science and advances in life quality leading to greater longevity and health. Yet with greater longevity, also comes terminal age-related illnesses and suffering (e.g., in cancer and dementia). First-world modern cultures worldwide have lost ceremonies, rituals,

10. C. Wesley, *Journal*, 1:271.
11. Lunn, "Becoming Truly Human," 18.
12. Payne, "Spiritual Maturity," 37.
13. Lunn, "Becoming Truly Human," 16–17.

celebrations, and spiritual practices that: (a) help process death, and (b) engage the community in the family's pain, compared with times past when disease, famine, pestilence, plagues, mortality, and infant death were common place.

"Fulton and Owen[14] have observed that for members of the generation born after World War II, individuals who generally lack first-hand experience with death, the phenomenon of death and dying has become abstract and invisible."[15] Durkin suggests that Americans, like members of many other societies, "attach fearful meanings to death, dying, and the dead."[16] It can be seen that faiths and cultures that are more accepting and open about the reality of death, are also therefore better able to discuss rituals and traditions surrounding dying and its preparation. Sincere discussion of death is denied in contemporary Western culture, especially in the First World where so much currency is given to autonomy and control, materialism and attachment, life-prolonging and beauty-prolonging procedures, and technologies venturing towards immortality.[17]

It is normative to use euphemisms and metaphoric language to describe death. Handling of dead people most often occurs in segregated spaces by professionals (e.g., in hospitals, by paramedic staff, coronial agencies, and funeral services). People who live far from the land are seldom confronted by death, even of food (animals and livestock), much less of humans, whereas some societies have traditionally held a much closer and more frank relationship with mortality, caring for the dying, and ceremonial processing of the dead, which perhaps demystifies and modifies the fear and denial of death.

Concurrently, the death and dying of unfamiliar or fictitious people in entertainment media is ubiquitous in crime, forensic and criminal drama, horror genres, the Day of the Dead, Halloween, and Gothic pop culture. However, in these scenarios, people are detached, sanitized, and desensitized from the actualities of death, and sometimes-unrealistic medical dramas. Exposure to these contemporary fables does not evoke genuine, personalized pain or suffering, and in turn may not challenge

---

14. Fulton and Owen, "Death and Society," 379–95.
15. Durkin, "Death, Dying," 43.
16. Durkin, "Death, Dying," 43.
17. DeSpelder and Strickland, *The Last Dance*; Leming and Dickinson. *Understanding Death, Dying*; Mannino, *Grieving Days, Healing Days*; Umberson and Henderson, "The Social Construction of Death," 1–15.

our conception of mortality, dying, afterlife, reconciliation, comfort, or safety.

According to DeSpelder and Strickland,[18] approximately one-third of television screening portrays death in some way. According to the US National Institute of Mental Health, violent murder is normalized on television.[19] Especially cartoons, manga and anime, frequently depict character deaths that can even be "reversed with no serious consequences to their bodily functions."[20] The now ubiquitous media coverage of global events such as celebrity funerals, terrorist disasters, and distant war-zones locate scenes of carnage and destruction in the average home almost instantaneously and daily.[21] War-tactics, visual propaganda, and retaliation are designed for the media. Casualties are dehumanized and shrouded in the propaganda of wartime media and a political narrative of "justice."

In the cinema, thanatological themes are popular across a range of genres from sci-fi interactions between alien or natural wildlife and humans, natural disasters, gruesome murder violence and mystery, serial killings, apocalyptic epics, the rise of "slasher" and horror popularity, and real-life depictions of murders and suicides.[22]

Thanatological themes are present in nearly every music style according to Durkin,[23] by which he is referring to requiems, funereal music, death narratives, elegies, etc.; but not particularly to music for the purpose of dying well. Opera stories and folk and popular ballads narrate tragedies and deaths in a range of circumstances, from the "notorious nineteenth-century 'Torture Doctor'"[24] to the popular music of the Baby Boomer's teenage years.[25] "In the 1950s, a musical genre referred to as 'coffin songs' became popular."[26] Other examples include Elton John's hit single "Candle in the Wind '97,"[27] sung at the funeral of Diana, Princess

18. DeSpelder and Strickland, *The Last Dance*.
19. Kearl, "Death in Popular Culture," 23–30.
20. Mannino, *Grieving Days, Healing Days*, 29.
21. Durkin, and Knox, "September 11th," 3–4.
22. Molitor and Sapolsky, "Sex, Violence, and Victimization," 233–344; Lewis, "The Killing Jokes," 251–83.
23. Durkin and Knox, "September 11th," 3–4.
24. Schecter and Everitt, *A–Z Encyclopedia of Serial Killers*, 185.
25. Kearl, "Death in Popular Culture," 23–30.
26. DeSpelder and Strickland, *The Last Dance*; Durkin, "Death, Dying,"
27. Merrin, "Crash, Bang, Wallop," 41–62.

of Wales, as well as John Tavener's (Classical Mystical) *Song for Athene*.[28] A long epitaph of composers and musicians have died (and been immortalized) in tragic and premature circumstances (e.g., John Bonham, Kurt Cobain, Jimi Hendrix, Buddy Holly, Janis Joplin, John Lennon, Bob Marley, Keith Moon, Jim Morrison, Elvis Presley, Bon Scott, Ritchie Valens, Prince, George Michael, rapper Lil Peep, and Chris Cornell).

According to Wass et al., "A number of professionals, their representative organizations such as the American Academy of Pediatricians and the National Education Association, various child advocacy groups, including the Parent's Music Resource Center, and others have suggested that such lyrics promote *destructive and suicidal behavior* in adolescents."[29] The continually rising suicide numbers in the Netherlands, where euthanasia is legalized, may also be viewed as normalizing death and perhaps inadequate alternate supporting therapies for pain and suffering such as quality palliative care or mental health treatment.

Heavy metal (and its variants such as Death Metal, etc.) and Rap are inextricably tied to death imagery and language, including bands such as Megadeath, Anthrax, Slayer, and Grim Reaper, and song titles such as "Suicide Solution," "Highway to Hell," and "Psycho Killer" or the Guns N' Roses cover song written by notorious killer, Charles Manson[30] that appear to idolize, glorify, and edify death and violence in their expression. The lyrics by Rap artists such as Snoop Dogg, Dr. Dre, Eazy-E, Puff Daddy, and Eminem are controversially overflowing with violence, murder, suicide, and devaluation of humanity, no longer merely a voice of the marginalized, racially peripheralized, and discriminated-against peoples of minority, color, poverty, and the ghettoes, the affluent Rap superstars have retained the language of oppression and morbidity that birthed the genre decades ago. The deadly impact of drug disputes, gangland shootings, and rival celebrity anti-establishment culture has revolted with the murder of Tupac Shakur and B.I.G.

Death and dying are prominent themes in literature and print media, the butt of ironic humor and dark sarcasm. The macabre, Gothic, and fascination with commodified death is represented and consumed in Dark Tourism—tours of cemeteries, ghost tours, Presley's Graceland home, anatomical and forensic museums, wax museums, battlefield sites,

---

28. Durkin and Knox, "September 11th," 3–4.
29. Wass, et al., "Adolescents and Destructive Themes," 200, emphasis original.
30. Schecter and Everitt, *A-Z Encyclopedia of Serial Killers*, 185.

disaster museums (such as Kobe Japan's Earthquake simulation), pretend combat scenarios such as Paintball and augmented reality and geocache games, combat toys, First-person Shooter Games, Ouija boards, voodoo dolls, and other cultic superstitious practices associated with fatalism, the occult, and death.

According to Durkin, many of the manifestations of death in U.S. popular culture deal with "the post-self," (i.e., "the reputation and influence that an individual has after his or her death"[31]) which is especially the case for deceased celebrities and public figures. The symbolic immortality of post-self hangs on to reputation, after he or she has died, a symbolical blur between the living and the dead, diminishing the "sting" or full finitude of death. Idolized dead celebrities and heroic figures can take on pseudo-religious adoration, from Elvis Presley to Che Guevara.

This seeming Janus-like, two-faced ambivalence between acknowledging and embracing the reality of death of the self and our closes friends and relatives, and colloquial ubiquity of normalizing, de-sensitizing death imagery is perhaps a disguise for very real fears in the Post-Christian essentially atheistic, hedonistic, materialistic world that has nothing to hope for beyond death and everything to cling on to in this world of attachments, possessions, achievements, and "earthly delights."

"Death is a disruptive event, not only for the individual who dies but for the larger social enterprise as well."[32] Consequently, all societies must construct mechanisms to deal with death's problematic impacts.[33] The "beliefs and practices of the members of a society toward dying and death are largely dependent upon that society's social organization."[34] Popular culture is a collective construction of meaning, a loose framework for interpreting and understanding life. Within this context, the Christian thinker holds an altogether different horizon, ultimacy, humility, juxtaposition of human finitude with God's eternity and the resurrection of the body in the Kingdom to Come, an eschatological hope in a condition that will resolve the tensions of materiality and morbidity by Jesus' resurrection that symbolizes the final overcoming of death. For people without an eternal hope, death, dying, and the dead "are traumatic and

---

31. Durkin and Knox, "September 11th," 3–4.
32. Durkin, "Death, Dying," 47.
33. Blauner, "Death and Social Structure," 378–94.
34. Pine, "Social Organization and Death," 149.

anxiety producing topics, and can be better confronted if they are socially neutralized."[35]

The thanatological saturation in popular media may inure individuals to death and dying, thus diluting or counteracting their anxiety about these phenomena.[36] Similarly, Wass et al. suggest that death-related themes in popular music might help adolescents confront their anxieties, given that death and dying are seldom discussed in the home or the classroom.[37] There remains a contradiction in that popular culture creates a surrogate conversation where there is none "at home" with the people who will likely be involved in the real-life event. Death depiction in media is a passive paradigm, not a reflective or philosophical one with capacity for personal moral and spiritual discovery, nor does it realistically prepare us for physical and emotional pain and potential suffering when it comes due to the impersonal nature of pop culture's characters. It is interesting that these genres of pop culture are so developed in the First World where realities of death are most removed from everyday experience, and in the countries with the most prominent rejection of traditional faiths and customs for coping with the disruption of death.

As yet, we do not see a permeation of conversation and acceptance of death in quotidian life, rather than avoidance, discreet silence, and aversion. It remains the case that the minority of people utilize Advanced Care Directive tools, and a minority of the population utilizes available palliative care services, which are expert in supporting end of life needs in a society that is simultaneously calling out for euthanasia and physician-assisted-death in an attempt to usurp control of how, when, and where one dies. If someone argues that the agenda of the pro-euthanasia debate is to reduce suffering, then they have not properly understood the scope and potential of palliative care services which afford comfort and safety, extensively ameliorate pain, and support the wide-ranging psycho-social and spiritual holistic aspects of humanness and personhood that interact in the prevention of suffering.

The majority of people in our society have not seen or touched a dead person, have not killed or touched an animal they will eat, taken their pets to the vet for euthanasia, etc. They may be fortunate to not be familiar with the smell of death, the smell of blood, infection, the pallor

---

35. Bryant, "Thanatological Crime," 9.
36. Bryant and Shoemaker, "Death and the Dead for Fun."
37. Wass, et al., "Adolescents and Destructive Themes."

of peripheral organ failure, the grey-blue skin or jaundiced eyes of a body shutting down, the rasping labored sounds of terminal breathing, the anxiety and hallucinations of someone approaching death. It's not that we should be shocked by these realities, but that we need to not be shocked when the time comes, so that we can overcome somatic and sensory responses to death and provide the dignity, love, care, and self-sacrifice for a loved-one when they are dying before us. The difficulty of this overcoming is precisely the reason that legitimizes beautiful techniques for supporting that process (such as the music vigil).

Where does this leave us? With popular culture inundated with death images and fear of authentic conversation about personal experience of dying, and an inadequacy of supports, rituals and "tools" for moving through the process of dying in a meaningful and memorable way that will be held sacred, special, and important for the family, friends, and others around. How can we have both a societal obsession with commodified "virtual" death and amnesia about the realities of sounds, smells, touch, and sight of a transitioning loved one?

The Problem with Dying Well

Death is often not well prepared for. The Advanced Care Directive, testament of preferences for end of life or care in the loss of agency, is currently not well utilized by Australians. It is intended to be a document to communicate wishes to paramedical and medical staff, as well as guardianship arrangements.

The greatest problem, however, is that many people do not know what to expect of death nor do they have the spiritual resources to work through the situation. Death can be "good"—calm, accepting, minimal, or medically controlled pain. But it can also be noisy, distressing, agitated ("terminal agitation"), with physical changes—pallor, facial tension, increased pain, irregular heart rate, feeling cold, upper respiratory gurgles, and labored breathing due to difficulty swallowing. It can be an existential and physical struggle and painful to watch, with monitoring equipment—anything but tranquil and spiritual—accompanied by hallucinations and confusion or delirium.

Pain

"Pain occurs in the physical, emotional, and spiritual realm."[38] Perception of pain is shaped by many aspects such as gender, culture, how pain affects the patient's life, stress or anxiety, previous experience with pain, outlook, and other psychological factors. Hence, the notion that different individuals have a different "pain threshold." People who are experiencing Post-Traumatic Stress Disorder (PTSD), financial, or other life instability and stress, or depression, for example, may perceive a greater impact of pain from injury or disease.[39]

Physical pain affects several measurable characteristics (e.g., blood pressure, immunoglobulin levels, and skin temperature).[40] Other indicators of pain can include moaning, quick or intermittent inhalation/exhalation, holding breath, muscle tension, tight jaw, facial grimaces, fisted hands, knees to chest, moodiness and restlessness, and sensitivity to light.[41]

Spiritual pain has many meanings and manifestations. It is possible for a person near the end of life to feel content, restored, at peace and to ameliorate spiritual pain. "Wholeness" for a dying person can come from coming to terms with their life and relationships with loved ones. Spiritual pain may also need attention in the presence of drug and alcohol abuse because dependency is a spiritual disease in which a person is trying to close a "hole in their soul."[42] "Music is a powerful way to demonstrate compassion without judgement."[43]

Milton Hay identifies the characteristics associated with spiritual suffering, including: pain, constant and chronic; insomnia; withdrawal or isolation from spiritual support system; conflict with family members, friends, or support staff; anxiety, fear, mistrust of love ones, friends, physicians, hospice staff; anger; depression; guilt, low self-worth, comments about self-loathing; hopelessness/feeling of failure with life; lack of sense of humor; unforgiveness; despair; and fear or dread.[44] Many of these characteristics correlate with the stages of death and dying in *The Tibetan*

---

38. Benson, *The Healer's Way Companion*, 19.
39. Beilharz, "Music Engagement and Therapeutic Music."
40. Benson, *The Healer's Way Companion*.
41. Beilharz, "Music Engagement and Therapeutic Music."
42. Benson, *The Healer's Way Companion*, 22.
43. Benson, *The Healer's Way Companion*, 22.
44. Hay, "Building Spiritual Assessment Tools."

Book of the Living and Dead.⁴⁵ A considerable concurrence of depression, anxiety, and loneliness may be experienced by people in palliative care due to their social isolation, uncertainty, and feelings of helplessness.

Spirituality has received attention in the health and mental health research literature in the past few years as a *protective construct*.⁴⁶ While difficult to define in empirical or quantitative terms, spirituality is often expressed as a private, individual-level concept that is characterized by perceptions, beliefs, and feelings about a sacred or divine higher power, universal spirit, or ultimate purpose⁴⁷ or even more broadly as a sense of existential well-being, which has been referred to as an understanding or belief in the meaningfulness of one's own life.⁴⁸ A related construct of religious well-being, on the other hand, is often defined through adherence to behaviors such as attending religious services or affiliation with a particular religious group.⁴⁹ Although slightly different, both are strongly related to positive mental health functioning.⁵⁰

Ancient Wisdom and Preparation for Dying

Grof posits,

> One of the major tolls modern humanity has had to pay for the rapid technological development following the scientific and industrial revolutions is a progressive alienation from our biological nature and loss of connection with the spiritual source. During the period of rapid evolution of materialistic science and precipitous technological progress, three basic areas that link humans to nature—birth, sex and death—were subjected to deep psychological repression and denial. At the same time, the spiritual awareness that had provided a sense of meaningful

---

45. Rinpoche, *The Tibetan Book*.

46. Staton-Tindall et al., "The Roles of Spirituality."

47. For example, Chida et al., "Religiosity/Spirituality and Mortality," 81–90; Green et al., "Stories of Spiritual Awakening," 325–31; Watkins, *Handbook of Psychotherapy Supervision*.

48. Arnette et al., "Enhancing Spiritual Well-being."

49. For example, Gorsuch, "Religious Aspects of Substance Abuse," 65–83; Taylor et al., "Religious Involvement and Suicidal Behavior," 478–86.

50. Dalmida et al., "Spiritual Well-being"; Rippentrop et al., "Relationship between Religion/Spirituality"; Taylor et al., "Religious Involvement and Suicidal Behavior"; Visser et al., "Spirituality and Well-being."

belonging to the cosmos was replaced by atheism, or superficial activities of decreasing vitality and relevance.[51]

Despite widespread public silence about death, isolated researchers have investigated and propagated a renaissance of interest in psychology of dying and near-death experiences.[52]

In contrast, the literature of ancient cultures that had a remarkably sharp awareness of the spiritual and philosophical importance of death abounds in eschatological passages and processes for approaching and processing death, both for the spirituality of the dying person and for the community surrounding them. Death is universal and yet a timely and natural death is shunned and avoided, un-pondered, and sometimes postponed or predetermined by unnatural means in Western, post-Enlightenment, First World cultures. There seems to be an aversion to conditions we cannot control in time and manner with technological advances or otherwise. Best et al. suggest that the current support for euthanasia and physician assisted dying in Australia arises for this reason: because people want to be able to control the timing, location, and circumstances of their death.[53] The ancient texts dedicated to the subject of death and dying are usually referred to as "Books of the Dead": Egyptian Book of the Dead, *Manifestation of Light;* the Tibetan Book of the Dead, *Bardo Thödol;* the Mesoamerican *Maya Book of the Dead* (C15th Codex Borgia); the Mesoamerican Toltec and Aztec material; and the European Christian medieval eschatological material known as *Ars morendi—The Art of Dying.*

"Books of the Dead" were used as guides in the context of sacred mysteries and spiritual practice. They described states of dying, mystical and liturgical practices to focus spiritual experience, preparation for the afterlife, and beginning of wisdom.

The Tibetan Book of the Dead, *Bardo Thödol,* arises from Tibetan Buddhism and documents an afterlife of either enlightenment or reincarnation, sharing a clearly delineated notion of states of dying—the physical and emotional changes that occur as a person experiences natural biological death, not incomparable with Elizabeth Kübler-Ross' observations published in 1970. The Tibetan Book of the Dead is a kind of manual for

---

51. Grof, *Books of the Dead,* 6.

52. For example, Kübler-Ross, *On Death and Dying;* Weisse, *The Vestibule;* Delacour, *Glimpses of Beyond;* Osis, *Death-Bed Observations;* Moody, *Life After Life.*

53. Best et al., "Conceptual Analysis of Suffering," 977–86.

the dying person and their teacher, to recognize the intermediary steps between death and life known as *bardo* states. These are dreamlike states, reminiscent of the deep ecstasy found in meditation, karmic illusions, and seeking favorable rebirth. Serious spiritual seekers can experience similar states through deeply focused meditation, remembering, sensing (e.g., touching), which are thought of as states of liberation. The *Bardo Thödol* makes numerous references to clear light and glorious, peaceful images of dazzling deities. In some ways, the descriptions of imagery share some of the Biblical bedazzlement of the Revelation to St. John in the heavenly throne room, of transcendent light and clarity, and serenity or comfort.

There is also a counter-image in the *Bardo Thödol* of dark awe, anguish, and terror for the unprepared and uninitiated—a hellish image of deistic wrath, "hungry ghosts" looking for souls to inhabit or possess, burning fire, and sinister red. A spiritual battle amongst celestial warriors and faith-protecting deities is described. This is said to occur between eight and fourteenth days post-death, which subsequently gives way to the ghost-like new form of the *bardo* body, which can penetrate matter, has no form of its own, and can "shape-shift." The positive or negative experience of this state depends on the karmic record of the deceased, according to the Tibetan tradition, all of which culminates in the final *Sidpa Bardo*, or scene of judgement, equivalent to the Christian Day of Judgment, that decides the future of the deceased.

The Mayan Death codices on pottery vessels depict an array of blood-curdling creatures and dragons, sacrifices, a hallucinatory serpent, and bloodletting.[54] Once again, a cosmic battle for the soul of the dead person is involved, a dialectic between the underworld of mythological creatures, disguise, and a plight of transformation to rebirth. In this curious myth there is, at once, sacrificial Christ-like imagery, Phoenix imagery, redemption by blood, and a human Creation story. This story is documented in the Fifteenth Century Codex *Borgia*,[55] sometimes known as the *Nahuatl Book of the Dead*.

The *Ars morendi* (Christian Book of the Dead), or the *Art of Dying*, dates from towards the end of the Middle Ages existing in many forms in Europe (Austria, Germany, Italy, and France). There was intense interest in death during this period, perhaps due to the frequent outbreaks of

---

54. Grof, *Books of the Dead*, 45.
55. Milbrath, *A Seasonal Calendar*, 139–62.

pestilence, famine, war, disease epidemics, and childhood disease that prevented people from reaching adulthood. Funeral rituals were a part of regular life. "Mass burials, burning of cadavers, public executions, even the immolations of heretics and alleged witches and Satanists were conducted on a large scale. According to some estimates, the victims of the Holy Inquisition alone exceeded three million."[56]

People were familiar with the death of relatives and friends. This pervasive death-awareness coincided with the blight of far-reaching corruption and social, political, and religious disintegration: the context of the Medieval *Ars morendi*. The document collection addressed death and fundamental "problems" of human impermanence. The portion concerned with the significance of death in life is named the *Ars vivendi* (*The Art of Living*). It emphasizes the right attitude towards death, contempt of the world and secular pursuits, possibly a Biblically derived eschatological hope and moral living, and the futility of material worldly pursuits, while the second portion addresses the needs of the dying and their spiritual and emotional support. A recurring theme is the contemplation of death (also found in some forms of Buddhism). It dwells on the certainty of death alongside the uncertainty of its timing and asserts that the awareness of death is the beginning of wisdom.[57] People should eschew harmful behavior and live in accordance with Divine law. A positive interpretation leads not to anxiety about death, but to productive and meaningful living. Contemplation of death and remembering mortality was motivational.

Many images from this period draw upon the apocalyptic imagery of Revelation in the Bible such as the horseman, Death, the trumpet sound that summons death, a "crossing" or river, Judgement, and the contrasting images of idyllic Elysium and tormenting Hell. As few people spoke Latin, which was still the language of the church, paintings and drawings were instrumental in Christian teaching. "Confrontation with death was seen as absolutely crucial, and avoidance was considered one of the major dangers the dying person faced."[58]

---

56. Grof, *Books of the Dead*, 58.
57. Grof, *Books of the Dead*, 62.
58. Grof, *Books of the Dead*, 70.

Re-thinking Palliative Care

Palliative care is a specialization in which quality of life and meaningful experience supersedes the approach found in other areas of therapy (such as curative, targeted, and physician-directed goal-oriented programs) in favor of focus on inner psychosocial, spiritual outlook, and physical comfort.[59] Creatively enhancing "the quality of living can help patients make sense of dying . . . [integrating] the physical, psychological, social and spiritual dimensions of their being."[60] Aldridge says that patients want "to be fully alive even in the face of an impending death,"[61] being in the presence of friends and family includes opportunities for expression and sharing experiences, which may be valuable to ameliorating suffering.

A *vigil* describes a tranquil time of watching, listening, waiting, and communion. When medical staff observe that a person in palliative care is transitioning into the terminal phase of life, family and friends, guardians, clergy, and close members of community are summoned to the home or hospital to accompany someone in this important stage. Alongside physical comfort, having the most treasured companions present is often the highest priority indicated in Advanced Care Directives. People do not want to feel alone or abandoned at the end of their life, yet reflection and transcendent thoughts are also significant.

Sonic resonance and music, for example, transcend focus and hearing is the last sense to fail as the body shuts down from its most peripheral organs and circulation towards the core. Music is therefore an effective way to connect when speech has gone or even if someone is semi-conscious or delirious. The way people die affects hospital and community staff and obviously is impressed on the memory of loved ones who are present.

Palliative Care affirms life, regards dying as a normal process, neither hastens nor postpones death, provides symptom relief, offers support for active living, and offers support to help families cope.[62] In other words, palliative care aims to help patients live until they die. However, it is well recognized that a group of people who are eligible for palliative care and supportive services do not use them, that it is a relatively new discipline sometimes overlooked by referrers, and that certain groups

---

59. Beilharz, "Music Engagement and Therapeutic Music," 2.
60. Aldridge, *Music Therapy in Palliative Care*, 9.
61. Aldridge, *Music Therapy in Palliative Care*, 24.
62. Best, "Palliative Care."

such as regional, low-income, people in Advanced Care Units, indigenous Australians, non-cancer patients, and people of particular ethnic backgrounds, miss out on palliative care services.

The Theological Imperative

The word *Thanatos* comes from the Greek and refers to the mythological figure who is the twin brother of Sleep (*Hypnos*) and the son of Night (*Nyx*). There are many kinds of thanatologists today—medical, academic, theological, and psychological. It is also a pastoral art, which takes the words of the Gospel seriously and turns toward the face of suffering without reserve.[63]

Suffering is an existential problem influenced by culture, physical, circumstantial, and psychological factors. For example, compare the pregnant woman's labor and the woman with cancer-pain. They may have the same degree of pain, yet they may experience different suffering due to factors such as hope, expectation, outcome, duration of pain, and meaning attributed to the pain. Diagnosis of life-threatening disease is a common trigger for the so-called "existential slap" (i.e., the need to adjust one's life story). According to Best, final human growth can *only* come when we know we are dying.[64] Spirituality (in the broad sense) in healthcare is the way that patients find meaning and purpose, connectedness to self, others, the significant, or the sacred. Spiritual robustness is related to resilience, wellbeing, and quality of life.

Examples of beneficial impacts of religion (faith) or spirituality on health include: stress reduction;[65] relief of depression;[66] recovery from illness;[67] prevention of substance abuse;[68] prevention of suicide;[69] prevention of heart disease and hypertension; relief of pain;[70] adjustment to disability; recovery from cardiac surgery; longevity; reduced incidence

---

63. See *The Chalice of Repose Project* (http://chaliceofrepose.org).

64. Best, "Palliative Care."

65. Krause and Tran, "Stress and Religious Involvement," S4–S13; Leserman et al., "The Efficacy of the Relaxation Response," 111–17.

66. Gartner, "Religious Commitment," 187–214; Koenig et al., "Religiosity and Remission of Depression," 536–42.

67. Levin and Vanderpool, "Religious Factors in Physical Health," 41–64.

68. Gorsuch, "Religious Aspects of Substance Abuse," 65–83.

69. Larson and Wilson, "Religious Life of Alcoholics," 723–27.

70. Kabat-Zinn, *Full Catastrophe Living*.

and longer survival with cancer; improved palliative care outcomes; counselling outcomes;[71] and coping with illness.[72]

As Jesus teaches in Matthew 25:34–40, we show our love for God, and Christ-likeness, when we give to and love strangers with unconditional compassion and provision for people we are not bound to and from whom we expect no reciprocity.

> Even to your old age and gray hairs
> I am he, I am he who will sustain you.
> I have made you and I will carry you;
> I will sustain you and I will rescue you. (Isa 46:4 NIV)

Needs in end-of-life care include: the social (e.g., isolation, loneliness, boredom) emotional (e.g., depression, anxiety, anger, fear, frustration); cognitive (e.g., neurological impairments, disorientation, confusion); physical (e.g., pain, shortness of breath); and spiritual (e.g., lack of spiritual connection, need for spiritually-based rituals).

The Bible is clear in the Old Covenant promises, the New Testament ministry of Jesus, and final restoration promised in the Revelation to John, that God's vision is for his people's soul to *abide in well-being* (Ps 25:13). God is the Creator and in control of circumstance (Isa 46:7), healing is part of God's plan for eschatological reconciliation of his faithful (Mal 4:2), and his vision of the New Kingdom (Rev 21:4). Both physical and spiritual healing were integral to Jesus' earthly ministry (Matt 4:24; 9:35) and a sign of the Holy Spirit acting through the disciples after Christ's resurrection (Acts 3:1–10; 5:12–16).

Conclusion

In conclusion, this chapter has identified some of the problems coping with and maintaining the spiritual significance of dying and living well until the very last breath. In so doing, this chapter has identified the paradoxical over-exposure to thanatological themes in popular media that has at once led to desensitization and normalization of death of action figures, entertainment heroes, and fictitious immortalization of celebrities, while failing to address the intimate reality of family relationships

---

71. Hassed, "The Essence of Healthcare," 957–60.
72. Hassed et al., "Enhancing the Health of Medical Students."

and conversations about genuine death experiences, plans for end of life, and demystification of palliative care.

The sanitization of death by removing the origins of primary industry, agrarian lifestyle, the widespread health and longevity in First World countries, which have all but eradicated famine, death in childbirth, plagues, and the like, together with the secularization of society generally, have eroded the death rituals and thanatological wisdom of ancient societies that provided social and communal means of recognizing and celebrating life at its conclusion and rituals intended to support grieving families and permit social empathy and mourning.

The ancient books of wisdom helped people prepare for death constructively and understand the spiritual significance of the final rite of passage, the final phase of spiritual growth in life-long sanctification understood by the Wesleys, by psychologists, and by ancient religious traditions, including the Christian faith. Whilst we live in a society capable of medicalizing and cushioning some factors of pain and suffering associated with death, and an era of pharmaceutical companies and other processes designed to immortalize the body with age-defying products and high quality medical care, and lifestyle factors increasing longevity, it has come with spiritual costs: the cost of detachment, outsourcing and downgrading the intimacy, dignity and uniqueness of death for individuals and their families; the cost of detracting from preparation through a phase of material divestment and spiritual focus, drawing nearer to God. The social unfamiliarity with the authenticity of deteriorating bodies and death has rendered our generation fearful and shocked when confronted with reality, immobilized by our own mortality and fears, thereby averse to the needs of the dying person before us, such as prayer, presence, fellowship, reconciliation, and contemplation. We have forgotten how to die well.

In drawing attention to the potential for growth, grace and dignity at the end of life, this chapter aims to redeem the end of life as a valuable spiritual transformative stage in a mature, flourishing life that ultimately recognizes the providence and protection of God for his faithful, without which the crucifixion and resurrection cannot fully be internalized. Christian Scripture is careful to present God's sovereignty without suggesting that it obfuscates human pain and suffering. Yet, God also promises the eschatological abiding of his people in his Kingdom—the renewed Heaven and Earth—and meanwhile provides his protection and unerring love. God's unconditional love does not marginalize or diminish the value of people in old age or decline. Ultimately, we need to concede that God has control over the time, place, and nature of the end of life, which will make life before it all the more bearable and meaningful.

Bibliography

Aldridge, David, ed. *Music Therapy in Palliative Care: New Voices*. Philadelphia: Kingsley, 1999.

Arnette, Natalie C., et al. "Enhancing Spiritual Well-being among Suicidal African American Female Survivors of Intimate Partner Violence." *Journal of Clinical Psychology* 63.10 (2007) 909–24.

Beilharz, Kirsty. "Music Engagement and Therapeutic Music." In *Textbook of Palliative Care*, edited by R. D. MacLeod and L. Block, 1–22. Cham: Springer, 2018. https://doi.org/10.1007/978-3-319-31738-0_39-1.

Benson, Stella. *The Healer's Way Companion: Soothing Music for Those in Pain, Volume I*. Seattle: NewGrail Media, 2003.

Best, Megan. "Palliative Care." Paper presented at the Society, Theology, Culture and Public Engagement Summer School of the Anglican Deaconess Ministries. Sydney, 2018.

Best, Megan, et al. "Conceptual Analysis of Suffering in Cancer: A Systematic Review." *Psycho-Oncology* 24 (2015) 977–86.

Blauner, Robert. "Death and Social Structure." *Psychiatry* 29 (1966) 378–94.

Bryant, Clifton D. "'Thanatological Crime': Some Conceptual Notes on Offenses against the Dead As a Neglected Form of Deviant Behavior." Paper presented at the *World Congress of Victimology*, Acapulco, 1989.

Bryant, Clifton D., and Donald Shoemaker. "Death and the Dead for Fun (and Profit): Thanatological Entertainment as Popular Culture." Paper presented at the AGM of the Southern Sociological Society. Atlanta, 1977.

Chida, Yoichi, et al. "Religiosity/Spirituality and Mortality. A Systematic Quantitative Review." *Psychotherapy and Psychosomatics* 78 (2009) 81–90.

Cruickshank, Joanna. *Pain, Passion, and Faith: Revisiting the Place of Charles Wesley in Early Methodism*. Lanham, MD: Scarecrow, 2009.

Dalmida, Safiya G., et al. "Spiritual Well-being, Depressive Symptoms, and Immune Status among Women Living with HIV/AIDS." *Women Health* 49.2/3 (2009) 119–43.

Delacour, Jean-Baptiste. *Glimpses of Beyond*. New York: Delacorte, 1974.

DeSpelder, Lynne Ann, and Albert Lee Strickland. *The Last Dance: Encountering Death and Dying*. 6th ed. New York: McGraw-Hill, 2002.

Durkin, Keith F. "Death, Dying, and the Dead in Popular Culture." In *Handbook of Death & Dying*, edited by C. D. Bryant and D. L. Peck, 43–49. Thousand Oaks, CA: Sage, 2003.

Durkin, Keith F., and Kristy Knox. "September 11th, Postmodernism, and the Collective Consciousness: Some Sociological Observations." Paper presented at the Annual Meeting of the Mid-South Sociological Association. Mobile, AL, 2001.

Erikson, Erik H. *The Life Cycle Completed: A Review*. New York: Norton, 1985.

Fowler, James W. *Stages of Faith: The Psychology of Human Development and the Quest for Meaning*. San Francisco: Harper & Row, 1981.

Fulton, Robert, and Greg Owen. "Death and Society in Twentieth Century America." *Omega* 18 (1987) 379–95.

Gartner, John. "Religious Commitment, Mental Health, and Prosocial Behavior: A Review of the Empirical Literature." In *Religion and the Clinical Practice of Psychology*, edited by E. P. Shafranske, 187–214. Washington, DC: American Psychological Association, 1996.

Gorsuch, R. L. "Religious Aspects of Substance Abuse and Recovery." In *Journal of Social Issues* 51 (1995) 65–83.

Green, L. L., et al. "Stories of Spiritual Awakening: The Nature of Spirituality in Recovery." *Journal of Substance Abuse Treatmeant* 15.4 (1998) 325–31.

Grof, Stanislav. *Books of the Dead*. London: Thames & Hudson, 2013.

Hassed, Craig. "The Essence of Healthcare." *Australian Family Physician* 34.11 (2005) 957–60.

Hassed, Craig, et al. "Enhancing the Health of Medical Students: Outcomes of an Integrated Mindfulness and Lifestyle Program." *Advances in Health Sciences Education: Theory and Practice* 14.3 (2008) 387–98.

Hay, Milton W. "Principles in Building Spiritual Assessment Tools." *American Journal of Hospice and Palliative Care* 6.5 (1989) 25–31.

Kabat-Zinn, Jon. *Full Castastrophe Living: Using the Wisdom of Your Body and Mind to Face Stress, Pain, and Illness*. Rev. ed. London: Random House, 2013.

Kearl, Michael C. "Death in Popular Culture." In *Death: Current Perspectives*, edited by John B. Williamson and Edwin S. Shneidman, 23–30. 4th ed. Mountain View, CA: Mayfield, 1995.

Koenig, H. G., et al. "Religiosity and Remission of Depression in Medically Ill Older Patients." *American Journal of Psychiatry* 155.4 (1998) 536–42.

Krause, Neal, and Thanh Van Tran. "Stress and Religious Involvement among Older Blacks." *Journal of Gerontology* 44.1 (1989) S4–S13.

Kübler-Ross, Elisabeth. *On Death and Dying*. London: Tavistock, 1970.

Larson, David B., and William P. Wilson. "Religious Life of Alcoholics." *Southern Medical Journal* 73.6 (1980) 723–27.

Leming, Michael R., and George E. Dickinson. *Understanding Dying, Death, and Bereavement*. 5th ed. New York: Harcourt College, 2002.

Leserman, Jane, et al. "The Efficacy of the Relaxation Response in Preparing for Cardiac Surgery." *Behavioral Medicine* 15.3 (1989) 111–17.

Levin, Jeffrey S., and Harold Y. Vanderpool. "Religious Factors in Physical Health and the Prevention of Illness." *Prevention in Human Services* 9.2 (2008) 41–64.

Lewis, Paul. "The Killing Jokes of the American Eighties." *Humor* 10 (1997) 251–83.

Lunn, Julie. "Becoming Truly Human: Charles Wesley's Understanding of Sanctification as Human Maturity and Its Implications for 21st Century Ministry." *Oxford Institute*, 2013. https://oimts.files.wordpress.com/2013/09/2013-2-lunn.pdf.

MacKinlay, Elizabeth. *The Spiritual Dimension of Ageing*. London: Kingsley, 2001.

Mannino, J. Davis. *Grieving Days, Healing Days*. Boston: Allyn & Bacon, 1997.

Merrin, William. "Crash, Bang, Wallop! What a Picture! The Death of Diana and the Media." *Mortality* 4 (1999) 41–62.

Milbrath, Susan. "A Seasonal Calendar in the Codex Borgia." In *Cosmology, Calendars, and Horizon-Based Astronomy in Ancient Mesoamerica*, edited by Anne S. Dowd and Susan Milbrath, 139–62. Boulder: University Press of Colorado, 2015.

Molitor, Fred, and Barry S. Sapolsky. "Sex, Violence, and Victimization in Slasher Films." *Journal of Broadcasting and Electronic Media* 37 (1993) 233–42.

Moody, Raymond. *Life After Life*. Sydney: Random House, 1975.
Osis, Karlis, and Erlendur Haraldsson. "Deathbed Observations by Physicians and Nurses: A Cross-Cultural Survey." *Journal of the American Society for Psychical Research* 71.3 (1977) 237–59.
Payne, Barbara. "Spiritual Maturity and Meaning-Filled Relationships: A Sociological Perspective." *Journal of Religious Gerontology* 7.1/2 (1990) 25–39.
Pine, Vanderlyn R. "Social Organization and Death." *Omega* 3 (1972) 149–53.
Rinpoche, Sogyal. *The Tibetan Book of the Living and Dead*. New York: HarperCollins, 1992.
Rippentrop, E. A., et al. "The Relationship between Religion/Spirituality and Physical Health, Mental Health, and Pain in a Chronic Pain Population." *Pain* 116.3 (2005) 311–21.
Schecter, Harold, and David Everitt. *The A–Z Encyclopedia of Serial Killers*. New York: Pocket, 1997.
Staton-Tindall, Michele, et al. "The Roles of Spirituality in the Relationship between Traumatic Life Events, Mental Health, and Drug Use among African American Women." *Substance Use & Misuse* 48.12 (2013) 1246–57.
Taylor Robert J., et al. "Religious Involvement and Suicidal Behavior among African Americans and Black Caribbeans." *The Journal of Nervous and Mental Disease* 199.7 (2011) 478–86.
Umberson, Debra, and Kristin Henderson. "The Social Construction of Death in the Gulf War." *Omega* 25 (1992) 1–15.
Visser, Anja, et al. "Spirituality and Well-being in Cancer Patients: A Review." *Psychooncology* 19.6 (2010) 565–72.
Wass, Hannelore, et al. "Adolescents and Destructive Themes in Rock Music: A Follow-Up." *Omega* 23 (1991) 199–206.
Watkins, C. Edwards, Jr., ed. *Handbook of Psychotherapy Supervision*. Chichester: Wiley & Sons, 1997.
Weisse, J. E. *The Vestibule*. Port Washington, NY: Ashley, 1972.
Wesley, Charles. *The Journal of the Rev. Charles Wesley: Volume 1*. Edited by Thomas Jackson. London: Mason, 1849.
———. *Preparation for Death* (1772). https://divinity.duke.edu/sites/divinity.duke.edu/files/documents/cswt/72_Preparation_for_Death_%281772%29.pdf.
———. *Scripture Hymns* (1762), Vol. 2. https://divinity.duke.edu/sites/divinity.duke.edu/files/documents/cswt/64_Scripture_Hymns_%281762%29_Vol_2.pdf.
Westmoreland, Diane Ruth. "Can Spiritual Maturity Be Nurtured in Northern English Anglican Congregations? An Exploration of Whether Parishioners Can Grow Spiritually through an Experiential Course on Prayer Using Methods Based in Ignatian Practice." PhD thesis, University of Durham, 2011.

9

Exploring Salvationist Understandings of Holiness in the Anthropocene

Matthew D. Seaman

Introduction

IN THE COMPLICATED AND contested spaces addressing issues of social change and climate change, fluidity and instability are common underlying themes. Pandemics, politics, and pollution are but a few of the areas of concern for many people across the globe. Along with the broader Christian church, The Salvation Army has been involved and impacted in various ways by these external fluidities and instabilities alongside various internal debates and complexities. In this paper, I aim to explore the intersections of some of these externally and internally contested aspects of Salvation Army thought and practice framed by the notions of practical holiness and of ecological care, and to share a selection of empirical research findings around these themes. I contend that a holistic view of humanity within God's creation must integrate ecological matters along with spiritual and social themes and concerns. Hence, one of the many questions that should be asked is: how might The Salvation Army as a movement, Salvationists individually—and indeed, the church more broadly—have failed to realize the practical ecological consequences of the call to holiness? In light of the wide array of human-caused ecological issues around the world, I suggest that if holy love is, in Wesley's words, to run "through all our tempers, words, and actions," and given the "all" must include what takes place within the physical world, then care and concern for the ongoing health and wellbeing of ecosystems and all of life is an essential part of the journey towards holy living for Salvationists and the wider body of the church within God's creation.

Holiness and the Anthropocene

The Salvation Army works within many areas of social, spiritual, and physical need in over 130 countries.[1] This includes supporting those experiencing challenges brought on by natural disasters, poverty, and addiction. The faith background of the Salvationist tendency toward practical action is a theological heritage primarily grounded within Wesleyan-Holiness teaching. The Wesleyan-Holiness tradition developed out of the practical theological work of John Wesley. Briefly, one of Wesley's descriptions of the life of holiness is: "the pure love of God and [hu]man—the loving God with all our heart and soul, and our neighbour as ourselves . . . love governing the heart and life, running through all our tempers, words, and actions."[2] The theme of holiness is infused throughout the theological heritage of The Salvation Army.

In terms of emphasizing and supporting the commitment to holiness within the movement, The Salvation Army's International Spiritual Life Commission (ISLC) of 1996–1998 affirmed: "We call Salvationists worldwide to restate and live out the doctrine of holiness in all its dimensions—personal, relational, social and political—in the context of our cultures and in the idioms of our day while allowing for, and indeed prizing, such diversity of experience and expression as is in accord with the Scriptures."[3] Furthermore, the ISLC stated: "We confess that at times

---

1. The Salvation Army, "Our Work, Worldwide." Furthermore, the identity of The Salvation Army is not entirely simple. The complexity can be gleaned from the various descriptors which have been used in different contexts: as faith-based organization (FBO), church denomination, Christian movement, charity, non-governmental organization (NGO), and business. Additionally, Hill, *Leadership in the Salvation Army*, xvii, notes that The Salvation Army's foundational deed poll and style guides capitalize the "T" in its legal name. This paper follows that naming convention.

2. J. Wesley, *Works*, 13:170.

3. Street, *Called to Be God's People*, 79.

we have failed to realize the practical consequences of the call to holiness within our relationships, within our communities and within our Movement."[4]

Perhaps the failure to realize the practical consequences of the call to holiness has more to do with the lack of understanding of what holiness means and the practical implications of the doctrine for our life in the world rather than any problem with the concept itself. And it is certainly timely that the relationship between holiness and ecological concerns needs to be articulated. Indeed, a growing number of scientists are certainly drawing attention to our effects on the planet. Indeed, humankind has forced such extensive and often negative changes upon ecosystems around the world that biologist Eugene Stoermer put forward the idea that a new era is taking shape. This new period has been labelled the Anthropocene.

Of course, in all societies past and present, humanity has impacted the planet in which we live, breathe, and have our being. These impacts have been through gathering, hunting, farming, or producing food; providing places of safety and shelter; or the transportation of goods and people. Some impacts have been minimal. However, throughout the past couple of centuries, particularly in the West and more recently in Asia, widespread industrialization has distinctly changed humanity's relationship with nature. With the increased rates of industrialization, capitalism, productivity, innovation, and human populations there is an ever-expanding range of products available to consume. The amount of energy and materials required to produce these commodities is therefore also increasing the amount of waste left from the creative process. Many have commented on the material and human waste stemming from the new industrialization. Indeed, The Salvation Army's co-founder, General William Booth, did just this within the publication of *In Darkest England and The Way Out*, published over 125 years ago.[5]

To list some known environmental changes and areas of concern due to anthropogenic causes is sobering. There have been huge losses in biodiversity caused by human activities. One report estimates that over the past few decades, vertebrate species populations worldwide have seen decreases of up to 50 percent.[6] Non-native invasive species, pollution,

---

4. Street, *Called to Be God's People*, 79.
5. Booth, *In Darkest England*; see also, Seaman, *Darkness and Deliverance*.
6. WWF, *Living Planet Report*.

disease, deforestation, overfishing, exploitation, habitat degradation, loss and change have all been contributors. Decreases in air, water and soil quality have been observed,[7] ozone depletion has occurred and oceans are becoming more acidic.[8] There have been vast increases in light and noise pollution[9] and chemical and nuclear contamination in both times of war and peace.[10] Other alarming human-caused environmental issues include the existence of "garbage patches" or "trash vortices" within all major oceans,[11] and that newborn babies can already test positive for a multiplicity of harmfully toxic chemicals and carcinogens.[12]

In addition to these monumental changes brought upon earth ecosystems by human activities, there now loom the potentialities of greater climate variability.[13] Before continuing, I acknowledge that not all are in agreement regarding human contributions to climate variability and change. Yet, with the significant risks and impacts if projections are even partly correct, it is wise, sensible, and responsible for all—including individual Salvationists and The Salvation Army corporately—to consider how the potentialities of climate change may affect all global neighbors and indeed the entirety of creation. However, even if these climate projections do not eventuate in full, as Wesleyan scholar Howard Snyder contends, caring for God's creation can be perceived as the first commission or call from God towards wholeness and holiness.[14]

It should be noted that individuals and sections of this Christian movement have recognized the link between spiritual, social, and ecological issues.[15] Taking note of other work around holiness and caring holistically for the entire Earth community[16] to the stated dimensions of

7. Ramanathan and Feng, *Air Pollution, Greenhouse Gases*; Hoekstra et al., *Global Monthly Water Scarcity*; Koch et al., *Solving the Global Soil Crisis*.

8. Joshi, *Ozone Depletion*; Schnoor, *Ocean Acidification*.

9. Gallaway et al., *Economics of Global Light Pollution*; Murphy and King, *Environmental Noise Pollution*.

10. Edelstein et al., *Cultures of Contamination*.

11. NOAA, *Marine Debris Program*.

12. PCP, *Reducing Environmental Cancer Risk*.

13. IPCC, *Assessment Reports*, AR1, AR2, AR3, AR4, and AR5.

14. Snyder, *Holiness and the Five Calls*.

15. E.g., The Salvation Army, "A Call for Climate Justice"; The Salvation Army, "Climate Change"; The Salvation Army, "Environmental Sustainability"; Barratt, "The Flourishing of All Things."

16. E.g., Snyder, *Holiness and the Five Calls*; Snyder and Scandrett, *Salvation Means Creation Healed*; Haynes, "Holiness"; Lodahl and Maskiewicz, *Renewal in Love*.

holiness articulated by the ISLC, I contend that the ecological must also be included. Hence, the question then becomes: how might The Salvation Army as a movement have failed to realize the practical ecological consequences of the call to holiness?

Indeed, in light of the wide array of human-caused ecological issues that we are faced with, I suggest that if holy love is, in Wesley's words, to run "through all our tempers, words, and actions" that take place within the physical world, then care and concern for the ongoing health and wellbeing of ecosystems and all of life is an essential part of the journey towards holy living within Salvationism and the wider body of the church.

Even with the recent growth in holiness literature, notwithstanding the work of Oord, Lodahl, Maskiewicz, Snyder, and a number of papers within Broward and Oord's edited volume *Renovating Holiness*,[17] ecologically-mindful writings around holiness appears to remain quite scarce. This is the case even more so within Salvation Army literature. Furthermore, within these texts there appears to have been little, if any, qualitative or quantitative practical theological research undertaken into the current views and practices around the topic of holiness of Salvationists and those within the wider Wesleyan-Holiness tradition, or even more specifically the relationships between holiness, ecology, and practical action. This work endeavors to add to the literature in this area and to engage Salvationists in deeper consideration of practical holistic holiness that is mindful of ecological issues.

Research Overview

In this chapter I include excerpts and research data from my recently completed doctoral project titled: "'To Turn the World Upside Down': An Empirical Study of Salvationist Understandings of Holiness in the Anthropocene." Essentially, the aim of the project was to examine the dimensions of holiness and its relationship with Salvationist faith and praxis, framed by the notion of the Anthropocene primarily from within an Australian context. Within a practical theological framework utilizing mixed research methods, people involved with The Salvation Army

---

17. Oord and Lodahl, *Relational Holiness*; Lodahl and Maskiewicz, *Renewal in Love*; Snyder, *Holiness and the Five Calls*; Snyder with Scandrett, *Salvation Means Creation Healed*; and a number of papers within Broward and Oord, *Renovating Holiness*.

were invited to reflect and respond to questions and emergent concepts regarding holiness and practical outcomes of living holy lives within a world that is increasingly experiencing the negative effects of humanity's consumptive habits. The project endeavored to provide an academic work that was theologically, socially, and ecologically compelling and also practically useful to Salvationists and the wider body of the church in navigating and reframing what it means to live holy lives in God's creation.

I considered the notion of holiness and the practical aspects of aiming to live a holy life were potentially important areas for Salvationists to consider in relation to their engagement with the physical world and the care of all of creation. Hence, this project raised questions such as: How might the practical outworking of holiness, both individually for Salvationists and corporately as The Salvation Army, respond to the interrelations between social, political, economic, and ecological issues? What are some of the extant barriers to Salvationist socio-ecological action? In a world that is increasingly experiencing the negative effects of humanity's destructive habits, what might a life of holiness mean for Salvationists in terms of the flourishing of the whole biosphere; that is, contributing to life in all its fullness? What might positive radical Salvationist actions, grounded in love and practical holiness look like? Are there more relevant ways for Salvationists and The Salvation Army to encourage and cultivate holy and holistic life within the household of God?

Data were gathered via interviews, surveys, and focus groups from people involved with The Salvation Army, primarily from within Australia. These mixed methods were used to complement each other and form a richer tapestry of data to examine. Following research ethics approval, consent, and permission to record forms were presented to participants. These documents also outlined the research project details which included noting the de-identification of personal information for privacy.

Semi-structured interviews were undertaken with twenty-one people involved with The Salvation Army. A balance of gender, age range, and relationship with The Salvation Army was generally maintained with the interview cohort. A list of prepared questions assisted in guiding the semi-structured interviews that took place at a convenient location of their choosing. Audio recordings and written notes were taken during the interviews to aid transcription and analysis. During this process, interviewee details and information was de-identified, and each interviewee was assigned a code based on the person's interview number, gender, and link with The Salvation Army.

Common qualitative research methods, such as those voiced by Swinton and Mowat,[18] were utilized and adapted. As the interview process proceeded, the first stage in analyzing this segment of data was verbatim transcription of the twenty-two hours of recorded interviews. This process offered deeper knowledge again of the interviewees and their thoughts. Initial data analysis stages included discerning the nature of the primary categories, themes, and sub-themes through coding or summarizing the data within paragraphs and sentences. As interviews continued, the emergent themes and concepts enhanced and informed the subsequent interviews and textual research throughout the remainder of the research process.

Questionnaires are widely used to obtain data that is more easily examined and analyzed for patterns and relationships. The positivist approach of much quantitative data collection aims to test theories by confirming or refuting exact hypotheses. However, this research project was not approached from such a perspective or testing a specific hypothesis. Rather, the data enhances and provides other beneficial perspectives. Quantitative and qualitative data were collected via online surveys. Quantitatively, questions were answerable either by using a five-point Likert scale or a yes/no response. Text boxes were provided for participants to input further thoughts or comments. It is acknowledged that there may also be a sampling bias when using online surveys as having access to technology is not ubiquitous or always equitable. Even so, gathering data from a larger population of Salvationists (n=90) was valuable. The self-reported associations participants have with The Salvation Army are soldier (33 percent), officer (23 percent), volunteer (17 percent), employee (14 percent), supporter (7 percent), and adherent (6 percent). It should be noted that more than one option could be selected, reflecting the potential for people being in more than one category. Reported age ranges of respondents were 18–35 (32 percent), 36–50 (38 percent), 51–65 (24 percent), and 65–80 (6 percent).

Focus groups were formed to discuss and delve deeper in theological reflection and to consider practical approaches and responses. The first small groups consisted of four participants meeting over the span of three weeks, with subsequent single meeting large focus groups containing up

---

18. Swinton and Mowat, *Practical Theology*, 68.

to nineteen participants. Focus groups were formed in response to the location, availability, and engagement of participants. Focus group data were collected via written text and digital audio recordings. Small group study guides were prepared and provided to most participants for feedback and recording personal reflections. The eight hours of audio recordings were subsequently transcribed for analysis along with the interview data. Focus group participants were also given particular codes.

It must also be noted that while the majority of respondents noted they were from an Australian context (63 percent), there are other predominately Western backgrounds represented in the collected data (Europe 17 percent and North America 16 percent).[19] As the majority of Salvationists do not live in Western countries, but rather within African and South Asian contexts, there is therefore an inherent contextual imbalance within the results of this project.

Research Findings

Several significant findings and themes emerged from the research, not all of which can be reported in this brief chapter. The first selection of findings outlined focus on broader Salvationist perceptions of holiness.

Participants were somewhat divided between two main camps. The first is that holiness as a term is still relevant and just needs more teaching, clarification, and explanation. For example, two online survey participants commented that they thought "the term 'holiness' is still vibrant and relevant" and "it's still fresh, but we should always clarify what we mean when using it." Numerous respondents acknowledged the usefulness of the term even if it is not well understood. For instance, "it does seem like an old-fashioned word, but I cannot think of a more descriptive word in modern language."

The second grouping perceived that holiness is often misunderstood, that it carries an amount of "baggage" and might need revisiting in terms of accessibility. Accessibility was at times linked to confusion or unhelpful connotations: "It needs to be described and expressed in fresh ways. To simply use the word 'holiness' is to encounter numerous negative stereotypes and to ensure misunderstanding." Others mentioned the undertone of legalism or traditions that has led to misperceptions of, or detachment from, holiness. For example, an online survey respondent

---

19. Participants who responded to the survey question: n=55.

noted they "think it is still relevant but needs to be spoken about in terms of God's amazing grace rather than a pharisaical keeping of rules in order to achieve it." Even with the divergence of opinion on nomenclature, there was an overwhelming sense that holiness is essential, both corporately and individually. For Salvationists individually, over 93 percent of respondents classed holiness as "essential," with nearly 5 percent selecting "useful." Whereas for The Salvation Army collectively the figures were only slightly different with over 89 percent regarding holiness as essential for the movement, with close to 8 percent considering it as useful.

When posed the survey question: "what words do you associate with holiness?" the list of responses was large and varied. Each respondent could input as many words or terms that they associated with holiness as they desired. For ease of reporting similar terms and words were collated into single groupings with variations recorded as collected. There were 156 separate items—a single word, a term, or a collation of similar terms—placed on the list. For brevity, only the most frequently mentioned themes (four or more mentions) are shared here with frequencies: Purity/pure/purification (22); Love/perfect love/God's love (14); Christlikeness/becoming like Jesus (12); Whole/Wholeness /Completeness (12); Righteous/righteousness (9); Clean/cleanliness/cleansed (8); Set apart (8); Sanctification/sanctified (7); Godliness/Godly (6); Grace (6); Jesus/Christ (6); Justice (5); Perfection (5); Discipline (4); Entire Sanctification (4); Freedom/set free (4); God/holy God (4); Holy Spirit (4); Obedience (4); and Separation/separate (4).

Notably, a few common terms found in Wesleyan-Holiness and Salvation Army literature were not frequently used by interviewees. For instance, the term "second blessing" was mentioned three times, while the terms "blessing of a clean heart" and "Christian perfection" were both only mentioned once each. This may indicate that ideas or ways of speaking on the notion of holiness have shifted.

There was a strong tendency for participants to speak of holiness as an amalgam of event(s) and process or journey (63 percent), with equal numbers favoring "event then process," or "event and process." Twenty-five percent felt it was more of a process or journey (some mentioned that this process *can* include events), with three percent saying it was neither an event nor process, and no participant viewing the state of holiness as a single crisis moment. Representative participant quotes give further depth, yet also show the differences in approach to the question of holiness as event and/or process:

- "A process which may be precipitated by and punctuated with a series of events."
- "It can be an event, but for most it's a process, marked by special events."
- "I think it is an event after a process. More like an ideal or a goal."
- "Holiness is a process that comes from an event—the event of meeting Jesus and asking Him into your life, the journey of holiness begins."
- "An event followed by a process of obedience. The event being a call from God or a revelation and a process of obedience and dedication to action."
- "A mix of event and process—and a unique journey for each Christian. As in any good relationship or in human growth and development or in any healing process, there are moments of breakthrough and many periods of slow and steady progress."
- "My personal experience is both process and event—moments or real divine encounter & calling, and the daily grind of working out that holiness in the reality of everyday life."
- "Neither. I believe that it is a state of being that can be achieved through accepting Christ however to fully attain it it's a process."
- "I'm unsure whether either of these words sit well with my understanding of holiness."
- "Holiness is all of life. Unity is not uniformity."

A common view of the outcome of embarking on the process of holiness was a tendency toward active and activated faith, with many also noting that practical holiness would often be considered radical within the cultural context. For instance, one participant shared that "Real Christianity is always a revolutionary movement and can often be most threatening to religious leaders and institutions. Holiness should always be world-transforming." Another additionally linked the idea of passivity to that of legalism: "Doesn't that whole quote give you the idea that holiness is an active thing, not a passive thing? And I think too often the churches present it as some sort of passive . . . the don'ts. If you want to be holy, you don't do this and you don't do this. Which makes it a passive, sit back and disengage. But actually, God's holiness is about engaging with the world."

There was a strong sense that participants perceived marked decline in radical action during The Salvation Army's 150-year existence. For example, when queried about The Salvation Army as a radical holiness movement specifically divided into 50-year groupings over its history (1865–1915; 1915–1965; 1965–2015), the responses were dramatic, with 74 percent of respondents strongly agreed that the Army was a radical holiness movement in the first 50 years, 18 percent agreed, and 8 percent were neutral/unsure. For the second 50-year period, only 15 percent strongly agreed, with the majority either agreeing (42 percent) or neutral/unsure (38 percent), and with 5 percent now disagreeing. For the most recent 50-year period, no respondents strongly agreed that The Salvation Army has been a radical holiness movement, with only 15 percent agreeing, 27 percent neutral/unsure, 42 percent disagreeing, and now 16 percent strongly disagreeing.

One online response mentioned they felt there were disconnects between historical and current Salvationist contexts: "These quotes are more historical anecdotes rather than accurate portrayals of today. We are resting on the laurels of our historical Railtons and Booths when it comes to revolutionary, holy, sacrificial living." Often associated with a decline in radicalism within The Salvation Army in a corporate sense was that of money. This correlation emerged most frequently during interviews rather than focus groups or online surveys. The following interviewee quote illustrates this perceived link: "I think our tie to, or dependence upon, both public funding in contracts and donations makes us walk a line of not being out at the front of social change." However, there was also clear interest in increased levels of radical holiness within The Salvation Army today from the majority of respondents. For example, in response to the question "should The Salvation Army be more radical in terms of practical holiness?" over 85 percent of participants selected either "strongly agree" or "agree."

Other participants also perceived that there have been shifts in Salvationist teaching, learning, and preaching around holiness. Correlations were drawn between less teaching and clarity around holiness with lower levels of focus on holiness. Shifts in worship practices have also been perceived as influencing the extent of holiness theology in Salvationist faith communities. This involves the widespread reduction in Sunday services, from two meetings—commonly termed as the "holiness" and the "salvation" meetings—to just one. As one participant noted, the common perception was that in "the holiness meeting . . . people are already saved, we're going to bring them into a further experience with God. The salvation meeting, we're bringing people off the street for their first introduction to Jesus." As another participant observed, "we're covering holiness and salvation in the one meeting." This practical shift in communal worship practices has occurred due to various factors that may include declining attendance and shifts in the focus on evangelization, which in turn may lessen the usefulness of a specific salvation-focused meeting. Whatever the causes may have been, shifts in worship practices have been perceived to affect the impact of theology in Salvationist faith communities. As one contributor expressed: "Even that kind of remedial understanding of what the words meant, we don't have an example of anymore. So, I think our own practice has made it a less relevant word for most people."

Further findings explored the range of positive aspects and perceived barriers that were expressed by participants when discussing the practicalities of aiming toward living a holy life that integrates ecological care. In terms of perceived barriers, primary themes of resistance, hindrance, and temptation emerged. Subthemes included: greed, self-centeredness, and inconvenience; lifestyle, finances, and consumerism; personal limitations, awareness, and anthropocentrism; political, structural, and theological influences. Positive themes around opportunities and entry points towards embracing the integration of ecological awareness within the notion of holy living were voiced and supported by most research contributors. The major themes reported included: love, wholeness, and justice; education, simplicity, and balance; personal and collective engagement; and experiencing the beauty of creation. As there were a significant number of participant quotes, only a brief overview of some of the main themes will now be shared.

Areas of resistance to embracing the inclusion of ecological care within the scope of holy living that emerged within the research project included observations around demographics, anthropocentrism, politics, correlations to environmental movements, theology, spiritual/physical dualism, and priorities. Speaking to the theme of lower prioritization placed on ecological holiness, evidencing a perceived divide between the spiritual and ecological, and providing an overarching sense of the general situation could be summed up in this online survey response: "I'm afraid that we don't have personal, spiritual holiness down yet. On the list of priorities of holiness, Environmental Holiness is way down that list."

Many participants conveyed a sense that the range of issues of concern and the available response options to these concerns can often be overwhelming. Furthermore, numerous participants revealed that they felt there is a finite ability for people and groups to act in holy ways continuously and constantly. Responses acknowledges wider structural issues and the enormity of the effort of living a holy life, yet also recognized the responsibility of taking on the process of care and of God's love and grace.

Perceived doorways to (eco)holiness were varied and included experiencing the beauty of creation, the notions of wholeness, love and justice, and by others seeing environmentally-mindful holiness being lived out effectively and consistently by Salvationists. Engaging in consistent ecologically perceptive action was advocated by numerous research contributors, both in relation to generally moving towards holiness and as a helpful opening for others who may not be currently aware or attentive to ecological aspects of holy living. Visions of personal holiness within the larger community of believers and the structures of The Salvation Army were also shared by participants.

The unencumbered, simple life was often highly admired and commended by respondents. For several respondents, the notion of holistic holiness included spending quality time and allowing space for God to speak. Furthermore, the life and example of Jesus featured consistently in responses and discussion on the topic of engaged, ecologically-aware holiness throughout the research project. The themes of love, holiness, and justice are deeply embedded within the scriptures and also within Wesleyan-Holiness theology. Participants took these themes and conveyed their concern that love, compassion and justice for the entirety of creation—not simply for humanity—would be a natural outflow of continued commitment to holiness.

Holiness was often considered as being contextually responsive to the issues faced by each Salvationist in their own situation and was commonly viewed as a journey into new areas of learning and faith and as encompassing all aspects of life. There was frequent focus on experiences, helps, habits, and tips for personal engagement toward more effective thought and action that integrates ecological matters and holiness. Numerous participants also spoke of their own experiences of awe and wonder at the beauty of creation and the way in which it has enhanced their own faith. The following quote from an online participant offers a view on the scope of holy living within God's creation, in terms of the gospel and the necessity of not engaging in harmful actions: "In Mark 16:15 we have the great commission to go into all the world and preach the gospel (good news) to all creation. This is an idea that is broader than just people. It seems to me to suggest that God's good news is somehow linked to the whole of creation. If the environment is to receive the gospel and be taken care of, then the destructive behaviors of humanity don't fit at all with any true form of holy living."

An optional online survey segment included fourteen questions that appeared in the 2011 Australian National Church Life Survey (NCLS). These questions were considered relevant to exploring Salvationist views on the importance of ecological matters to faith and action. The survey measures were slightly modified to incorporate Salvationist terminology such as "corps." As this second section of the online survey was optional, the total number of respondents (n=49) was lower than the main body of the survey (n=90). A brief overview of some of the question responses will be noted in order of the highest proportion where respondents "strongly agreed" and "agreed" with question statements:

- Non-human creation praises God (97 percent);
- God is present in nature (95 percent);
- Christians have a responsibility to be active on environmental issues (93 percent);
- Humanity's role is to help all life thrive (91 percent);
- Creation care is an essential part of the Church's mission (86 percent);
- We need to care for earth for the sake of humans (86 percent);
- Humanity created to rule over nature (63 percent);
- The most important aspect of ecological care is human flourishing (28 percent).

Concluding Thoughts

Within the Anthropocene, it appears that a complex and multidimensional existential crisis is unfolding. With the levels of ecological destruction and the potentialities of further climate upheavals on one hand, and the dissatisfactions that are expressed with the apparent need and demands placed on continued consumption on the other, there is growth in the number of people who are questioning the value, logic, and health of the current pervasive model of growth, wealth, and consumption.

Moving forward within the Anthropocene can be described as a "wicked" problem, that is, a confluence of pronounced complexity, definite uncertainty, and value divergence. Hence, there is not one preeminent theory or clearly indicated course of action. Furthermore, terms such as "nature," "environment," "sustainability," and the discourses around them are certainly contested, heterogeneous and therefore have the potential to be divisive in social and political spheres.[20] Factors such as apathy, fear, the lack or misrepresentation of information, having a purely spiritual focus on holiness where the body is seen as being against the spirit, or focusing on political or financial concerns, can mean that, for many, the easiest option is to continue with "business as usual." Of course, that avenue is not amenable to those who understand that "business as usual" will very likely result in increased ecological degradation and human inequalities. Consequently, action could be taken in ways that either stays within the bounds of societal norms, moves beyond current societal norms in passive or gradual forms, or moves beyond current societal norms in radical oppositional forms of the current systems.

Kahan argues for the removal of "culturally antagonistic meanings" that have become "entangled" in environmental debates.[21] The literature explored within the project, together with the insightful views of the research participants, constitutes a compelling case that for followers of Christ, practical holistic holiness—as a response to God's love and grace—is a key frame through which caring for all of God's creation can be stripped of competing ideologies or political notions that do not sit well with holy living.

Different models, ideas, and practices will emerge as the best way forward for particular local contexts through continuing considerate conversations around the most helpful actions that individual Salvationists and The Salvation Army as a movement can take in terms of embodied, practical, and ecologically-mindful holiness. Along with Krasny and Tidball, I contend that there is a definite need for more positive instances

20. Wells, *Dreams of Sustainable Capital*.
21. Kahan, *What You "Believe."*

where people are actively working to recreate or "rebuild the health of their community while restoring the health of their local environment."[22] Krasny and Tidball further suggest that there is a critical message in these "civic ecology" practices, that "Humans are not separate from the environment that surrounds us . . . we are part of nature, and in coming together to heal our local environments, we also heal our communities and ourselves."[23]

There are a multitude of movements, groups, and individuals who take practical approaches that move away from "business as usual" models and bear in mind the holistic relational impetus between the social, ecological, and economic that can be instructive for Salvationists on the journey toward holistic holiness. For example, Ivanko and Kivirist provide one way forward past a business-oriented society.[24] For the "entrepreneur," Ivanko and Kivrist argue that the prime value belongs to money; environmental and social costs are externalized; the crucial stakeholders are stockholders; and the common view that "bigger is better." Whereas for the "ecopreneur," the primary values are the flourishing of life, purpose, meaning, and fulfilment. Environmental and social costs are either imbedded or internalized. The business stakeholders include nature, communities, and future generations with preferences for smaller scale, simpler, and adaptable solutions. Ivanko and Kivirist raise the specter of the four horsemen of the apocalypse and their related horrors of pestilence, war, famine, and death and make a connection to four ecologically-related fears: climate change, ecological collapse, peak oil, and debt. They then bring a positive spin by directing these four fears into motivation for positive change and hope that a holistic approach to life is both necessary and possible.[25]

There are also a variety of models that may assist Salvationists and The Salvation Army to promote a holistic view of life within the biosphere. Circles of Sustainability is one such practical, collaborative tool for engaging in "making our cities, locales and organizations more sustainable, resilient, adaptable and liveable."[26] The process within the Circles of Sustainability framework involves examining four main

22. Krasny and Tidball, *Civic Ecology*, xiii.
23. Krasny and Tidball, *Civic Ecology*, xiii.
24. Ivanko and Kivirist, *Ecopreneuring*, 25.
25. Ivanko and Kivirist, *Ecopreneuring*, 33.
26. Circles of Sustainability, "Circles of Social Life."

domains of a local community: economics, ecology, politics, and culture. Each primary domain contains seven subdomains. Three other stages outlined in the Circles of Sustainability model lend themselves to assist Salvationists making positive, ecologically-holy impacts. First, the process circle stage provides pathways for moving forward with projects. Second, engagement circles consider the ways in which civil society (inclusive of faith-based groups), governance institutions, business organizations, and research-based entities can interact and collaborate. Third, knowledge circles do not prioritize empirical analysis, but look to "sensory experience (feeling), practical consciousness (pragmatics), reflective consciousness (reflection) [and] reflexive knowing (reflexivity)" to enhance engagement throughout the processes.[27] For Salvationists and The Salvation Army corporately, considering integrating practical holiness into these and other extant models is reasonable and sensible. Yet, there are deeper personal issues that also require attention.

Acknowledging and praising God for the gift of a beautiful creation is an indispensable aspect of following in the way of Jesus. Yet, praise, words, and faith that do not result in practical love and care for God's loved creation appear hollow and equally "actions without the words that convey purpose are empty."[28] There is serious need for Christian thoughts, words, and deeds to "co-inhere" and to convey love, hope, healing, and wholeness for all of God's loved creation.

It is a complex task to consider the holistic embodiment of holiness, to consider the varying impacts of individual and collective consumerism on those who are poor and marginalized, on local ecosystems, and the global biosphere. How might a particular action impact and effect change spiritually, physically, and ecologically, both personally and collectively? Practically caring for all of God's creation, both for the glory of God and as a response to God in Jesus Christ and the Spirit's outpouring of holy love, can encompass so many personal and communal actions. Recycling; supporting sustainable practices and policies in all aspects of individual, community, and corporate life; reducing consumerist mentalities, energy usage, and ecological footprints are but some of the areas that can be considered as practical holiness. As Howard Snyder observes: "These are not mere secondary or peripheral ethical concerns, nor are they primarily political issues. They are good old-fashioned holiness

---

27. Circles of Sustainability, "Knowledge Circles."
28. Cameron et al., *Talking About God in Practice*, 14.

issues."[29] Similarly, Emily Haynes speaks, originally to the Church of the Nazarene, around these inherently holistic holiness issues:

> If we ... could finally start to believe that holiness is really about living a life of wholeness, then we could change the world with God. If our "distinctive doctrine" started to be translated as insistence that God cares about every part of our lives, then we would start to look very different from everyone else. We might shop at thrift stores to be able to afford to give clothes to those who need them. We might start to grow our own food as a way to connect to the soil and educate our neighbors about how they can free themselves from a corrupt system. We might create alternative societies where people have common possessions and pay off each other's debts. A life of wholeness ... a life of holiness will allow us to do weird things that no one else can explain, but everyone wants to be a part of.[30]

Everyday choices, noted by Haynes, Snyder, and others, inform and flow forth from what can be described as a *habitus*. A personal *habitus* is socially constructed and influenced by cultural, ecological, emotional, religious, and other such factors. A *habitus* is described by Forrester as "a disposition of the mind and heart from which action flows naturally, in an unselfconscious way."[31] Dispositions of the mind and heart that flow naturally also sit within the sphere of holiness and holy living. There is close interrelatedness between the journey towards holiness and the natural outflow of inner dispositions. Dispositions that are often considered integral to a holistic Christian worldview and holy lifestyle, termed "fruit of the spirit" in Galatians 5:22–23, include and embrace the rich and deep concepts and related living out of love, joy, peace, patience, kindness, goodness, faithfulness, gentleness, and self-control within the finite boundaries of life in this world.

At the heart of the Christian way of life is an outpouring of, and disposition towards, love, peace, justice, hope, and practical wisdom. Practical theologies must take into account the complex fusion of global and local conditions and aim to provide positive, sensitive, accessible, theologically-sound, and practical thinking towards praxis to assist in the formation and adoption of an increasingly holistic personal *habitus* in community. Spiritual and personal formation of the individual, which

---

29. Snyder, *Holiness and the Five Calls*, 143.
30. Haynes, "Holiness," 84.
31. Forrester, *Truthful Action*, 5.

can also be described as the journey toward holiness, occurs within the bounds of community. As Kaoma avers, holistically living out the gospel of Jesus cannot help but "envision an interdependent community of all creatures intricately and inextricably connected to a single sacred web of life in Christ."[32] Being aware of and carefully involved in particular communities, ecosystems, and watersheds[33] are crucial to the flourishing of life, as our personal lives are always lived in relation to others and the entirety of life on Earth.

Personal journeys inform and influence, and in turn are informed and influenced by, the communal theology and praxis of the wider Church, both locally and globally through the communication and sharing of new insights and helpful knowledge. For example, worship and preaching provide opportunities for reflection on and exhortation to ecologically-attentive and practical holiness.[34] This can then lead toward deeper personal formation and holy transformation toward holistic (eco) holiness in community. Cone states that, like personal transformation, changing "communities involves a change of *being*. It is a radical movement, a radical reorientation of one's existence in the world. Christianity calls this experience conversion."[35]

Viewed in negative terms, there are consequences when transformation, conversion and the journey towards holiness is unbalanced, impractical, incomplete, or not holistic. As Wall argues, the toleration of unholy words and actions "subverts the internal integrity and external witness of the church as God's holy people."[36] Furthermore, Ayre contends that "the challenge for the holiness of the Church now is to acknowledge the sinfulness and profanity of the church itself, and re-conceive what 'holy' means in this context."[37] To use a Wesleyan term, for those who have become "backsliders" from a holistic, all-encompassing perspective on holiness, there is grace and hope towards being restored to a vision of holistic holiness permeating all of life.

It is my hope that this project and the short overview within this chapter are useful contributions to the literature and also to the practices

---

32. Kaoma, *Creation Care*, 8–9.

33. Myers, *Watershed Discipleship*; Seaman, "(Re)discovering Watershed Discipleship."

34. E.g., Rhoads, *Earth and Word*; Spiller, *Sermon on the Environment*.

35. Cone, *A Black Theology of Liberation*, 103.

36. Wall, *Reading Paul with Acts*, 145.

37. Ayre, *Where on Earth is the Church?*

of the church, that it may create a "potentially transformative resonance" with the reader in their current context.[38] That these works may provide a positive, practical theological contribution to the conversation around exploring relevant ways for Salvationists, The Salvation Army, and the wider body of the church that encourages and cultivates holy, sacramental, sustainable, and holistic life within what can be termed the Anthropocene—that it may assist toward continued personal and communal conversions, *metanoias*, "radical reorientation[s] of one's existence in the world"[39] that broadens the scope of holy living to include practical, ecologically-mindful actions. That followers of Jesus may take seriously the responsibility to pursue dynamic *habitus* and contextual postures of holiness that inherently integrate practical care, concern, and compassion for all of God's loved creation, of renewing one's own mind, and partnering in love and hope with neighbors, nations, and nature towards restoring and reconciling all things on earth and in heaven, by making peace through Jesus, the holy creator of all things (Col 1:20). There are potentially far-reaching and positive impacts of practical, holistic holiness—the living out of the fruit of the Spirit—on the world as a whole. There is hope that the world, that is, the hearts and lives of people, societies, and the flourishing of the entire biosphere, will be positively enriched through practical, loving expressions of holiness to all of creation.

Bibliography

Ayre, Clive. "Where on Earth is the Church? The Nature, Mission, Governance and Ministry of the Church." In *Christian Faith and the Earth: Current Paths and Emerging Horizons in Ecotheology*, edited by E. Conradie et al., 137–56. London: Bloomsbury T&T Clark, 2014.

Barratt, Ingrid. "The Flourishing of All Things." https://www.salvationarmy.org.nz/article/flourishing-all-things.

Booth, William. *In Darkest England and The Way Out*. Atlanta: The Salvation Army, 1942.

Broward, Josh, and Thomas J. Oord, eds. *Renovating Holiness*. Nampa, ID: SacraSage, 2015.

Cameron, Helen, et al. *Talking About God in Practice: Theological Action Research and Practical Theology*. London: SCM, 2010.

Circles of Sustainability. "Circles of Social Life." http://www.circlesofsustainability.org/.

———. "Knowledge Circles." https://www.circlesofsustainability.org/circles-overview/knowledge-circles/.

38. Swinton and Mowat, *Practical Theology*, 47.
39. Cone, *A Black Theology of Liberation*, 103.

Cone, James H. *A Black Theology of Liberation*. 40th Anniversary ed. Maryknoll, NY: Orbis, 2010.

Edelstein, Michael R., et al. *Cultures of Contamination: Legacies of Pollution in Russia and the U.S.* Bingley, UK: Emerald Group, 2007.

Forrester, Duncan B. *Truthful Action: Explorations in Practical Theology*. Edinburgh: T&T Clark, 2000.

Gallaway, Terrel, et al. "The Economics of Global Light Pollution." *Ecological Economics* 69 (2009) 658–65.

Harley, Alan. "Is The Salvation Army Really a Holiness Movement?" *Word and Deed* 11.2 (2009) 5–18.

Haynes, Emily JoAnn. "Holiness: The Most Hipster Doctrine." In *Renovating Holiness*, edited by Josh Broward and Thomas J. Oord, 81–85. Nampa, ID: SacraSage, 2015.

Hill, Harold. *Leadership in the Salvation Army: A Case Study in Clericalisation*. Milton Keynes, UK: Paternoster, 2006.

Hoekstra, Arjen, et al. "Global Monthly Water Scarcity: Blue Water Footprints versus Blue Water Availability." *PLoS One* 7.2 (2012) e32688. https://doi.org/10.1371/joural.pone.0032688.

Intergovernmental Panel on Climate Change (IPCC). *First Assessment Report*. 1990. https://www.ipcc.ch/reports/?rp=ar1.

———. *Second Assessment Report*. 1995. https://www.ipcc.ch/reports/?rp=ar2.

———. *Third Assessment Report*. 2001. https://www.ipcc.ch/reports/?rp=ar3.

———. *Fourth Assessment Report*. 2007. https://www.ipcc.ch/reports/?rp=ar4.

———. *Fifth Assessment Report*. 2014. https://www.ipcc.ch/reports/?rp=ar5.

Ivanko, John, and Lisa Kivirist. *ECOpreneuring: Putting Purpose and the Planet before Profits*. Gabriola Island, BC: New Society, 2008.

Joshi, Dina K. "Ozone Depletion: A Challenging Global Pollution Issue." *International Journal of Science, Environment and Technology* 2.4 (2013) 654–60.

Kahan, Dan. "What You 'Believe' about Climate Change Doesn't Reflect What You Know; It Expresses *Who You Are*." *The Cultural Cognition Project at Yale Law School Blog*, April 23, 2014. http://www.culturalcognition.net/blog/2014/4/23/what-you-believe-about-climate-change-doesnt-reflect-what-yo.html.

Kaoma, Kapya J., ed. *Creation Care in Christian Mission*. Oxford: Regnum, 2015.

Koch, A., et al. "Soil Security: Solving the Global Soil Crisis." *Global Policy* 4.4 (2013) 434–41.

Krasny, Marianne E., and Keith G. Tidball. *Civic Ecology: Adaptation and Transformation from the Ground Up*. Cambridge: MIT Press, 2015.

Lodahl, Michael, and April C. Maskiewicz. *Renewal in Love: Living Holy Lives in God's Good Creation*. Kansas City: Beacon Hill, 2014.

Murphy, Enda, and Eoin King. *Environmental Noise Pollution: Noise Mapping, Public Health, and Policy*. Burlington, MA: Elsevier, 2014.

Myers, Ched, ed. *Watershed Discipleship: Reinhabiting Bioregional Faith and Practice*. Eugene, OR: Cascade, 2016.

National Oceanic and Atmospheric Administration (NOAA). *Marine Debris Program*. http://marinedebris.noaa.gov/.

Oord, Thomas J., and Michael Lodahl. *Relational Holiness: Responding to the Call of Love*. Kansas City: Beacon Hill, 2005.

President's Cancer Panel (PCP). *Reducing Environmental Cancer Risk: What We Can Do Now, 2008–2009 Annual Report*. National Cancer Institute, 2010. https://deainfo.

nci.nih.gov/advisory/pcp/annualreports/pcp08-09rpt/pcp_report_08-09_508. pdf.

Ramanathan, V., and Y. Feng. "Air Pollution, Greenhouse Gases and Climate Change: Global and Regional Perspectives." *Atmospheric Environment* 43.1 (2009) 37–50.

Raymond, Jonathan S., and Roger J. Green. "Our Historical Heritage of Holiness." *Word and Deed* 13.2 (2011) 5–18.

Rhoads, David M., ed. *Earth and Word: Classic Sermons on Saving the Planet*. New York: Continuum, 2007.

The Salvation Army. "A Call for Climate Justice." https://issuu.com/isjc/docs/climate_ justice_full.docx.

———. "Climate Change." https://www.salvationarmy.org.au/masic/guidelines-for-salvationists/climate-change/.

———. "Environmental Sustainability." https://www.sarmy.org.au/en/Social/ JustSalvos/Issues/Environmental-Sustainability/.

———. "Our Work, Worldwide." http://www.salvationarmy.org/ihq/zones.

———. "The Salvation Army International Positional Statement: Caring for the Environment." https://s3.amazonaws.com/cache.salvationarmy.org/bd8885f7-16a9-4ab7-bcee-c035301e2f9e_English+Caring+for+the+Environment+IPS.pdf.

Schnoor, Jerald L. "Ocean Acidification." *Environmental Science and Technology* 47.21 (2013) 11919. https://doi.org/10.1021/es404263h.

Seaman, Matthew, ed. *Darkness and Deliverance: 125 Years of the Darkest England Scheme*. Nambour, QLD: Chaordic Creative, 2016.

Seaman, Matthew. "(Re)discovering Watershed Discipleship." *Thought Matters* 8 (2019) 11–24.

———. "'To Turn the World Upside Down': An Empirical Study of Salvationist Understandings of Holiness in the Anthropocene." PhD Thesis, University of Queensland, 2018.

Snyder, Howard A. "Holiness and the Five Calls of God: Holiness in Postmodernity." In *The Holiness Manifesto*, edited by Kevin Mannoia and Don Thorsen, 129–51. Grand Rapids: Eerdmans, 2008.

Snyder. Howard A., with Joel Scandrett. *Salvation Means Creation Healed: The Ecology of Sin and Grace*. Eugene, OR: Cascade, 2011.

Spiller, Catherine. "Sermon on the Environment." In *Environmental Justice*, Just Salvos Information Pack, edited by M. Seaman et al., 6–7. Melbourne: The Salvation Army Australia Southern Territory, 2016. https://www.sarmy.org.au/Global/ SArmy/Social/justsalvos/images/2016/Environmental%20Justice/Just-Salvos-Environmental-Justice-Resource-Pack.pdf.

Street, Robert. *Called to Be God's People: The International Spiritual Life Commission, Its Report, Implications and Challenges*. London: The General of the Salvation Army, 1999.

Swinton, John, and Harriet Mowat. *Practical Theology and Qualitative Research*. London: SCM, 2006.

Wall, Robert. "Reading Paul with Acts: The Canonical Shaping of a Holy Church." In *Holiness and Ecclesiology in the New Testament*, edited by Kent Brower and Andy Johnson, 129–47. Grand Rapids: Eerdmans, 2007.

Wells, Peter. "Dreams of Sustainable Capital: Environment and Discourse in the Social Production of Space." Honors Thesis (BA), University of Queensland, 2012.

Wesley, John. *The Works of John Wesley: Volume 13: Doctrinal and Controversial Treatises II*. Edited by Paul Wesley Chilcote and Kenneth J. Collins. Nashville: Abingdon, 2013.

World Wildlife Fund (WWF). *Living Planet Report 2014: Species and Spaces, People and Places*. Gland, CH: WWF International. 2014. http://assets.worldwildlife.org/publications/723/files/original/WWF-LPR2014-low_res.pdf?1413912230&_ga=2.257748939.110608558.1606351290-1389553635.1606351290.

10

How Relationality Facilitates Human Flourishing

A Neurobiological and Christological Conversation

EMMA E. MOORE

Introduction

ANDREA AND NINO PISANO's marble sculpture, *La Madonna del latte* was composed in the fourteenth century and is now displayed in the National Museum of Saint Matthew in Pisa, Italy.[1] This art piece is reflective of popular medieval iconography of *Madonna and Child*. It depicts Christ gazing at Mary while suckling at her breast. You may notice how the two study one another with eye contact. The baby tenderly holds his mother's breast with his hands. Mary's arms encircle the Christ-child. The infant receives touch, milk, and gaze from his mother. What we see here is an important aspect of Christ's human nature. He is a vulnerable, dependent person. He is recipient of his mother's care, nourishment, and protection. He is reaching out to touch his mother and in return, he receives her touch. He is recipient and benefactor of relationality.

1. Pisano and Pisano, "Le collezioni del Museo."

Drawing together this Christological perspective and key aspects of Interpersonal Neurobiology, in this paper I will explore how relationality is intrinsically linked to human flourishing. While much has been written about relationality between people and God through contemplative practices and how these contribute to the flourishing of human life, this paper will only examine relationality between people. The first part of this paper will explore emerging research of how the human brain is shaped by relationships. In the second part our attention will turn to a Christocentric focus, examining how Christ was both giver and receiver of relationality and exemplar for human flourishing. I will return to the *Madonna del latte* to consider the paradox of how self-giving and sacrifice facilitate human flourishing. And finally, I will consider the neurobiological data coupled with the Christological perspective to discuss the implications for Christian faith and practice.

Defining Flourishing

In their book on wellbeing, psychology of religion scholars Martin Dowson, Stuart Devenish, and Maureen Miner trace the philosophical and psychological approaches to wellbeing and human flourishing. They conclude that there are two aspects to human flourishing.[2] The first is the internal aspect of actualization and the second the external aspect of altruism. "Actualization refers to the ongoing and achieved realization of the individual's human potential across developmental domains (physical, emotional, intellectual and spiritual). Altruism refers to the deployment of the individual's realized potential to the benefit of others."[3] Philosopher, Alasdair MacIntyre highlights that people who are dependent upon others are most successful at being effective "independent practical reasoners." For MacIntyre, this is the goal of human development.[4] This understanding of human flourishing is expounded upon by bioethicist Stephen Post who describes true flourishing as the extent that a life is marked by giving and love, expressed in compassion and mutuality.[5] The neuroscience of human flourishing is relatively new. Known as positive neuroscience, researchers are discovering that

2. Miner et al., *Beyond Wellbeing*.
3. Miner et al., *Beyond Wellbeing*, 15.
4. MacIntyre, *Dependent Rational Animals*, 99.
5. Pope, "Jesus Christ and Human Flourishing."

the flourishing life is marked by social bonds, altruism, resilience, and creativity.[6] Across the disciplines, human flourishing is connected to relationality.[7] And I want to argue that flourishing is enhanced for those who are embedded in a web of relationships that are marked by mutual attunement, attachment, self-giving and sacrifice.

The Neuroscience of Human Flourishing and Relationality

In his work in the area of Interpersonal Neurobiology, neuropsychologist Daniel Siegel explores the impact that relationality has upon the human brain's capacity to flourish. Defined as attunement and attachment to others, relationality has the potential to create new neurons and new synaptic connections, particularly in the limbic system, which can strengthen the brain, creating cognitive health and altering the physiology of the brain.[8] This feature of the brain's architecture demonstrates that the brain is malleable, capable of adapting and changing, significantly impacted by extrinsic factors such as life experiences, education, and relationships. This factor is known as neuroplasticity and the system that is most influenced and shaped by relationality is known as the attachment system.[9] In infancy and childhood, a person is motivated to seek proximity to those caring relationships in order to build communication, empathy, emotional regulation, memory, and trust. The developing brain of the child seeks out the mature brain of the caring adult in order to organize and regulate itself. The caregiver provides a circle of security that allows the child's personhood and identity to be formed. Certain processes take place in the brain triggering certain behaviors. For example, if a fearful child is firmly embraced and comforted by the caring adult, neurotransmitters flood the brain and neural integration is achieved, creating a sense of security, connection, and reward. If the caregiver is consistent in meeting the child's needs, the brain consistently produces these neurotransmitters and further neural integration occurs, enabling

---

6. Greene et al., *Positive Neuroscience*, 2–4.

7. For more information on the impact of contemplative practices upon the brain refer to: Newberg and Waldman, *How God Changes Your Brain*; Ricard, "Inner Experience and Neuroscience," 15–25; Shukla et al., "Neurotheology-Matters," 1486–90.

8. Costandi, *Neuroplasticity*, 145–47.

9. Siegel, *The Developing Mind*, 14.

the child to regulate their emotions, make sense of the world, and develop trust and the feeling of deep attachment.[10] In addition, the child becomes more confident to explore the world and move into adulthood as a flourishing person. However, even if secure attachment does not take place in infancy or childhood, the neuroplastic nature of the brain allows the system of attachment to be shaped and reformed through significant and intentional relationships all throughout life. In adult to adult relationships, secure attachment helps to increase resilience, compassion and empathy, the capacity to love and forgive.[11]

Coupled with attachment is the need for the human brain to "feel felt" by other people.[12] This is known as emotional attunement. According to Siegel, attunement is a requirement for the human person to survive and to flourish.[13] An aspect of human behavior that increases emotional attunement is eye-contact. The human mirror-neuron system generates activity that allows the person to feel known, enhancing compassion, and communication between people when eye-contact and intentional gazing takes place.[14] In his research on how communication shapes the brain, neuroscientist Andrew Newberg developed a strategy called Compassionate Conversation that was designed to enhance the mirror-neuron system and strengthen emotional attunement. This practice involved two people sitting in close proximity, making eye-contact, and engaging in mindful but spontaneous conversation, while holding compassionate thoughts about one another. It was reported that the participants did experience an increase in activity in the mirror circuitry of the brain, which led to greater emotional attunement.[15] Newberg reported, "After practicing Compassionate Communication with strangers, both men and women were more likely to share personal information and were more willing to listen to personal disclosures. They felt closer to each other and were more willing to be emotionally supportive and socially affectionate. Thus, Compassionate Communication appears to be an effective strategy for generating interpersonal understanding and peace."[16] Neuroscience is

10. Brown et al., "Human Relationality," 99.
11. Siegel, *The Developing Mind*, 21.
12. Hollingsworth, "Neuroscience and Spirituality," 850.
13. Siegel, *The Mindful Brain*, 317.
14. Newberg and Waldman, *How God Changes Your Brain*, 217.
15. Newberg and Waldman, *How God Changes Your Brain*, 218.
16. Newberg and Waldman, *How God Changes Your Brain*, 218.

demonstrating that relationality and human flourishing are intrinsically connected. Those brains that feel "felt," attuned, and attached to others are the brains that flourish.

The Example of Christ

Taking into consideration the neuroscience of human flourishing and relationality, we turn now to the Incarnation. In her work on the trinity and Christian life, Catholic theologian, Catherine Mowry LaCugna said, "Human beings are created in the image of the relational God and gradually are being perfected in the image (*theosis*)."[17] She referred to the communion of the divine and human natures of Christ and to Paul's claim that Christ is the image of God (2 Cor. 4:4). She continued, "Christian Theology looks to the person of Jesus Christ to see both who God is, and who we are. . . . He is the exemplar of human nature."[18] As the example of human nature, the life of Christ demonstrates that the measure of flourishing is intrinsically connected to the extent of communion with God and with others. The gospel accounts demonstrate that Jesus' purpose and sustenance originated in and was maintained by his proximity to the other persons in the godhead, which was described by the early church fathers as like a loving dance or *perichoresis*. "*Perichoresis* means being-in-one-another and . . . provides a dynamic model of persons in communion based on mutuality and interdependence."[19] Theologian John Jefferson Davis outlines three aspects of the perichoretic nature of the Triune God.[20] These aspects are shared interiority, reciprocal empathy, and, what Davis calls, the "*Thou-Thou*" relationship, which he draws from the concept of the *I-Thou* relationship in philosopher Martin Buber's personalist work.[21] Shared interiority speaks of each person of the godhead participating openly and mutually in the inner-life of the others. Reciprocal empathy refers to the affinity and insight shared within the Trinity and the "*Thou-Thou*" relationship describes the interdependent respect, openness, transparency, and trust between the persons of the godhead where each person allows themselves and the other to be known

17. LaCugna, *God for Us*, 292.
18. LaCugna, *God for Us*, 293.
19. LaCugna, *God for Us*, 271.
20. Davis, "What is Perichoresis," 146.
21. Buber, *I and Thou*.

as a *thou*. Davis suggests that the concept of perichoresis is not only a way of understanding the Trinity, but it is also a framework for understanding the ultimate purpose of the incarnation of Christ.

The Gospels paint a portrait of Christ seeking proximity to others (e.g., John 1:14). His proximity to people was marked by mutual giving and receiving in relationships where there was shared conversation, eye-contact, and touch. For instance, Jesus saw, heard, and shared a meal with Zacchaeus (Luke 19:1–10). On another occasion, Jesus saw and heard the man who had been possessed by demons (Luke 8:26–39). Jesus saw, heard, and received touch from the woman who had a reputation for being a sinner (Luke 7:36–50). In this account of Jesus being anointed by the sinful woman, the relationality that was shared between Jesus and the woman—the amalgamation of Jesus' proximity to the woman and the woman's *agape* love displayed in touch and acts of honorable hospitality—were defined as salvific for the woman. Jesus states, "I tell you, her sins, which were many, have been forgiven; hence she has shown great love" (Luke 7:47).[22] What this and other Gospel stories demonstrate is the relational nature of Jesus; he was attuned to others, orientated otherward, living in solidarity with others, especially with those who were relegated to the margins of society. However, what the Lukan story also demonstrates is that Jesus benefited from interdependence where he was both giver and receiver of relationality. He not only gave of himself, but he was recipient of the woman's *agape*.

This is what the *Madonna del latte* sculpture demonstrates. In the act of breastfeeding, important formation of attachment takes place between the mother and the child as mother responds to the needs of the infant. Neural integration takes place in the child's brain as the mother responds to the needs of her child. In addition, the mirror neuron system is activated, creating a sense of attunement between mother and infant. The pituitary gland in the brains of mother and child produces the hormone oxytocin which creates a secure attachment, deep trust and a sense of self for the child and enhances the woman's capacity to nurture and form an emotional connection to her child.[23] Both child and mother benefit from this relationship. The mother experiences feelings of love and warmth, her blood pressure and stress levels lower and she becomes

---

22. *Sozo* can also be translated as healing and wholeness and is the same word used in Luke 19:9 and Luke 8:36 to define Jesus' interaction with Zacchaeus and the man possessed by the demon (Strong, *A Concise Dictionary of Greek*, 70).

23. Cozolino, *Neuroscience of Human Relationships*, 121.

more focused while the infant is nourished by the mother's self-giving and sacrifice. Feminist theologian, Jeannine Fletcher captures this in a profound way. "The woman who has committed herself to nurturing her child in this way must follow through on the giving. And she herself is the gift. All that sustains the child has been produced within her. . . . This is sacrifice. It is self-giving that empties the self."[24] This sculpture compels us to consider the mutual giving and receiving nature of relationality. However, it suggests to us that self-denial and sacrifice are also part of what it means to be human, to be part of a web of relationships and part of what it means to flourish.

Perhaps the ultimate example of how self-denial and sacrifice facilitate flourishing is in Jesus' acts of selfless love. Paul describes Jesus in his letter to the Philippians as self-emptying and self-giving, becoming a servant of all and becoming obedient to death on the cross (Phil 2:6–8). The crucifixion and resurrection of Jesus expressed the full meaning of Jesus' proximity to human life, signifying Jesus' love and solidarity in suffering with people, the hope for life to be restored and renewed and affirming that people are created to love and to be loved in the same manner that Jesus loved.[25] As the prime example of human nature, Jesus demonstrated that human flourishing is associated with mutual giving and receiving in relationships of proximity. However, Jesus' example illustrates that sacrifice, self-denial, and laying down one's life for others are also indicative of relationality and can facilitate human flourishing.

Conclusion

Both the example of Christ and the examples drawn from neuroscience indicate that people flourish in relationships that are marked by proximity to others who see, hear, and touch them. Those people that make up an individual's web of relationships and the quality of those relationships are a significant factor in how a person flourishes. In terms of Christian faith and practice, those people who commit themselves to a relationship or a small group of relationships where there is interdependence, mutuality, understanding, and trust, where conversation is mindfully compassionate and spontaneous, when the individuals can participate in

24. Fletcher, *Motherhood as Metaphor*, 56.
25. World Council of Churches, *Christian Perspectives on Theological Anthropology*, 22.

intentional gazing or eye-contact, and appropriate touch, the potential for the person to flourish increases. Christian practices that prioritize the fostering of friendship and the sharing of life are practices that can foster attachment and attunement and facilitate the flourishing of human life.

I have argued in this paper that the flourishing life is one that is embedded in relationships of proximity and mutuality, where everyone is able to engage in eye-contact, compassionate conversation, and is able to give and receive touch. This relationality has the potential to shape the human brain, resulting in individuals who are more inclined towards compassion, empathy, and forgiveness. The Christocentric perspective reveals that, along with these qualities and characteristics, relationality is also costly to the self, requiring sacrifice, self-denial, and suffering. However, as one gives of self for the other, the other may flourish and give of self. It is this mutual giving and receiving that is aptly reflected in the very nature of the perichoretic God and is a model for human relationships.

Bibliography

Brown, Warren S., and Brad D. Strawn. *The Physical Nature of Christian Life: Neuroscience, Psychology, and the Church*. New York: Cambridge University Press, 2012.

Brown, Warren S., et al. "Human Relationality, Spiritual Formation, and Wesleyan Communities." In *Wesleyan Theology and Social Science: The Dance of Practical Divinity and Discovery*, edited by M. Kathryn Armistead et al., 95–109. Newcastle upon Tyne: Cambridge Scholars, 2010.

Buber, Martin. *I and Thou*. Translated by Walter Kaufmann. New York: Scribner's Sons, 1970.

Costandi, Moheb. *Neuroplasticity*. Cambridge: MIT Press, 2016.

Cozolino, Louis. *The Neuroscience of Human Relationships: Attachment and the Developing Social Brain*. New York: Norton and Company, 2014.

Davis, John Jefferson. "What is 'Perichoresis'—and Why Does it Matter? Perichoresis as Properly Basic to the Christian Faith." *Evangelical Review of Theology* 39.2 (2015) 144–56.

Fletcher, Jeannine Hill. *Motherhood as Metaphor: Engendering Interreligious Dialogue*. New York: Fordham University Press, 2013.

Greene, Joshua, et al., eds. *Positive Neuroscience*. New York: Oxford University Press, 2016.

Hollingsworth, Andrea. "Neuroscience and Spirituality: Implications of Interpersonal Neurobiology for Spirituality of Compassion." *Zygon* 43.4 (2008) 837–60.

LaCugna, Catherine Mowry. *God for Us: The Trinity and Christian Life*. San Francisco: HarperCollins, 1973.

MacIntyre, Alasdair. *Dependent Rational Animals: Why Human Beings Need the Virtues*. Chicago: Open Court, 1999.

Miner, Maureen, et al. *Beyond Wellbeing: Spirituality and Human Flourishing*. Charlotte: Information Age, 2012.

Newberg, Andrew, and Mark Robert Waldman. *How God Changes Your Brain: Breakthrough Findings from Leading Neuroscientists*. New York: Ballantine, 2009.

Pisano, Andrea, and Nino Pisano. "Le collezioni del Museo." Direzione regionale musei della Toscana. http://www.polomusealetoscana.beniculturali.it/index.php?it/205/le-collezioni-del-museo.

Pope, Stephen J. "Jesus Christ and Human Flourishing: An Incarnational Perspective." Paper presented at the Yale Centre for Faith and Culture. New Haven, December 2014.

Siegel, Daniel J. *The Developing Mind: Toward a Neurobiology of Interpersonal Experience*. New York: Guildford, 1999.

———. *The Mindful Brain: Reflection and Attunement in the Cultivation of Well-Being*. New York: Norton and Company, 2007.

Strong, James. *A Concise Dictionary of the Words in The Greek New Testament*. Madison: World Bible, 1890.

World Council of Churches. *Christian Perspectives on Theological Anthropology: A Faith and Order Study Document*. Geneva: World Council of Churches 2005.

11

"Let Our Anger Cease"

George Te Ara as a Case Study of the Encounter between Human Trauma and Gospel Healing

PETER G. BOLT

THE STORY OF THE Whangaroan Māori "George" Te Ara (?1790–1825) provides a case-study of a traumatized individual struggling to grasp the healing potential of the Christian gospel as it entered his world. George's presence figured in the decision to found the first Wesleyan Mission in New Zealand at Whangaroa in June 1823 and, with all his changeable "moods," George was a major reason for the mission's close in January 1827—despite him dying almost two years earlier.

Cultural factors might provide the kindling, but the spark for historical events comes from the principal actors, operating within a tangled web of relationships exerting both influence and pressure.[1] Owens argued for more personal causes of the meteoric collapse of the WAMS station, before exploring the psychology of the missionaries. However, from the Māori side, they were confronted by a long-term trauma survivor, who seemed unpredictable, volatile, and highly dangerous. To honor

---

1. Owens, "Wesleyan Mission," i–ii, iv; Owens, *Prophets*, 127.

George's memory, this essay seeks tell his trauma narrative with more empathy, softening his usual negative portrayal in the European sources.

On Christmas Day 1814, as the Church (i.e., not the Wesleyan) Missionary Society established a station at the Bay of Islands, Samuel Marsden preached to an assembled crowd of Māori on the Christmas text: "Behold I bring you good news of great joy" (Luke 2:10).[2] We do not know whether he also spoke on the next words to the shepherds declaring "peace on earth" (Luke 2:14), but they would have been in his mind. For Marsden had come determined to bring peace in a concrete way to this "uncivilized" country.[3]

Four days earlier, Marsden had spent the night on a beach with the warriors from Whangaroa, at war with the people of the Bay of Islands at the time (see Figure 1). George Te Ara was amongst them, who already knew Marsden, having previously visited Parramatta.[4] When Marsden spoke of peace, George readily agreed. He did not want to fight any more. He wanted the war to stop.[5]

---

2. See Bolt and Pettett, *Launching Marsden's Mission*; Pettett, "Samuel Marsden."

3. God established the penal colony of NSW "to make a way for His Missionary servants—for them that should bring glad tidings—that should publish peace to the Heathen world" (Marsden, "Account of First Visit," 332).

4. Marsden, "Account of First Visit," 356, cf. 358; Marsden, "Account to Pratt," 467. His brother Te Puhi may have also visited Parramatta, since Marsden claimed to know him well (Marsden, "Account of First Visit," 336). Given that Berry, "Particulars of a Late Visit," 305, (cf. Dillon, *Narrative*, 1:215–16), clearly puts him on the *Star* after Wilkinson took command for her second cruise (Hainsworth, *Sydney Traders*, 230, cf. 80, 125–26, 132, 151–52), George was in Sydney to meet Marsden between her arrival on 31 December 1806 (*Sydney Gazette*, 4 January 1807) and Marsden's departure for England on 10 February 1807, before himself sailing on the *Elizabeth* in March (Hainsworth, *Sydney Traders*, 229). On this reading, Dillon was mistaken that Wilkinson returned him to Whangaroa in the interim.

5. Marsden, "Account of First Visit," 355; Marsden, "Account to Pratt," 466.

Figure 1: Map of Northlands

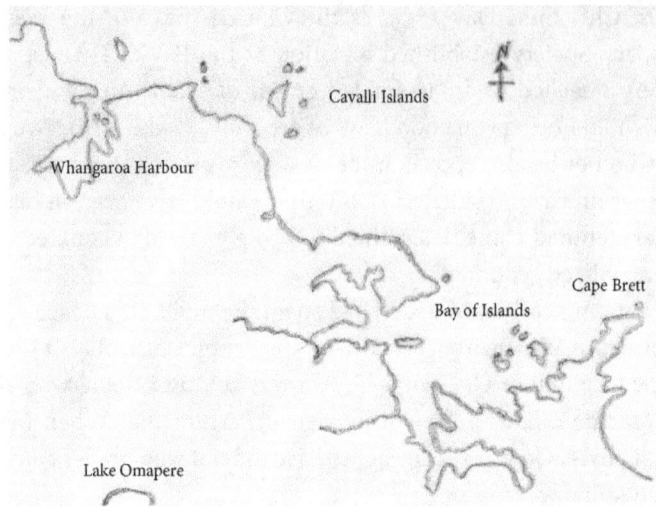

Nine years later, on 6 November 1823, after the WAMS mission had begun at Whangaroa in June, George dictated a letter (see Figure 2). He was still at war. His letter was a cry of the heart, delivered through a twice-repeated, simple request, dramatically standing out with all the force of a troubled soul: "Let our anger cease."

The fact that the cry is *unelaborated* is significant. To understand the phenomenon of headhunting, Rosaldo criticized ethnographies for "eliminat[ing] intense emotions," rather than exploring "the cultural force of emotions."[6] George's simple *cris de coeur* is emblematic of the broader, far-reaching story of George's life. It encapsulates his trauma, just as surely as it encapsulates his desire for things to be different.

---

6. Rosaldo, "Grief and a Headhunter's Rage," 172, 175. His 1974 publication arose from thirty months of anthropological study of the Ilongot of northern Luzon, Philippines, in 1967–1969 (168).

Figure 2: The Letter from George Te Ara, Annotated[7]

Letter	Comments
Wesleydale. Whangaroa, New Zealand	WAMS mission station
Nov 6, 1823	Five months after establishment
	Ended Jan 1827
My friend,	
Part 1: Request for Reconciliation	
Let our anger cease (*Ka mutu ranga*) for the killing of Cap$_n$ Thompson, and all his men.	Request
I came from Port Jackson on board his ship and he flogged our three.	Provocation
As soon as his ship was at anchor, I went on shore and told my tribe, the tribe at Whangaroa, the Kiddu Kiddu [Keri Keri], Tippoonah [Te Puna], and the tribe at Shukianga [Hokianga]	Report to Māori community
and they all came to this Place and killed Cap$_n$ Thomson and his crew.	Revenge
In a little time after, a Ship came from England to revenge the loss of the *Boyd*, when Tippahee [Te Pahi], his son [Mytye], and Duaterra [Ruatara] were killed.	Counter revenge from English community
That is enough.	Satisfaction
Let our anger cease.	Request repeated
Part 2: Request for Ratification of Reconciliation	
and as a token of this I have given a New Zealand Matt to Mr White for you.	Gift Exchange: - George's is done
You give me a Fowling piece to shoot Birds for food.	- England's is still to come
That will do. no more from you,	(potential) Satisfaction
Closing Greeting	
Friend George	

7. Te Ara, "Open Letter." The letter is preserved both in Māori and in English translation.

Wensleydale

The letter was dictated at "Wesleydale," the Wesleyan Auxiliary Missionary Society mission station established at Whangaroa, the natural harbor where, in mid-December 1809, the *Boyd* was destroyed as an act of revenge, and her crew killed and eaten.[8]

Founded on 5 July 1820,[9] the Wesleyan Auxiliary Missionary Society's (WAMS) first missionaries, Samuel Leigh and his new bride, arrived in the Bay of Islands on 21 February 1822 to live with CMS, while awaiting the rest of the team to arrive.[10] After settling on "Wesley Dale,"[11] the party anchored at Whangaroa on Thursday evening, 6 June 1823 and after breakfast the next day, Samuel Leigh and William White set off for George's place, passing the wreck of the *Boyd* on the way.[12]

Whangaroa was home to two separate people-groups. The Ngāti Pou, about six hundred people under the chief Te Pere, occupied the island at the harbor's entrance, and the Ngāti Uru, who were about two hundred strong and located up the Kaeo river at the western end of Whangaroa harbor, under the shared leadership of brothers Te Puhi, Ngahuruhuru, and George.[13]

George and Te Puhi "were not only willing but anxious that the missionaries should settle amongst them."[14] The next week they set up camp near where *HMS Dromedary* had landed in 1820, and commenced building a log house. By 13 July the missionaries had moved in[15] and across 1824 the building continued: they opened a school, commenced chapel services, had frequent visits from shipping and from the CMS missionaries, and they had good and frequent contact with the Māori, especially with George, who was "much in their company."[16] But at the beginning of

---

8. See Bolt, "The *Boyd* Set-Back."
9. WAMS, Early Notes; WAMS, Minutes; *Sydney Gazette*, 1 July 1820.
10. Owens, *Prophets*, 22; Blacket, *Missionary Triumphs*, 66.
11. Blacket, *Missionary Triumphs*, 68. On 4 April 1822, Leigh informed Marsden that he would go to Whangaroa "after the war has ended" (Leigh to Marsden, 4 April 1822).
12. Owens, *Prophets*, 39.
13. Clover, *Collision*, 63, cf. 5.
14. Owens, *Prophets*, 34, 38, 40; Doak, *Burning*, 149.
15. Owens, *Prophets*, 40–41.
16. Owens, *Prophets*, 51–52, 56–57.

1825, things turned sour,[17] and George died in April. Things picked up a little, but by 1826 they got much worse and the missionaries were spending more time with their crops than they were preaching the gospel. By January 1827, the mission at Wesleydale was all over.[18]

George dictated his letter on 6 November 1823, five months after the mission began. When Samuel Marsden arrived in August for his fourth visit to New Zealand, he had called in at Whangaroa. In poor health, Leigh planned to return with him to NSW and it was agreed that George's niece would also travel with them. They were delayed by shipwreck and by November, White also decided to visit NSW. On the eve of departure, White wrote down this letter dictated to him by George.[19]

The Request for Reconciliation

The letter encapsulates both George's trauma and his desire to be at peace. Part 1 is a request for reconciliation, the establishment of peace where presently there is only hostility. This desire for reconciliation is demonstrated in the opening and closing greeting. The word "friend" at the beginning is a respectful address (*e koro ma*), but the word "friend" at the end refers to a blood relative (*tau whanaungu*). George's request hopes to move the recipient from being hostile, towards being treated as kin.

"Let our anger cease."

The request is twice given, once at the beginning, once towards the end. The word translated "anger" (*ranga*) means "to avenge a death." "Let our blood vengeance cease." What is lying in the background here is the Māori concept of *utu*: "reciprocity of resources, equality in gift exchange; satisfaction for wrongs committed."[20]

---

17. Owens, *Prophets*, 57. For a report of the missionaries' version of events, see *Sydney Gazette*, 28 April 1825.

18. Despite their own self-blame, the subsequent history of the WAMS personnel shows that they were not failures elsewhere; see Clover, *Collision*, 69–72.

19. The *Dragon* left on 14 November 1823 (Owens, *Prophets*, 46). According to Turner to WMS, 30 January 1824, White left on 5 November 1823, which would have been when he embarked. This would therefore mean the letter was dictated on board ship.

20. Clover, *Collision*, xlii. For *tuku*, gift exchange, see the examples in Parkinson, "Tuku."

Ethnographers and historians preferring their *etic* grand themes and generalizations to the personal agency of individuals have tended to overlook, ignore, or trivialize *utu* as a motive for the attack on the *Boyd*.[21] Since *utu* is what George and his people constantly spoke about, as recognized at the time by shrewd Europeans like Marsden,[22] an *emic* approach to anthropology allows those from within the culture to speak for themselves. Following Rosaldo, it is not always in the rituals, the grand themes, that you find the deep reasons. George's simple statement, "let the anger cease," is a clue—perhaps *the* clue—to the spark that lit the fire.

The translation "our" anger, hints at George feeling he is caught up in a cycle of *utu*; one from which he wishes to escape. But you only escape when *utu* is satisfied. The letter is trying to point out that this has occurred, so now the cycle of vengeance can stop. The blood loss has been satisfied by further blood loss. Let it be enough. Let the anger cease.

After part 1 presents the request, part 2 speaks of the gift exchange to seal the deal. This is thoroughly part of Māori practice, in which *utu* satisfaction can involve gift exchange. But George also knew it was part of the Christian culture of the English. Back at Christmas time 1814, after he'd told Marsden he didn't want to fight anymore, the new commitment to peace was also sealed by the exchange of gifts.[23] Now he tells the recipient of his letter that he has started the gift exchange. He has given missionary White a New Zealand mat, and all he asks for in exchange is a fowling piece to shoot birds for food. That will do. No more required from you. With the fowling piece, satisfaction will be completed, and the cycle of *utu* will be completed.

---

21. E.g., Mansfield-Smith, "Trade and Violence," explicitly rejects *utu* as a sufficient motive for the *Boyd*, being insufficient and "too simplistic," and preferring to relegate it to "myth" (e.g., 52, 82–83, 85, 120).

22. E.g., Marsden, "Journal, 1823," October 13: "When they have lost a near Relation in Battle their minds continually dwell upon the death of their friend, having nothing to occupy them— If they are able to revenge the death of their friend they will attempt it as soon as possible, if not they will think on their loss for years, and mourn over it, and if at any future period they can obtain satisfaction during their life they never will lose an opportunity— Their wounded feelings never appear to be healed, and they feel it a sacred duty which they owe to their departed relations to punish those by whose hands they have fallen."

23. Marsden, "Account of First Visit," 359; Marsden, "Account to Pratt," 469.

The Provocation

What started it all? George recalls how the blood vengeance cycle in which he still felt trapped first got going. The killing of Captain Thomson and the crew of the *Boyd* happened at Whangaroa in December 1809. Despite the bad press it gave the New Zealanders, it was provoked by Thomson, on a voyage from Sydney, flogging George—along with two other Whangaroans and another New Zealander.[24] George had already spent some three years sailing on two other ships, and since their voyages were not profitable, he hadn't been paid for his work so he already felt hard done by.[25] When he fell ill on the voyage back to New Zealand and couldn't work, Captain Thomson had him severely flogged.[26] When George protested that he was a chief and it was not right to flog a chief, Thomson just mocked him, saying that he was not a chief, but just a *cookee* (a slave).[27] Because of the captain's failure to protect him, the entire crew mocked him for the rest of the voyage. After arriving at Whangaroa, Thomson stripped George of everything he had, and, adding further shame and humiliation, he returned George to his people with his back badly gouged by the flogging and stark naked.

This event contains all the elements required to create a traumatized individual.[28] The flogging was completely unexpected and therefore came as a surprise. Being tied to the rigging made it inescapable and rendered George helpless to do anything about it. Because of its extreme brutality—even on a normal, healthy man, let alone someone already stricken with sickness—it was tantamount to a life-threatening situation. Sudden, inescapable, life-threatening. These are the elements to produce

---

24. According to King et al. to Pratt, 4 October 1810, Thomson flogged three natives; Marsden to Pratt, 25 October 1810, says four New Zealanders were flogged, but perhaps one was not a Whangaroan?

25. Dillon, *Narrative*, 1:217. He sailed on the *Elizabeth* and then, for a second time on the *Star*. See n. 4 above.

26. For this version, see, e.g., Kendall to Pratt, 6 September 1814. Alternatively, Dillon, *Narrative*, 1:218, reports that the cook accused George of theft to cover up his mistake in throwing overboard a dozen pewter spoons, resulting in a flogging from the particularly powerful boatswain "performed his office with severity." The accounts, of course, may dovetail.

27. Dillon, *Narrative*, 1:219.

28. George's trauma narrative may have begun earlier. How was he affected during his visit to Fiji with the *Elizabeth*, 26 April 1808 to 10 September 1808, when four of the crew had been murdered by the natives? (*Sydney Gazette*, 23 October 1808).

simple PTSD.[29] The sustained mockery of the victim by captain and crew added to the psychological trauma already created in this young man, who had innocently (naively?) ventured abroad on a grand adventure to see the world of the white man.[30]

One isolated event of flogging would already be sufficient to create a case of simple PTSD, but this event also had the elements that play a key role in producing complex PTSD—a condition that sufferers find much more difficult to recover from, if they recover at all. It was a massive breach of trust. On the little "world" that was shipboard life, George had entrusted himself to the captain's care. Thomson betrayed his fiduciary obligations to George, and the "betrayal of what is right" is arguably the "moral injury" at the core of long-term psychological trauma.[31]

This betrayal of what is right even according to English standards was made worse by Thomson's mockery of George as a slave not a chief. Flogging him despite him being a chief also offended against the Māori standards of what is right. Such violation of the fabric of a person's moral world, produces the moral injury that lies at the heart of complex PTSD.[32]

Meditating upon the contrast between *menis*, indignant wrath, associated with the heroic warfare of Homer and the "indignant rage" of Vietnam PTSD sufferers, Shay hears

> the word *dignity* hidden in the word *indignant*. It is the kind of rage arising from social betrayal that impairs a person's dignity through violation of "what's right." . . . the rage that ruptures social attachments . . . choking-off of the social and moral world.[33]

And with Thomson's flogging, George's traumatizing had only just begun.

---

29. See Herman, *Trauma and Recovery*, 33–50.

30. An initial naivety is also recognized as a precondition for PTSD. Cf. Shay, *Achilles*, 10, 184–86, on the loss of innocence.

31. Shay, *Achilles*, 15, notes the "fiduciary assumption," that an army (as other human organizations) "is ultimately a moral structure, a *fiduciary*, a trustee holding the life and safety of that soldier. The need for an intact moral world increases with every added coil of a soldier's mortal dependency on others."

32. Shay, *Achilles*, 20: "moral injury is an essential part of any combat trauma that leads to lifelong psychological injury. Veterans can usually recover from horror, fear, and grief once they return to civilian life, so long as 'what's right' has not also been violated."

33. Shay, *Achilles*, 21.

Report to the Māori Community

By the time George got onshore, it was already obvious that a severe injury had been done to him and to his people. As he reports in his letter, he immediately told his tribe at Whangaroa what had happened. His father Peepee, the chief, and his elder brother Te Puhi were outraged at the white man's offence.

George also said he reported what happened to the tribes at Keri Keri and at Te Puna, both at the Bay of Islands, and to the people at Hokianga, over on the West coast. For sure, all of these tribes eventually found out and were ultimately affected by what happened at Whangaroa, but only George's tribe were there on the spot, and there is no way they could have all assembled by the third day after the ship arrived to join the revenge. This slip of the tongue in his later report probably shows us how things had become tangled in George's troubled mind. He knows that all these tribes had been caught up in the aftermath of the *Boyd* affair, and he mistakenly implicates them in the initial event, because he carries a burden of guilt for the event that changed everybody's life so dramatically for 14 years.

The Revenge

Once the Whangaroans heard of Thomson's offences and witnessed the obvious signs on George's body, revenge was inflicted quickly. According to the Māori custom of *utu*, one violent act demands satisfaction through another.

With a greater awareness of trauma, it is now known that this too is a traumatizing experience. In cultures that say, "don't get sad, get mad," grief gives way to revenge. Or better put, revenge becomes the sanctioned form of grief. This strategy, however, actually prevents those who are raging for revenge from ever grieving properly, so doing further damage to their soul.[34] This was brought to the attention of trauma therapists through the work of Rosaldo's ethnographical study of headhunters, which is easily transferable to cannibals.

---

34. Cf. Rosaldo, "Grief and a Headhunter's Rage"; Shay, *Achilles*, 53–54, to describe his combat "berserker," for whom "the sense of being already dead may contribute to the berserker's complete loss of fear. . . . It may also be the prototype of the loss of *all* emotion that defines for combat post-traumatic stress disorder the prolonged states of numbness—the inability to feel love or happiness or to believe that anything matters."

> The rage born of devastating loss animates the older men's desire to raid. This anger at abandonment is irreducible in that nothing at a deeper level explains it. Although certain analysts argue against the dreaded last analysis, the linkage of grief, rage, and headhunting has no other known explanation.[35]

Similarly, like the headhunter "says that rage, born of grief, impels him to kill his fellow human beings. He claims that he needs a place 'to carry his anger,'"[36] cannibalism can be regarded as a highly dysfunctional way of grieving.[37] It is grief turned into rage. And, again, without proper grieving, such grief turned into rage further traumatizes the soul. Westerners, even grief therapists, tend to minimize the rage in grief, even while encouraging an awareness of it.[38] But the trauma therapists have also seen its relevance for those suffering PTSD. Shay notes "the rapid transformation of grief into rage," and that for many "replacement of grief by rage has lasted for years and become an entrenched way of being."[39]

To ask this personal question normalizes such responses into the realm of an understandable response, given how trauma effects the universals of our biology.

> The combat veterans that I treat are neither feral men nor lifelong misfits. Therefore, we need to ask whether the berserk rage that emerged out of their grief is a product of acculturated emotional responses (as, for example, the concept of vendetta), or whether it is a reaction that every human being in every age and society would experience in a similar circumstance. We simply don't know enough to settle this question now. I believe that the emergence of rage out of intense grief *is* a biological universal and that long-term obstruction of grief and failure to communalize grief can lock a person into chronic rage.[40]

---

35. Rosaldo, "Grief and a Headhunter's Rage," 175.

36. Rosaldo, "Grief and a Headhunter's Rage," 167, admitting that bereavement cannot be reduced solely to anger (171).

37. Cf. Smith, "Peopling of the North," 6: "it was not for hunger that we ate human beings, no, we ate our enemies in order to satisfy our hearts full of hatred." Also quoted by Doak, *Burning*, 177n3.

38. Rosaldo, "Grief and a Headhunter's Rage," 171–72.

39. Shay, *Achilles*, 53.

40. Shay, *Achilles*, 54–55.

Three days after the *Boyd*'s arrival,[41] George's tribe lured Captain Thomson off the ship and upriver to where the spars were being collected. There they killed him and the boats' crews. Disguising themselves in the dead mens' clothing, the Whangaroans returned to the *Boyd* at dusk and, by this subterfuge, they were able to get on board. They proceeded to kill everyone, all the crew and passengers. To finish the revenge to the utmost, as was usual in such a reprisal, all the dead were duly cooked and eaten.[42]

But before it all finished, George was struck by further tragedy. After the killing, the Māori found some much prized muskets on the ship and broke open a keg of gun powder. Trying out a musket, George's father snapped the flintlock over the powder, which exploded, killing him and several others, and burning the *Boyd* to the waterline. George's father was killed as he acted to avenge him.[43] George was never able to forget that his dad lost his life for him—because of him. More guilt. More trauma.

About seventy people died and only four people survived the attack: a woman who had been kind to George, her infant, another child, and a cabin boy who had also been kind to George. It appears that it was George who rescued them from his tribe's vengeful fury.

With one atrocity being answered by another, *utu* could have been satisfied and it could have stopped there. But it did not.

Counter-Revenge from the English Community

On 31 December 1809, after rumors of the attack reached him at the Bay of Islands, Alexander Berry, supercargo of the ship *City of Edinburgh*, brought some men around to Whangaroa to see if they could rescue the survivors and any property that might remain. According to Berry, with the assistance of "Matingaro," a local, they were successful in doing both.

Although Alexander Berry's report of the *Boyd* went viral,[44] and although he never changed his story across the next sixty years, it got some

---

41. Pattison et al. to Ship's Masters, 6 January 1810.

42. The link between cannibalism and revenge was also clearly made from the *emic* description of Maretu of the pre-Christian practice on his own island of Rarotonga in his early lifetime: "it was revenge which caused the eating of human flesh" (Maretu, *Cannibals and Converts*, 33, 40; cf. 41–42). See also Rosaldo, "Grief and a Headhunter's Rage," 171–72.

43. *Sydney Gazette*, 1 September 1810 and 25 August 1810.

44. Cf. Bolt, "The *Boyd* Set-Back," 65n25.

facts seriously wrong—perhaps even deliberately.[45] He blamed Te Pahi from the Bay of Islands (whom he had found reasons to dislike) for the incident. However, as better information emerged it became clear that Te Pahi had accidentally happened to be there the next morning, and unsuccessfully tried to save some of the crew who had escaped into the rigging.[46]

It is also difficult to get at what actually happened when Berry recovered the surviving persons and property—although it came out over time. In Berry's earliest report, the rescue and recovery apparently occurred easily "by gentle measures."[47] A decade later, however, he revealed that he had strong-armed the two Whangaroan brothers[48] in order to rescue the survivors and property, threatening to shoot them and holding them captive with a pistol to the head.[49] After what George had been through, that would be sufficient to traumatize him further. But in another account a further decade on, the story got even worse.[50] When he became impatient for the return of Betsey Broughton, Berry had turned to the chief next to him in the boat and threatened to kill him if she didn't turn up soon, putting his sword against his chest. The chief—probably George—"[dropped his head] upon his shoulders and he began to blubber and sob."[51] With no touch of human sympathy, Berry is unashamed of the brutality he perpetrated on an already damaged soul, but instead he mocked him for his tears.[52]

---

45. Cf. Bolt, "The *Boyd* Set-Back," 64n21. He gave accounts of the *Boyd* from 1810 through to 1873; cf. Berry, "Passages."

46. Cf. Bolt, "The *Boyd* Set-Back," 64–69.

47. Berry, "Particulars of the Destruction, 1818," 405.

48. I have assumed that "the two chiefs" to whom Berry constantly refers without naming were Te Puhi and George Te Ara, despite Berry later declaring that "both [George] and family were of such inferior rank, that it was perfectly unnecessary for me to have the least communication with them in the recovery of the prisoners, &c." (Berry, "Particulars of a Late Visit," 405).

49. Berry, "Particulars of the Destruction, 1827," 346–49.

50. Berry, "Supplement," 10–13.

51. Berry, "Supplement," 6.

52. Shay, *Achilles*, 63, 67: "American military culture in Vietnam regarded tears as dangerous but above all as demeaning, the sign of a weakling, a loser"; "If military practice tells soldiers that their emotions of love and grief—which are inseparable from their humanity—*do not matter*, then the civilian society that has sent them to fight on their behalf should not be shocked by their 'inhumanity' when they try to return to civilian life."

After having already recovered persons and property, to "avenge the massacre," Berry then put the two chiefs through what he called "a farcical tragedy"—which was, in fact, a mock execution. After having them tied and tried, he declared them guilty of death and had two men level the muskets to kill and gave the order to fire. But he had only loaded the muskets with powder. He then made the chiefs the slaves of another Māori, adding further offence to "what is right," which would have caused further moral injury to the already traumatized George.

But the white man's revenge did not even stop with Berry's brutalizing of Thomson's victim. Having formed the opinion that Te Pahi of the Bay of Islands was the perpetrator of the attack on the *Boyd*, Berry wrote that opinion in a report he sent to Sydney, which then reverberated around the world, before he left with the survivors for South America, leaving a copy of his report at the Bay of Islands.

About March 1810, after hearing Berry's report, a group of whaling captains thought they would take their own *utu* on behalf of the *Boyd*. They raided Te Puna, Te Pahi's island, and slaughtered every man, woman, and child they found (perhaps as many as 60 people). Despite being innocent, Te Pahi received wounds in the raid which soon killed him.

And, of course, the *utu* did not stop there—it couldn't stop there. What did Te Pahi and his tribe at Te Puna in the Bay of Islands have to do with Whangaroa and the *Boyd*? From their point of view this was an unprovoked attack from English sailors. But they knew it was a reprisal for the *Boyd*, so their vengeance was directed against the Whangaroans. And so, from March 1810 until December 1814 when Marsden slept on the beach with George and his warriors, the warfare continued. And, at least in his own mind, responsibility for all of this was heaped on George's head.

As a further consequence of the attack on the *Boyd* and the turmoil it caused amongst the Māori, English shipping, which had previously been so frequent, now ceased altogether, removing the advantages of timber supply, trade, and exchange that the Māori valued so highly.[53] No English captain wanted to visit New Zealand, anytime or anywhere. From the Māori point of view, this was an economic disaster. This added fuel to the fires of vengeance already blazing between the Bay of Islands and

---

53. Owens, *Prophets*, 36–37. Because no vessel would go into Whangaroa for three years, when Marsden purchased the *Active*, he had difficulty engaging a captain (Marsden, "Account of First Visit," 337). When Fairfowl appeared before Commissioner Bigge in May 1821, he believed that no South Sea whalers had visited since the *Boyd*.

Whangaroa. When Marsden came at Christmas time, 1814, George told him he did not want to fight anymore. He wanted peace. But despite that moment and the gift exchange on board Marsden's ship the peace did not last long at all, and the vengeance didn't stop.

With the rise of Hongi Hika from Keri Keri harnessing the power of the musket to wipe out any tribe not his own, up and down the coast, even in the 1920s, the Whangaroans still lived in fear of Hongi wiping them out for their actions in 1809, which scared off the English shipping and threatened his musket supply.

The Whangaroans had become the objects of the wrath of the other tribes. And perhaps that is why George thought he told the tribes at Keri Keri, Te Puna, and Hokianga. They were all now angry at Whangaroa. No, with the massive self-blame of a trauma survivor, since he had caused the *utu* to start in the first place, in his mind they were all now angry at him.

Notice, too, George's perception of the whalers' counter-revenge. "A ship came from England." The Māori knew the origins of the shipping that began arriving on their coasts with Captain Cook. Several of them had taken a voyage to see England, where they had been treated like royalty and some had even met the king. After the *Boyd*, the Māori feared his displeasure.[54] When George himself was first placed on an English ship in late 1806, his father had put him on board so he could go to England.[55] But all he got was the bitter cold of the Antipodes Islands, Port Jackson for a time, and long years of shipboard work for which he was never paid. Now George saw the *utu* cycle begun by him being flogged, not as a minor skirmish between individuals. "A ship came from England"—he had triggered an international war!

Perhaps here we have the hint at the recipient of the letter. The manuscript is labelled by the National Library of Australia "an open letter," but why would George be writing such a letter to an untargeted audience, like some armchair critic writing a "letter to the editor"? He had someone particular in mind. In fact, his opening address uses the singular, "my friend," using the term of respectful deference that younger men would

---

54. Notice the initial report from Pattison et al. to Ship's Masters, 6 January 1810: "The natives of the Spar district . . . seem much concerned on account of this unfavourable event; and, dreading the displeasure of King George have requested certificates of their good conduct in order to exempt them from his vengeance; but let no man (after this) trust a New Zealander."

55. Dillon, *Narrative*, 1:215–16; see n. 4 above.

use for their elders (*e koro ma*). Perhaps he had King George in mind?[56] Missionary William White is about to go to Port Jackson and, since the letter now sits in the archive amongst Governor Brisbane's papers, he probably gave it to the King's representative in NSW.

A decade after the *Boyd*, George and the Whangaroans still lived in fear of the English ships continuing to exact revenge. In 1820, it was not a couple of whalers that entered their harbor, but the Naval frigate *HMS Dromedary*, with her big guns and fifty-seven soldiers on board. The Whangaroans were filled with fear. They could not understand why a ship that just wanted timber like all the others, needed so many guns and so many soldiers armed with the dreaded muskets.[57] They thought England had come for more revenge. They were glad to see the ship on her way. When she left, George had done all he could to help, collecting timber, showing hospitality. He'd even given Captain Skinner a preserved Māori head, and told him it was one of the warriors who had attacked the *Boyd*.[58] But was all of that enough? Would the *utu* stop?

George was also convinced that he would be hung if he ever returned to Port Jackson. At the time of his letter, as Marsden prepared to return, he put his niece on board as something of a test. If she were not hung, he would then venture to Sydney again![59] When this arrangement was brokered in August 1823, this prospect alarmed her father, Te Puhi. He told Marsden, "We are reconciled to you, but we can't believe you are reconciled to us, but will demand sacrifices in return for the *Boyd* people." After hearing this man express his fear fourteen years after the event, Marsden commented in his journal that

> it will be impossible to remove the fears of these people until they have some proof we will not avenge the loss of the *Boyd*. Their religion will not allow them to pass over such an act unpunished. They cannot believe our religion will allow us to forgive.[60]

---

56. King George III had died on 29 January 1820, to be replaced by King George IV. But these facts would be irrelevant to the distant George Te Ara. Cf. the letter to King William IV dictated by Titore to William Yates, in Parkinson, "Tuku," 57.

57. Fairfowl, "Dr. Fairfowl's Evidence," 550–58.

58. Such was the fascination with George, that the head, known as Watangheon, was displayed in Liverpool as his own, several years before he died! (*Liverpool Mercury*, 14 June 1822).

59. Marsden, "Journal, 1823," August 16.

60. Marsden, "Journal, 1823," August 18.

When George formulated his letter to go on the same ship as his niece, what was in his mind? He had been flogged by an English captain. His tribe had taken revenge on that English ship. Another ship "came from England" to exact counter-revenge on poor old Te Pahi, and this had led to more revenge from the rival Māori tribes. George wanted it all to stop. So, on the banks of the Kaeo river at Wesleydale, he dictated his request for reconciliation to the king of England himself.[61]

This might explain another set of mistakes in George's letter. When the English ships destroyed Te Puna, yes, Te Pahi was wounded and subsequently died. But George referred to Te Pahi's more famous son Mytye [Matara], who had been to England,[62] he was not killed in the March 1810 raid. How could he be? He died of natural causes nine days before the *Boyd* was attacked.[63] And Ruatara, the friend of Marsden who was instrumental in bringing the CMS mission to the Bay of Islands, and who had also visited England, didn't die until March 1815, four days after Marsden left for Port Jackson (i.e., on 5 March 1815).[64] But in George's mind, these men who had been to England and so, he thought, would have been known to King George the recipient of his letter; these men who were such significant chiefs, were also killed in the English counter-revenge. Surely their deaths were sufficient *utu* for King George? Surely this cycle of vengeance that sat so heavily on George's shoulders could now come to an end? Isn't it *now* enough? Let our anger cease.

Gift Exchange

As the sign of *utu* being satisfied, George initiated the gift exchange usual to the Māori,[65] and what he had also experienced with Marsden's attempt

---

61. Cf. the (later) *Gazette* comment that the mission had originally been situated in his territory because he "wished for a restoration of amity between himself and the English" (*Sydney Gazette*, 28 April 1825).

62. Berry left Sydney on 26 January 1808, before spending three months at the Bay of Islands for repairs and refitting (*Sydney Gazette*, 17 September 1809). The *City of Edinburgh* brought Ceroni and Matara, a son of Te Pahi, back to the Bay of Islands from London via Port Jackson (Berry, "Particulars of a Late Visit," 306; Berry, "Particulars of the Destruction, 1827," 333). Te Pahi informs him of the epidemic at Wangaroa, and of his inheritance. Matara dies within a few months of his arrival.

63. Marsden to Pratt, 25 October 1810.

64. Marsden, "Account of First Visit," 337.

65. E.g., Owens, *Prophets*, 92–93.

to bring peace at Christmas 1814. With his letter, he had given William White "a New Zealand matt." All he wanted in return was for the English king to send a fowling piece to shoot birds for food.[66] Not much to ask. "That will do. No more from you." Stop the warships! Let the trading ships return. Send the missionaries with their trade and protection and cultural exchange. Let this recurring nightmare be over, so that Whangaroa, George's outer world, could be at peace. More importantly, so that George's inner world might also find peace, from the trauma from which he had not been permitted release. Since 1809 he had not had the space to grieve. His grief was turned into vengeance, and when grief transforms into rage, it inflicts even more psychological damage.[67]

I wonder whether the king of England, or his representative, the Governor of NSW, ever sent George the fowling piece that would have made all the difference? Of course, King George never got the letter, and neither Governor Brisbane, nor, sadly, missionary William White (who was not exactly brimming over with EQ or cultural sensitivity) would have seen the importance of this request. It would have seemed rather trivial to them. I suspect that when White returned in February 1824, George would have been disappointed yet again. Another "betrayal of what is right." Where is the exchange gift of equal value to the New Zealand matt? Where is the English gift signifying the warfare was over and George can be at peace? If it did not come, this would be a further traumatizing event.

Sixteen months after he wrote this letter, George was dead. Although the missionaries declared 1824 a pretty good year, they also noticed the growing indifference of the Māori to their Christianizing efforts.[68] No doubt George was interfering in the background, but by the end of the year and the beginning of 1825 his internal troubles came to a head. By February 1825, he was severely ill and his body visibly wasting away. From George's traumatized perspective, he saw everything as some kind of vengeance falling on him. Giving the missionaries another chance, he

---

66. Perhaps reflecting a form of affection for the missionary, George used to accompany White shooting (Owens, *Prophets*, 55). In *tuku*, there is an expectation of a reciprocal gift exchange (cf. Parkinson, "Tuku," 61).

67. Shay, *Achilles*, 59–60, notices that "there was no safe time to mourn. Allowing one's attention to turn inward to grief could result in one's own death and the death of others. . . . [A] degree of security from enemy attack is essential for griefwork to proceed. . . . If you cannot let down your guard, you cannot grieve."

68. Owens, *Prophets*, 59–60.

asked them for medicine, but it did not help and probably even made him worse. Early in March and while George was sick,[69] another "English" ship arrived, *The Mercury*,[70] and the locals started plundering it for muskets.[71] They only stopped after the intervention of missionary White and they were left, once again, with exacerbated fears of reprisals from the English, vengeance from other tribes for loss of shipping, and especially from Hongi, for threatening the supply of muskets, and withdrawal of the missionaries with all their advantages.

With the weight of the world upon his shoulders now for fifteen years, on his sickbed George had a clear view of the cause of it all. His father had been blown up in the explosion, during the attack on the *Boyd* that he had initiated because of George. And yet never in the long and difficult years since, had George exacted *utu* for his father's death.[72] Now he realized this was what he needed to do.

From his sickbed, George arranged for chief Hau Hau from Hokianga to plunder the missionaries at Whangaroa after he died, perhaps killing them too. When the missionaries heard this, due to their own traumatic fears, they began removing their property to CMS at the Bay of Islands, assuming the mission would be abandoned.[73] But by abandoning the mission, to George's traumatized brain, they were also abandoning him, and without missionaries as a protective influence, abandoning him to the further wrath of Hongi locally and the English king more distantly. All because he had failed to avenge his father, and so he arranged for the missionaries' destruction.

When he died on 17 April 1825, the missionaries hid, but nothing much happened and so they eventually returned.[74] Tensions subsided, and things seemed to be settling down. But it was only a matter of time before the warring Māori around them also swept over the mission, with

---

69. Owens, *Prophets*, 62–63.

70. Hall's diary 1 March 1825: "this day the *Mercury* entered Whangaroa" (as cited in Doak, *Burning*, 152). However, Hall mentions that "the morning [after] being the Sabbath," but the first was a Tuesday. According to Captain Edwards, she entered on Saturday the 5th (*Sydney Gazette*, 28 April 1825).

71. Owens, *Prophets*, 61.

72. Cf. Maretu's reflections on Rarotongan cannibalism: "word was handed down through all the families of the victims, generation by generation, that they seek revenge for those deeds" (Maretu, *Cannibals and Converts*, 40).

73. Owens, *Prophets*, 64.

74. Owens, *Prophets*, 65.

the Whangaroans themselves joining the Hokianga and Keri Keri tribes in plundering idyllic Wesleydale. Fearing for their lives, at 6 am on 10 January 1827, the missionaries fled to the Bay of Islands, and then on to Port Jackson.[75] The first WAMS mission in New Zealand was abandoned, as were the people of George Te Ara.

Conclusions

George Te Ara entered documentary history as a bad guy and has retained that position ever since.[76] He is the Whangaroan trouble-maker, regarded as something of a nutcase whose wild moods and erratic behavior disrupted the missionaries' peace and contributed in a major way to the total collapse of the mission.

But despite history's best efforts to ignore them, hints of another side of George continue to poke through the sources, for those with eyes to see. From beginning to end, despite the warfare and his erratic behavior, he seems to have wanted the conflict to stop. He wanted peace for his people and country, and, I suggest, this traumatized soul really wanted to find peace within.

He was the one who rescued the four survivors of the *Boyd*. Despite Berry's account, he handed them over along with the *Boyd* property. He sobbed during Berry's abuse. After five years of war with the Bay of Islanders, when Marsden arrived George declared that he did not want to fight any more; he wanted peace. He willingly went through the gift exchange with Marsden to seal that peace.

When Samuel Leigh arrived with the WAMS missionaries, George enthusiastically wanted them to live amongst his people, and from then

---

75. For a summary of the end, see Owens, *Prophets*, 94, 102. They arrived in Sydney on 9 February 1827. The next Sunday they gave an account to a packed crowd and, within weeks, Turner submitted his resignation.

76. E.g., Mansfield-Smith, "Trade and Violence," 85: "Te Ara, with his rage and paranoia, was a very unbalanced individual. There is no doubt that external influences provided him with a focus for *utu*. However, it is likely that he would have created his own focus out of violence and delusion, whether or not he had ever sailed in the *Boyd*"; and, again "Te Ara George was a highly volatile, perhaps mentally unbalanced character" (120).

on, he supported and protected them—at least, in his own way[77]—and even his detractors knew he wanted them to reconcile with the English.[78]

Then there was this letter, a cry from the heart: "Let our anger cease." But, from his point of view, his cry went unanswered, and the anger never ceased; it was with him until he died. As was his own grief transformed into rage.

The missionaries were clear that George was never a convert. This was understandable, not only because he had caused them distress by his erratic behavior, but also because he had specifically denied any interest in the gospel, saying "I do not wish to hear about Jesus Christ. I wish to hear about tommyhawks, etc." They imagined that rather than receiving Christ's salvation, he had gone to hell.[79]

Each of the missionaries had their own conversion story and, as usual in the evangelical revival tradition, each of their conversions was preceded by some kind of personal crisis. But despite having an elaborate conversion narrative to tell, from all reports their conversion never brought them the perfection they were looking for. They continued to be afflicted with their own forms of human weakness, both moral and psychological.[80] I guess they found it easier to excuse their own human weaknesses than they did those of George.

But what about George? The "betrayal of what is right" shatters the trauma sufferer's ability to trust.[81] The shattering of trust has devastating consequences, inhibiting or preventing human connection, the ability to love, to form intimate relationships. And this, in turn, leads to withdrawal, isolation, and a secrecy that turns the trauma survivor in on themselves. This "demonic anxiety" and "inclosing reserve" (to use Kierkegaard's terms, meditating on Mark 1:24)[82] then creates further dysfunction. In addition, the betrayal of the moral universe (justice) and

---

77. Owens, *Prophets*, 92: George "had in his own way protected them."

78. *Sydney Gazette*, 28 April 1825.

79. Hobbs, Journal 17 April 1825, cited in Owens, *Prophets*, 64, 76.

80. E.g., White had a violent temper and was known to the Māori as an angry man, prone to physical punishment (Clover, *Collision*, 63); the missionaries' diaries show they were often under distress, and display signs of mental disorder (68). Cf. Marsden, "Journal, 1823," August 15.

81. Herman, *Trauma and Recovery*, 51–53. Kolk, *Body*, 18, 134, 141, 150, 158, 163, 253. This, of course, makes therapy difficult.

82. See further, Bolt, "Kierkegaard."

the shattering of trust makes it very difficult for the trauma survivor to put their trust in a loving God—or his messengers.[83]

If we desire an elaborate conversion narrative from George Te Ara—a testimony—then we, like the missionaries, will be disappointed. But if we listen to this simple unelaborated cry of the heart, "let our anger cease," and feel its force, then maybe we are getting in touch with the deeper reality of this man. He knew Marsden and the WAMS missionaries were preaching salvation in Christ and modelling the peace and reconciliation Christ promised.

Both Rosaldo's Filipino headhunters and Maretu's Cook Island cannibals knew that the Christian gospel brought them a new way of grieving that would cancel out the need for their previous barbaric practices.[84] George also wanted the peace that the white men spoke about. And yet the long-term traumatic scars caused him by other white men made it hard for him to trust and seemingly impossible for him to find the healing that Christ promised, and that he longed for.

But on the other hand, George's rather tragic story reminds us that the Son of God became incarnate *in* a world and *for* a world of broken people, and that broken people grasp hold of salvation often rather tenuously and because of their brokenness often hold onto it only with great difficulty. While the healing promised by the message of Christ is tremendously attractive, sometimes the very brokenness that so badly needs healing, becomes an almost insurmountable blockage inhibiting individuals from ever finding that healing. That seems to be the case with George Te Ara.

But if his cry from the heart also indicates a heart turning towards his Savior, then despite everything else, by the grace of God alone, perhaps we will see him in heaven after all.

Bibliography

Berry, Alexander. "Particulars of the Destruction of a British Vessel on the Coast of New Zealand, with Anecdotes of a New Zealand Chief." *The Edinburgh Magazine and Literary Miscellany; A New Series of the Scot's Magazine, January to June 1818.*

---

83. E.g., Herman, *Trauma and Recovery*, 52, 94, 121: "loss of sustaining faith"; Shay, *Achilles*, 148.

84. Rosaldo, "Grief and a Headhunter's Rage," 168–69; Maretu, *Cannibals and Converts*, 41.

Vol. II, 403–8. Edinburgh: Printed for Archibald Constable and Co., 1818. https://archive.org/details/edinburghmagazi22unkngoog/page/n413/mode/2up.

———. "Particulars of the Destruction of a British Vessel on the Coast of New Zealand, with Anecdotes of Some New Zealand Chiefs." In *Adventures of British Seamen in The Southern Ocean: Displaying the Striking Contrasts Which the Human Character Exhibits in an Uncivilized State*, compiled by H. Murray, 323–53. Edinburgh: Printed for Archibald Constable and Co., 1827. https://babel.hathitrust.org/cgi/pt?id=nyp.33433082431606&view=1up&seq=4.

———. "Particulars of a Late Visit to New Zealand, and of the Measures Taken for Rescuing Some English Captives There." In *Edinburgh Magazine and Literary Miscellany, January to June 1819. Vol. IV*, 304–14, 405–9. Edinburgh: Printed for Archibald Constable, 1819. https://babel.hathitrust.org/cgi/pt?id=hvd.32044092547678&view=1up&seq=7.

———. "Passages in the Life of a Nonagenarian." *Sydney Morning Herald* (25 and 27 December 1873) 3–4.

———. "Supplement to the Printed Account of the Destruction of the *Boyd* Showing How I Avenged the Massacre." In *The Boyd Massacre*. 1829. https://nla.gov.au/nla.obj-1342447855/view.

Blacket, John. *Missionary Triumphs among the Settlers in Australia and the Savages of the South Seas. A Twofold Centenary Volume*. London: Kelly, 1914. https://babel.hathitrust.org/cgi/pt?id=uc2.ark:/13960/t6nz83t20&view=1up&seq=4.

Bolt, Peter G. "The *Boyd* Set-Back to Marsden's Mission: The View From New South Wales." In *Launching Marsden's Mission: The Beginnings of the Church Missionary Society in New Zealand, Viewed from New South Wales*, edited by Peter G. Bolt and David B. Pettett, 61–78. London: Latimer Trust, 2014.

———. "Kierkegaard on Anxiety." In *The Consolations of Theology*, edited by Brian S. Rosner, 77–108. Grand Rapids: Eerdmans, 2008.

Bolt, Peter G., and David B. Pettett, eds. *Launching Marsden's Mission: The Beginnings of the Church Missionary Society in New Zealand, Viewed from New South Wales*. London: Latimer Trust, 2014.

Clover, Gary A. M. *Collision, Compromise and Conversion during the Wesleyan Hokianga Mission, 1827–1855*. Nelson, NZ: Clover, 2018.

Dillon, Peter. *Narrative and Successful Result of a Voyage in the South Seas Performed by Order of the Government of British India, to Ascertain the Actual Fate of La Pérouse's Expedition, Interspersed with Accounts of the Religion, Manners, Customs, and Cannibal Practices of the South Sea Islanders*. 2 vols. London: Hurst, Chance, and Co., 1829. https://archive.org/details/dli.granth.71286.

Doak, Wade. *The Burning of the Boyd: A Saga of Culture Clash*. Auckland: Hodder & Stoughton, 1984.

Fairfowl, Dr. "Dr. Fairfowl's Evidence to Commissioner Bigge, May 1821." In *Historical Records of New Zealand (HRNZ)*, edited by Robert McNab, 2 vols., 1:550–58. Wellington: Mackey, 1908. https://archive.org/details/historicalrecord01mcnauoft/page/550/mode/2up.

Hainsworth, D. R. *The Sydney Traders: Simeon Lord And His Contemporaries, 1788–1821*. Melbourne: Melbourne University Press, 1981.

Herman, Judith. *Trauma and Recovery. The Aftermath of Violence—from Domestic Abuse to Political Terror*. New York: Basic, 1997.

Kendall, Thomas. Letter to Reverend Josiah Pratt, 6 September 1814. Marsden Online Archive. https://marsdenarchive.otago.ac.nz/MS_0054_066.

King, John, et al. Letter to Reverend Josiah Pratt, 4 October 1810. https://marsdenarchive.otago.ac.nz/MS_0498_236#page/1/mode/1up.

Kolk, Bessel van der. *The Body Keeps the Score: Mind, Brain and Body in the Transformation of Trauma*. London: Penguin, 2014.

Leigh, Samuel. Letter to Reverend Samuel Marsden, 4 April 1822. Marsden Online Archive. http://www.marsdenarchive.otago.ac.nz/MS_0057_078.

Mansfield-Smith, Gaylene. "Trade and Violence: Early European Contact in New Zealand and the Massacre of the Boyd." MLitt. thesis, University of New England, 1997.

Maretu. *Cannibals and Converts: Radical Change in the Cook Islands*. Translated and edited by Marjorie Tuainekore Crocombe. Suva, Fiji: Institute of Pacific Studies University of South Pacific, 1983.

Marsden, Samuel. "Journal: Reverend Samuel Marsden's Journal from 2 July 1823 to [30] November 1823." Marsden Online Archive: http://www.marsdenarchive.otago.ac.nz/MS_0177_003.

———. Letter to Reverend Josiah Pratt, 25 October 1810. Marsden Online Archive. http://www.marsdenarchive.otago.ac.nz/MS_0498_237.

———. Letter to Josiah Pratt, 20 June 1815. 73 folios. "The Following Is the Account of Mr Marsden's First Voyage to New Zealand." Marsden Online Archive. http://www.marsdenarchive.otago.ac.nz/MS_0055_004. Printed in *CMS, The Missionary Register for MDCCCXVI* [1816], 461–471, 500–523. London: Seeley, 1816. https://archive.org/details/1816CMSMissionaryRegister.

———. "Rev. S. Marsden's Account of his First Visit to New Zealand. Observations on the Introduction of the Gospel into the South Sea Islands: Being my First Visit to New Zealand in December 1814." In *Historical Records of New Zealand (HRNZ)*, edited by Robert McNab, 2 vols., 1:331–99. Wellington: Mackey, 1908.

Owens, John M. R. *Prophets in the Wilderness: The Wesleyan Mission to New Zealand, 1819–27*. Auckland: Auckland University Press, 1974.

———. "The Wesleyan Mission to New Zealand, 1819–1840." PhD thesis, Victoria University of Wellington, 1969.

Parkinson, Philip G. "Tuku: Gifts for a King and the Panoplies of Titore and Patuone." *Tuhinga* 23 (2012) 53–68. https://www.tepapa.govt.nz/sites/default/files/tuhinga.23.2012.pt6_.p53-68.parkinson.pdf.

Pattison, S., et al. Letter to Ship's Masters, 6 January 1810. In *Historical Records of New Zealand (HRNZ)*, edited by Robert McNab, 2 vols., 1:293–95. Wellington: Mackey, 1908.

Pettett, David. "Samuel Marsden—Christmas Day 1814. What Did He Say?" In *Te Rongopai 1814, "Takoto te Pai!" Bicentennial Reflections on Christian Beginnings and Developments in Aotearoa New Zealand*, edited by Alan Davidson et al., 72–85. Auckland: Anglican General Synod, 2014.

Rosaldo, Renato. "Grief and a Headhunter's Rage." In *Death, Mourning, and Burial: A Cross-Cultural Reader*, edited by Robbin Anronius, 167–78. Malden, MA: Blackwell, 2004.

Shay, Jonathan. *Achilles in Vietnam: Combat Trauma and the Undoing of Character*. New York: Atheneum, 1994.

Smith, S. P. "The Peopling of the North: Notes on the Ancient Maori History of the Northern Peninsula and Sketches of the History of the Ngati-Whatua Tribe Of Kaipara, New Zealand: 'Heru-Hapainga.'" *Supplement to the Journal of the Polynesian Society* 5 (1896) 1–22. http://www.jps.auckland.ac.nz/document/Volume_5_1896/Supplement_to_the_Journal_of_the_Polynesian_Society-_The_peopling_of_the_North%3A_notes_on_the_ancient_Maori_history_of_the_northern_peninsula_and_sketches_of_the_history_of_the_Ngati-Whatua_tribe_of_Kaipara?action=null.

Te Ara, George. Open Letter dictated at Wesleydale, Whangaroa, 6 November 1823. National Library of Australia: MS 4036.

Turner, Nathaniel. Letter to Wesleyan Missionary Society (WMS), 30 January 1824. In *Historical Records of New Zealand (HRNZ)*, edited by Robert McNab, 2 vols., 1:619–21. Wellington: Mackey, 1908.

WAMS. Vickery Summary, Early Notes on Methodism in Australia, compiled by E. Vickery (UCRHS: M 287.94 MET/NSW VIC).

———. Wesleyan Missionary Society Sydney, Minutes of Quarterly Meeting 1815–1831 (UCRHS: M287.94 MQM) [Emily G. Pickering transcription; original in Mitchell Library].

12

Aspects of Believers' Flourishing in Paul's Language of Call/Calling

Rob A. Fringer

Introduction

When considering the life of Paul, it is hard to ignore his radical transformation from persecutor to proclaimer. This once devout Pharisee who was committed to embracing the fullness of the Torah as part of his participation in God's covenant, suddenly shifted his full attention to Christ recognizing him as the long-awaited Messiah who had ushered in a new age. When thinking about Paul's Damascus Road Experience (DRE), also known as his Christophanic (*Christos* + *phaneroō*) experience, many people quickly move to the three accounts in Acts (9:1–19; 22:1–21; 26:4–18). However, Paul himself references this experience numerous times with varying degrees of detail (1 Cor 9:1–17; 1 Cor 15:1–11; 2 Cor 3:1–4:6; Eph 3:1–13; Phil 3:4–14; cf. 1 Tim 1:11–17).[1] Scholars have often been quick to emphasize that Paul does not use his regular conversion language of "repentance" (*metanoia/metanoeō*) and "turning" (*epistrephō*) when speaking about this event.[2] Instead, Paul

---

1. This paper will focus on the ten generally agreed upon epistles of Romans, 1 Corinthians, 2 Corinthians, Galatians, Ephesians, Philippians, Colossians, 1 Thessalonians, 2 Thessalonians, and Philemon.

2. See Longenecker, "A Realized Hope," 25–26.

frames his experience around his divine calling to apostleship and speaks often of this calling in the opening of his letters (e.g., Rom 1:1; 1 Cor 1:1; cf. 2 Cor 1:1; Gal 1:1; Col 1:1).[3] Nevertheless, there is ample evidence to show some immediate[4] and significant transformation took place in light of his encounter with Christ.[5] Thus, we can confidently say that Paul was both converted and called.[6]

This dual reality of conversion and calling does not negate the pertinent question of why Paul overwhelming prefers the language of "call" and "calling" (*klētos/klēsis/kaleō*), and moreover, why he utilizes this same language for all believers. Paul employs this word-group forty-seven times: four times to speak about his own calling; thirty-one times to speak about believers' calling; and an additional twelve times to speak about believers' calling in a way that is inclusive of himself. In other words, the language of call/calling is not unique to Paul but includes many elements to which all believers benefit.

This paper will briefly explore Paul's "call/calling" language utilizing Galatians as a primary example of Paul's larger theological understanding of this phenomenon. First, it will show a connection between Paul's "calling" and the "calling" of Isaiah's Servant. Second, it will show how Paul parallels his own calling and that of the Galatians. Third, it will argue for a larger thematic connection between the Isaianic Servant's calling and Paul's extension of this calling to all believers. Finally, it will make some measured assertions about the depth of Paul's call language as it pertains to believers' flourishing.

Paul's Calling and Isaiah's Servant

Galatians contains Paul's lengthiest and most significant Christophanic reference (Gal 1:11–24), which sits within Paul's largest autobiographical narrative, encompassing nearly all of the first two chapters of this epistle. With respect to this reference, multiple scholars have emphasized Paul's paralleling of his account to the so-called Suffering Servant passages

---

3. Stendahl, *Paul among Jews*, 7–23.

4. Kim, *Origin of Paul's Gospel*, 56. This does not discount the strong possibility that Paul's transformation continued and that it may have taken years for him to develop his understanding of how Christ functioned in connection to the law.

5. Segal, *Paul the Convert*.

6. Chester, *Conversion at Corinth*. Cf. Gaventa, "Conversion," 342–54: who argues neither of these categories are fully appropriate.

of Isaiah.[7] Galatians 1:15 is almost definitely an allusion to LXX Isaiah 49:1b[8] (cf. Jer 1:5[9]) (See Table 1).

In addition to the verbatim quotation of four words, "from my mother's womb," and the shared use of the verb "to call" (*kaleō*), there are multiple other connections between the larger contexts of these two passages including: (1) Paul's self-description as servant/slave in Galatians 1:10 (cf. Rom 1:1; Phil 1:1; 2 Cor 4:5), which correlates with the moniker of servant/slave given to the figure in Isaiah 49:3, 5; (2) Paul's reference to the churches in Judea glorifying God "in me," that is "in Paul" (Gal 1:24), which fulfils the prophetic promise that God would be glorified "in you," that is "in the servant" (Isa 49:3); (3) Paul's call to proclaim Christ among the nations (Gal 1:16), which matches the servant's call to be "a light for the nations" (Isa 49:6; cf. 49:8b); and (4) Paul's reference to having gone to Jerusalem to make sure he had not run in vain (Gal 2:2), which correlates to the servant's grieving over labor given in vain (Isa 49:4).

TABLE 1

	Paul		Isaiah's Servant
Gal 1:15	the one who had set me apart from my mother's womb (*ek koilias mētros mou*) and called me (*kalesas*) through his grace	Isa 49:1b	from my mother's womb (*ek koilias mētros mou*) he called (*ekalesen*) my name
Gal 1:10	servant/slave (*doulos*)	Isa 49:3, 5	servant/slave (*doulos*)
Gal 1:24	they glorified God in me (*edoxazon en emoi ton theon*)	Isa 49:3	I will be glorified in you (*en soi doxasthēsomai*)
Gal 1:16	that I might proclaim him among the nations (*hina euangelizōmai auton en tois ethnesin*)	Isa 49:6	a light for the nations (*eis phōs ethnōn*)
Gal 2:2	in vain (*eis kenon*)	Isa 49:4	I labored in vain (*kenōs ekopiasa*)

---

7. Harmon, *She Must and Shall*, 105–15; Stanley, "Theme of the Servant," 385–425; Dinter, "Paul and Prophet Isaiah," 48–52; Beker, *Paul the Apostle*, 115–16; Ciampa, *Presence and Function*, 94–95; Newman, *Glory-Christology*, 206–7.

8. Sandnes, *Paul*, 61–65; Aernie, *Paul among the Prophets*, 136–37; Harmon, *She Must and Shall*, 78–79.

9. Segal, *Paul the Convert*, 13–14; Jervis, *Galatians*, 43; Witherington, *Galatians*, 105.

Many scholars believe that here, and in other places, Paul sees himself (or wants others to see him) as fulfilling the Servant's role; he has been called to carry out God's mission, specifically to the Gentiles, and will enviably suffer in this task.[10] This view, however, does not take the whole of Galatians into account; nor does it acknowledge Paul's numerous other references to Isaiah (especially chapters 40–66)[11] in many of his other epistles. As a point of reference, Paul directly quotes Isaiah thirty-one times, which is more than any other OT book.[12] Furthermore, scholars have identified an additional fifty allusions to Isaiah (in the undisputed letters).[13]

When examining Paul's use of Isaiah, we see that Paul regularly makes clear that Christ, and Christ alone, is the Singular Servant of Isaiah, who suffered, died, was resurrected, and exalted. This is most clearly revealed in the Christological hymn of Philippians 2:6–11, which echoes multiple sections of Isaiah.[14] (See Table 2)

---

10. See n. 7 above.

11. E.g., Hays, *Conversion*, 25–49; Wilk, *Die Bedeutung des Jesajabuches*; Wagner, *Heralds of Good News*; Shum, *Paul's Use of Isaiah*; Moyise and Menken, *Isaiah in the New Testament*, 117–58; Gignilliat, *Paul and Isaiah's Servants*.

12. Koch, *Die Schrift*, 21–23, lists twenty-eight; Hays, *Conversion*, 46–47, lists thirty-one; Silva, "OT in Paul," 631, lists twenty-seven, with Psalms the next closest at twenty-three. Furthermore, Harmon, *She Must and Shall*, 11n41, believes: "Of the thirteen Pauline letters, only Philemon lacks an Isaianic citation, allusion, or echo."

13. Hays, *Conversion*, 25–26.

14. Cf. Bauckham, *Jesus and the God*, 201–10; Gorman, *Inhabiting the Cruciform God*, 31; Wright, *Faithfulness*, 680–83; Ware, *Paul and the Mission*, 224–26; Cerfaux, "L'hymne au Christ," 425–37.

Table 2

Philippians 2:6–11	Isaiah 52–53; 45
Christ Jesus, 6 who, though he was in the form of God, did not regard equality with God as something to be exploited,	
7 but emptied himself, taking the form of a slave, being born in human likeness. And being found in human form,	53:12 because he poured out himself ... 53:2 he had no form or majesty (cf. 52:14)
8 he humbled himself and became obedient to the point of death—even death on a cross.	53:12 ... to death
9 Therefore God also highly exalted him and gave him the name that is above every name,	53:12 Therefore I will allot him a portion with the great 52:13 he shall be exalted and lifted up and shall be very high
10 so that at the name of Jesus every knee should bend, in heaven and on earth and under the earth,	45:23 To me every knee shall bow,
11 and every tongue should confess that Jesus Christ is Lord, to the glory of God the Father.	45:23 every tongue shall swear

Also, of great significance is the connection Paul makes between Christ and the Isaianic Servant in Galatians 1:4 and 2:20 (see Table 3; cf. 1 Cor 15:3b), which harkens back to an important theological concept found in Isaiah 53.[15]

Table 3

Gal 1:4	(the Lord Jesus Christ), who gave (*dontos*) himself for our sins (*hyper tōn hamartiōn hēmōn*)
Isa 53:6	and the Lord gave (*paredōken*) him over for our sins (*tais hamartiais hēmōn*)
Isa 53:12	and he bore the sins (*hamartias*) of many, and because of their sins (*hamartias*) he was given over (*paredothē*)

15. Ciampa, *Presence and Function*, 51–61; Harmon, *She Must and Shall*, 56–66; Bruce, *Galatians*, 75; Longenecker, *Galatians*, 7; Hays, "Galatians," 203; Rohde, *Paulus an die Galater*, 35; Fee, *Galatians*, 19, also proposes Isa 53:4.

Within Christian circles, it is quite common to take for granted the doctrine of atonement or more specifically the idea of vicarious suffering, that one person's suffering could take away another person's suffering by atoning for their sins. However, this important theological understanding, was not mainstream within the Judaisms of Jesus' day. While there are traces of this idea in various OT books, it is not until Isaiah 53 that this concept comes together in a way reminiscent of that found in the Christian faith.[16]

The significance of Isaiah 53 as a foundation for Paul's understanding of Christ's work is reinforced by Paul's multiple other allusions to Isaiah 53 in places where he refers to Christ's vicarious suffering (e.g., Rom 4:24–25; 5:15–19; 1 Cor 15:3–4; Phil 2:7–9; cf. Eph 5:2, 25). It is further supported by the recognition that Isaiah 53 was a significant text for the apostolic church's understanding of the person and work of Christ (e.g., Mark 10:45; Matt 20:28; Luke 22:37; John 1:29, 36; 1 Tim 2:6; Titus 2:14; Heb 9:28; 1 Pet 2:21–25; 3:18).[17]

Therefore, if Christ is the Isaianic Suffering Servant, then what is Paul's role? To answer this question a very brief look at the Isaianic Servant is necessary.

Excursus: Isaiah's Suffering Servant/s[18]

In both the Hebrew and Greek texts of Isaiah, the word Servant (Hebrew: *ebed*; Greek: *pais* [fourteen times[19]]; *doulos* [nine times[20]]; *douleuō* [seven times[21]]; *therapeuō* [once[22]]) is used thirty-one times in Isaiah 40–66: twenty times in the singular, which are all located in chapters 40–53, and eleven times in the plural, which are all located in chapters 54–66. The abrupt and decisive shift from the singular to the plural as well as

---

16. Spieckermann, "Vicarious Suffering," 1–15. Also see Scharbert, "Stellvertretendes Sühneleiden," 190–213, for an argument against viewing Babylonian traditions as a background for the phenomenon of *Stellvertretung* found in Isa 53.

17. Stuhlmacher, "Isaiah 53," 147–62; Hofius, "The Forth Servant Song," 163–88; Stanley, "Theme of the Servant," 386–412; Gignilliat, "Who is Isaiah's Servant?," 125–36.

18. This excursus is a slight revision from my previous work: Fringer, *Paul's Corporate Christophany*, 46–49.

19. Isa 41:8, 9; 42:1, 19; 43:10; 44:1, 2, 21(bis), 26; 45:4; 49:6; 50:10; 52:13.

20. Isa 42:19; 45:14; 48:20; 49:3, 5, 7; 56:6; 63:17; 65:9.

21. Isa 53:11; 65:8, 13(thrice), 14, 15.

22. Isa 54:17.

the ambiguous identity of the Servant can be confusing until one understands the three shifts in identity that take place in these chapters.

First, chapters 40–48 continually designate the singular servant collectively as Israel or Jacob,[23] whose main role was to bring justice to the nations (Isa 42:1, 3, 4) because God had given them as "a covenant to the people, a light to the nations" (Isa 42:6). Here we must remember the covenant between God and Abraham in Genesis 12:3 where God promises that in Abraham, "all the families of the earth shall be blessed." This theme of being a blessing or a light to the nations is repeated throughout the OT (e.g., Gen 12:3; 22:18; 28:14; Isa 2:2–4; 25:6–8; 56:6–8; Ezek 39:7; Zech 8:20–23; Mic 4:1–3) and is a significant aspect of Israel's calling, or mission. However, it quickly becomes evident that Israel has not and cannot fulfil this divine calling. In the words of Goldingay, "It is . . . because Israel cannot fulfil the servant role which is her responsibility, that . . . The picture of the servant has become a role seeking for someone to fulfil it."[24]

Second, this "someone" is introduced in chapter 49 and remains consistent throughout chapter 53. Though still named Israel (Isa 49:3), this Servant[25] is clearly represented as an individual who speaks in the first-person singular about being called by God (Isa 49:1–5) "to raise up the tribes of Jacob and to restore the survivors of Israel" and to be "a light to the nations, that [God's] salvation may reach to the end of the earth" (Isa 49:6). The Servant becomes representative of the whole. The Servant does not replace Israel; rather, the Servant "remains inseparable from Israel—but as a faithful embodiment of the nation Israel who has not performed [her] chosen role."[26] The exact (historical) identity is not the primary goal of the texts.[27] In fact, there are places where the lines are blurred to such an extent that one might see God as the Servant (e.g., Isa 49:7; 51:4–6; 53:13).[28] Almost metaphorically, the Servant represents the suffering God has endured at the hands of Israel's disobedience and reveals that part of the Servant's role is to awaken Israel to embrace her calling and embody her covenant commitment (Isa 51:9; 52:1–2).

This constitutes third and final shift in the identity of the servant; namely, an expanded return to the collective servant, here represented

---

23. Wilcox and Paton-Williams, "The Servant Songs," 82–84.
24. Goldingay, "Arrangement of Isaiah," 292.
25. Here, Servant with a capital "S" represents the individual servant.
26. Childs, *Isaiah*, 385.
27. Westermann, *Isaiah 40–66*, 93; Gignilliat, "Isaiah's Servant," 134; Seitz, "How is the Prophet Isaiah," 239. Cf. Clines, *I, He, We, and They*, 33, 46.
28. Wilcox and Paton-Williams, "The Servant Songs," 95.

with the plural in chapters 54–66 (e.g., Isa 54:17; 55:6). The plural "servants" is foreshadowed in Isaiah 53:10 as the singular Servant's suffering results in "offspring" or "seed" (Hebrew: *tzera*; Greek: *sperma* cf. Isa 44:3) who prolong his days.[29] This "prolonging" of days does not refer to the Servant's escape from death but to his offspring who turn (or repent) from their transgressions and receive the same righteousness (Isa 53:11), same Spirit (Isa 59:20–21; cf. 11:2; 42:1), same mission[30] (Isa 61:1–2, 9; 62:2, 10–12), and potentially the same suffering (Isa 57:1–2)[31] as the Singular Servant. Isaiah 65–66 concludes with a glorious picture of God's faithfulness and restoration of his creation, in which the servants of the Servant hold a special place (Isa 65:8–9, 12–15; 66:14).[32]

Paul's Christophanic experience resulted in a significant theological dilemma. If Jesus was the prophesied messiah, then the Scriptures must contain evidence for a suffering messianic figure who would bear the sins of both Jews and Gentiles. In the oracles of Isaiah came an exegetical revelation—a basis for a universal Suffering Servant Savior. Furthermore, in Isaiah, Paul formed an understanding of his calling to be one of the servants of the Servant, Christ (Gal 1:10). In other words, Paul did not view himself as the singular Servant, but as one of many offspring of this Servant.

Parallels between Paul's and the Galatians' Calling

Paul appears to go to great lengths to help the Galatians understand their own experience in line with his, as evidenced by the similarities in language and imagery (see Table 4). First, Paul begins this epistle by affirming that both he and the Galatians have been *called* by God through *grace* (Gal 1:15; 1:6). This truth of their shared calling is the foundation for the rest of Paul's claims about the Galatians call experience. Second, just as Paul *received* his gospel by divine revelation (Gal 1:12), the Galatians *received* the Spirit through believing what they heard (Gal 3:2). This "hearing" is a reference to Paul's proclaimed gospel, the *to euangelion to euangelisthen*, which Paul understands as revelation from God.[33] Third,

29. Beuken, "Theme of Trito-Isaiah," 67–87, argues the question driving Isaiah 56–66 is: "who are his offspring, in whom does he go on living?" (73).

30. Childs, *Isaiah*, 446; McKenzie, *Second Isaiah*, lvii.

31. Seitz, "Isaiah 40–66," 490–91; Gignilliat, *Paul and Isaiah's Servant*, 116–17.

32. Beuken, "Theme of Trito-Isaiah," 76–85.

33. Fringer, *Paul's Corporate Christophany*, 61–64; cf. Sturm, "Paul's Use of *Apokalyptō/Apokalypsis*," 248.

both Paul and the Galatians *see* Jesus Christ (Gal 1:12; 3:1). Based on Paul's Christophanic references in 1 Corinthians 9:1 and 15:8, we can confidently make a thematic link between *apokalypsis* (revelation) and *horaō* (to see). Both are revelatory language that Paul utilizes to express the phenomenon of seeing Christ post-ascension.

Fourth, Paul's reference to Christ being formed "in you," in reference to the Galatians (Gal 4:19) echoes his own experience of having Christ revealed "in me," that is, in Paul (Gal 1:15, 16). Christ "in" the believer is participatory language whereby the believer "in Christ" is being transformed by Christ and is carrying out Christ's mission in the world (cf. Gal 2:19–20).[34] Additionally, Paul may be using the motherhood language of "my children" and "labor pains" (Gal 4:19) to more intimately connect the Galatians calling to his own. "Paul now provides the motherly womb, but it is Christ who is being formed in the Galatians."[35] The fifth and final connection is somewhat removed from Paul's Christophanic experience, but sits within the larger autobiographical narrative and has already been shown to be tied to Paul's allusion to Isaiah 49. Paul mentions the possibility that both his and the Galatians' calling may be in vain (*kenon*; Gal 2:2) or for nothing (*eikē*; Gal 3:4). These two, *kenon* and *eikē*, are synonyms, and Paul uses them in an identical way in his Christophanic reference in 1 Cor 15 (vv. 2, 10).

TABLE 4

	Paul's Experience		The Galatians' Experience
Gal 1:15	(God) Called (*kalesantos*) me through his grace (*karitas*)	Gal 1:6 (cf. 5:8)	The one who called (*kalesas*) you in grace (*kariti*)
Gal 1:12	I did not receive (*parelabon*) (my gospel) from a human source … but through a revelation (*apokalypseōs*) of Jesus Christ	Gal 3:2 (cf. 3:5)	Did you receive (*elabete*) the Spirit by doing the works of the law or by believing what you heard? (*ex akoēs pisteōs*)
Gal 1:12	through a revelation (*apokalypseōs*) of Jesus Christ	Gal 3:1	It was before your eyes (*ophthalmous*) that Jesus Christ was publicly exhibited

---

34. Cf. Harmon, *She Must and Shall*, 119.
35. Fringer, *Paul's Corporate Christophany*, 71.

Paul's Experience		The Galatians' Experience	
Gal 1:15,16	God, who had set me apart from my mother's womb . . . was pleased to reveal his Son in me (*apokalypsai ton huion autou en emoi*)	Gal 4:19	My little children, for whom I am in labor until Christ is formed in you (*morphōthē Christos en hymin*)
Gal 2:2	I went up in response to a revelation. . . . in order to make sure that I was not running, or had not run, in vain (*kenon*)	Gal 3:4	Did you experience so much for nothing? (*eikē*)—if it really was for nothing (*eikē*)

The Galatians' Calling and Isaiah's Servant

The five points above show significant intentionality on Paul's part to bring together his and the Galatians callings, which are both represented as revelatory experiences that call the receivers to some type of active participation. Additionally, each of these can be seen as alluding to or echoing passages from Isaiah 40–66 (see Table 5). Points 1, 2, and 3, with their references to calling, motherhood imagery, and vain effort, point back through Paul's Christophanic reference to Isaiah 49:1–6. If this Isaianic connection is intentional, then Paul believes the Galatians share a similar, general calling to be servants of the singular Suffering Servant Savior, Christ.

This radical claim may be reinforced by the recognition of another connection between the Galatians' calling and an Isaianic Servant passage (point 4 in Table 5). In Galatians 3:2, 5, Paul twice contrasts "doing the works of the law" with "believing what you heard" as the means by which the Galatians have received the Spirit. The latter phrase, "believing what you heard" (*ex akoēs pisteōs*), is most likely an allusion to Isaiah 53:1a, "who has believed our report" (*tis episteusen tē akon hēmōn*).[36] Paul references this same passage as part of a similar argument in Romans 10:16–17; where he writes: "But not all have obeyed the good news; for Isaiah says, 'Lord, who has believed our message?' So faith comes from what is heard, and what is heard comes through the word of Christ." Isaiah 53:1, in its contexts, fits Paul's Galatians' argument well as "hearing" is directly connected to revelation (*apekalypsthē*) from the Lord (Isa 53:1) and the proclamation of the gospel by God's messenger (Isa 52:7).

---

36. Harmon, *She Must and Shall*, 129–32; Hays, *Faith of Jesus Christ*, 128–31; Bruce, *Galatians*, 149.

If Paul does have this final so-called Servant Song (Isa 52:13—53:12) in mind here, then, Galatians 3:1b (point 5 in Table 5) which states, "It was before your eyes (*ophthalmous*) that Jesus Christ was publicly exhibited," may be echoing Isaiah 52:10, which says, "And the Lord shall reveal (*apokalyptō*) his holy arm before all the nations, and all the ends of the earth shall see (*ophthalmous*) the salvation that comes from God" (cf. Isa 40:5). Paul would be viewing Christ as God's "holy arm" and his crucifixion as God's means for salvation. In other words, what the Galatians have *seen* is a revelation from God, which has led to their own salvation. Lest we forget, the singular Servant's salvation, righteousness, and mission are extended to the many servants of the Servant just a few verses later in Isaiah 53:10–11.

TABLE 5

	The Galatians		Isaiah's Servant
Gal 1:6 (cf. 5:8)	The one who called (*kalesas*) you in grace (*kariti*)	Isa 49:1b	he called (*ekalesen*) my name
Gal 4:19	My little children, for whom I am in labor until Christ is formed in you (*morphōthē Christos en hymin*)	Isa 49:1b, 5a	from my mother's womb (*ek koilias mētros mou*)
Gal 3:4	Did you experience so much for nothing? (*eikē*)—if it really was for nothing (*eikē*)	Isa 49:4	I labored in vain (*kenōs ekopiasa*)
Gal 3:2, 5	believing what you heard (*ex akoēs pisteōs*)	Isa 53:1a	who has believed our report (*tis episteusen tē akon hēmōn*)
Gal 3:1	It was before your eyes (*ophthalmous*) that Jesus Christ was publicly exhibited	Isa 52:10	And the Lord shall reveal (*apokalyptō*) his holy arm before all the nations, and all the ends of the earth shall see (*ophthalmous*) the salvation that comes from God

To summarize, we have seen how Paul intentionally aligns his and the Galatians' callings and how both are also connected to the Isaianic Servant. Paul seeks to help the Galatians understand that all believers are called by God through a divine revelation, either directly or via the proclaimed gospel, and that this calling includes being transformed by the actions of the Servant and taking on aspects of the Servant's mission; in other words, they become servants of the Servant. In what follows, we will briefly highlight three important elements of Paul's call language that are based on the groundwork laid above and that pertain to believers' flourishing.

Aspects of Believers' Flourishing

The language of "human flourishing" is relatively new, but the concept is not. Some have traced it back to the Greek philosopher Aristotle (384–322 BC) and his writings on *eudaimonia*,[37] which has often been translated in English as "happiness," but is better represented by the more robust terminology of "human flourishing."[38] Nevertheless, the concept is much older than Aristotle and could arguably be traced back to God's creation. Therein, we find God's mandate for humanity to "be fruitful and multiply" (Gen 1:28), God's inauguration of Sabbath rest (Gen 2:1–3), and God's proclamation that relationship and community are essential to humanity's wellbeing (Gen 2:18–24). As the Genesis narrative continues (as well as the whole of the Scriptures), it becomes evident that true human flourishing is only possible in relationship with this God; thus, we can speak of "believers' flourishing." As Pennington eloquently states,

> true human flourishing is only available through communion with the Father God through his revealed Son, Jesus, as we are empowered by the Holy Spirit. This flourishing is only experienced through faithful, heart-deep, whole-person discipleship, following Jesus' teachings and life, which situate the disciple into God's community or kingdom.[39]

Post-fall, human flourishing is integrally tied to the burgeoning eschatological reality ushered in by the Christ event, and we participate in this new creation reality (2 Cor 5:17) by walking according to the Spirit. As Paul writes, God "will give life to your mortal bodies also through his Spirit that dwells in you" (Rom 8:11). Thus, we are to "lead a life worthy of the calling to which (we) have been called" (Eph 4:1).

Paul articulates a vision of human flourishing that is dependent upon our connection to God and our acceptance and participation in God's calling upon us. Below, we will briefly look at three aspects of

---

37. Hurka, "There Faces of Flourishing," 44–46; Haybron, *Happiness*, 11, see also 70–76.

38. Pennington, "Biblical Theology of Human Flourishing," 2–3.

39. Pennington, *Sermon on the Mount*, 14–15.

believers' flourishing that are connected to Paul's understanding of call/calling: salvation, corporate healing, and incarnation.

Calling and Salvation

The two most prevalent ways *kaleō* is utilized in the LXX and in Graeco-Roman antiquity are (1) "to name, designate, [and] give a title to," and (2) "to summon or invite."[40] It is rarely if ever used to denote conversion.[41] Nevertheless, Chester has shown how Paul develops the concept of calling *as* conversion,[42] and how he is more focused on the "before and after of calling, [the] from what and to what, rather than on the event itself."[43]

This is seen in Paul's reference to his own calling. His earlier life in Judaism as a Pharisee and persecutor of the church (Gal 1:13–14) is juxtaposed with his being set apart to proclaim Christ among the Gentiles (Gal 1:15–16). He goes so far as to say that he has "been crucified with Christ; and it is no longer [he] who live[s], but it is Christ who lives in [him]" (Gal 2:19–20).[44] This same dichotomy is highlighted in the Galatians' calling but in negative terms. They are in danger of turning from their calling (Gal 1:6; 5:7–8) and returning to their former life where they did not know God and were enslaved to things that were not gods (Gal 4:8–11). Positively, we are told that their "hearing" resulted in believing, which resulted in their receiving of the Holy Spirit (Gal 3:1–5). It is obvious that for both Paul and the Galatians, a radical transformation or conversion has taken place.

Both "callings" are said to have taken place in/through the grace of God. This highlights God's action as agent of this gift of calling,[45] which is functioning metaphorically to express God's salvation. Additionally, Hussey reminds us that "[c]all is not just the inception of the salvation but an ongoing reality for the Galatians (and for Paul). Call relates not just to salvation but also to sanctification."[46] Acceptance of God's call upon

---

40. Chester, *Conversion at Corinth*, 60; cf. Hussey, *Soteriological Use of Call*, 19–20.
41. Chester, *Conversion at Corinth*, 64–77.
42. Chester, *Conversion at Corinth*, 77–106.
43. Chester, *Conversion at Corinth*, 61.
44. McFarland, "The One Who Calls," 160–65, views Gal 2:18–21 as containing a corporate "I" that includes the Galatians.
45. See Barclay, *Paul and the Gift*, 358–60.
46. Hussey, *Soteriological Use of Call*, 64.

one's life is the first step toward true human flourishing. When believers embrace their calling, a new reality is opened before them that includes transformation into the image of God (2 Cor 3:18). Salvation includes "strip[ping] off the old self with its practices and [clothing oneself] with the new self, which is being renewed in knowledge according to the image of its creator" (Col 3:10–11).

Calling and Corporate Healing

The use of *kaleō* as a metaphor for corporate healing should be seen as an extension of *kaleō* as a metaphor for salvation. It includes immediate and ongoing individual and corporate transformation, and it includes the continuation of the singular Servant's mission to be a blessing to the nations. Personally, Paul's calling included his being made righteous through the death of Christ, allowing him to live by faith in the Son of God (Gal 2:20–21). Paul's calling enables him to participate in the Servant's righteousness (Isa 53:11), and through this participation to be healed. But this healing is not for him alone, just as the Servant's suffering was not an end in itself, but a means to a greater end, the bearing of humanity's sin.

Paul's calling is tied to his commission to proclaim Christ among the nation (Gal 1:16; cf. 2:9), which is a continuation of the Servant's calling (Isa 49:6) and a fulfilment of Israel's calling (Isa 42:6) that harkens all the way back to God's covenant with Abraham (Gen 12:3). Through Paul's proclamation of the Gospel to the Gentiles, Paul prolongs the Servant's mission, extending the Servant's range (Isa 53:10) that God's "salvation may reach to the end of the earth" (Isa 49:6). Thus, the Galatians are themselves recipients of the Servant Christ's righteousness and of God's healing through Paul's obedience to his calling.

While many have emphasized OT prophetic call as the foundation for Paul's own calling,[47] these same people would, nevertheless, not make the equivalent assertion concerning believers' calling, even though they share similar, and often identical, language. Here, it should be clearly stated that Paul's calling to apostleship is unique, and does, at least in part, appear to coincide with some of the OT prophets. Nevertheless, if we can move beyond seeing Paul as the singular Isaianic Servant and assign that reality to Christ, then it seems likely that Paul is intentionally

---

47. Fredriksen, "Paul and Augustine," 15–17, 30; Sandnes, *Paul*, 49–70; Aernie, *Paul among the Prophets*, 136–39.

aligning elements of his and believers' calling in such a way as to invite them to embrace their identity as servants of the Servant and, in so doing, to embrace, in general terms, the Servant's mission to bring salvation and healing to others through their obedience (cf. Isa 56:6–8). This is reflected in Galatians 5:13–14—"For you were called to freedom, brothers and sisters, only do not use your freedom as an opportunity for self-indulgence, but through love become slaves to one another. For the whole law is summed up in a single commandment, 'You shall love your neighbor as yourself.'"

"Neighbor" is not limited to unbelievers; it also refers to the community of believers, the body of Christ. The Galatians' calling includes recognizing other believers' transgressions and seeking to "restore such a one in a spirit of gentleness" (Gal 6:1), and Paul tells them to "work for the good of all, and especially for those of the family of faith" (Gal 6:10). An integral part of our corporate healing is incorporation into the body of Christ. Therein, we become one with Christ and with other believers (Gal 3:28), bringing together what was broken in the Fall. We flourish together or we suffer together (1 Cor 12:26). This is beautifully summed up in Ephesians 4:15–16—"[S]peaking the truth in love, we must grow up in every way into him who is the head, into Christ, from whom the whole body, joined and knit together by every ligament with which it is equipped, as each part is working properly, promotes the body's growth in building itself up in love."

In one sense, we could argue that just as the Servant Christ brings corporate healing to others through his suffering, death, and exaltation, so too the many servants, who are the body of Christ, bring healing to Christ through their transformation and participation in his mission. Paul may hint at this when he writes: "I am now rejoicing in my suffering for your sake, and in my flesh I am completing what is lacking in Christ's afflictions for the sake of his body, that is, the church" (Col 1:24). The bodily presence of Paul as he embraces his calling "to make the word of God fully known" (Col 1:25) helps to "present everyone mature in Christ" (Col 1:28).[48] In the calling of Paul and all believers to be "ambassadors for Christ" entrusted with a "ministry of reconciliation," we are enabled to "become the righteousness of God" (2 Cor 5:18–21), and to thus extend the Servant's mission of healing the whole creation (Isa 65:17–25; 66:22–23; Rev 21:1–7), which is inherently tied to its Creator.

---

48. Cf. Garland, *Colossians/Philemon*, 118–23.

Calling and Incarnation

Finally, within the larger context of Paul's use of *kaleō* in Galatians, there are some images of Christ's incarnation as part of Paul's and the Galatians' calling. First, the birthing language connected to both Paul and the Galatians callings (Gal 1:15; 4:19) reflect Christ's incarnation in as much as they allude to the Isaianic Servant who was called before he was born and was "formed in the womb to be a servant" (Isa 49:1, 5). Second, Paul's language of Christ living in him (Gal 2:20) and of Christ being formed in the Galatians reflects an embodiment of Christ in the believer. Just as the believer lives "in Christ," so too, Christ dwells in the believer, incarnating himself within the believing community. This is the process of salvation and sanctification that is part of the believers' calling.

Third, the believers' protracting of the Servant's mission can itself be seen as an incarnation of the Servant through the obedience of the servants. Thus, Paul evidences his willingness to suffer significantly for the sake of the Galatians, which he recognizes as an inevitable part of his calling (Gal 2:19–20; 4:12–15; 5:11). Likewise, the Galatians are called to use their freedom to embody God's love (Gal 5:13–14), to live out the fruit of the Spirit (Gal 5:22–23), and to bear one another's burdens (Gal 6:2). These things are not done in their own strength. They are done through the Spirit as Christ's life and the Father's love is incarnated through the believer. In the words of the late Archbishop of Canterbury Michael Ramsey, "We do not know the whole fact of Christ incarnate unless we know his church, and its life as part of his own life. . . . [T]he Body is the fullness of Christ, and the history of the Church and the lives of the saints are acts in the biography of the Messiah."[49]

Conclusion

This short chapter has only scrapped the surface of the depth of Paul's understanding of his own and believers' callings. It has indevoured to show the inclusiveness of Paul's understanding of calling, which came about through his Christophany and his subsequent re-reading of Scripture, especially Isaiah. The final section on the aspects of believers' flourishing was merely a glimpse into the significance of salvation, corporate healing, and incarnation; it needs further development. Nevertheless, it provides

---

49. Ramsey, *Glory Descending*, 102.

us with hope and challenge to allow God to transform us and use us in our world. May we, through the power of the Holy Spirit, lead a life worthy of the calling to which we have been called (Eph 4:1).

Bibliography

Aernie, Jeffrey W. *Is Paul Also among the Prophets? An Examination of the Relationship between Paul and the Old Testament Prophetic Tradition in 2 Corinthians*. Library of New Testament Studies 467. London: Bloomsbury, 2012.

Barclay, John M. *Paul and the Gift*. Grand Rapids: Eerdmans, 2015.

Bauckham, Richard. *Jesus and the God of Israel: God Crucified and Other Studies on the New Testament's Christology of Divine Identity*. Grand Rapids: Eerdmans, 2009.

Beker, J. Christiaan. *Paul the Apostle: The Triumph of God in Life and Thought*. Philadelphia: Fortress, 1980.

Beuken, W. A. M. "The Main Theme of Trito-Isaiah: 'The Servants of YHWH.'" *Journal for the Study of the Old Testament* 47 (1990) 67–87.

Bruce, F. F. *The Epistle to the Galatians*. New International Greek Testament Commentary. Grand Rapids: Eerdmans, 1982.

Cerfaux, Lucien. "L'hymne au Christ—sérviteur de Dieu (Phil. 2.6–11 = Is. 52.13—53.12)." In *Recueil Lucien Cerfaux*, vol. 2, 425–37. Bibliotheca Ephemeridum Theologicarum Lovaniensium 6–7. Gembloux: Duculot, 1954.

Chester, Stephen. *Conversion at Corinth: Perspectives on Conversion in Paul's Theology and the Corinthian Church*. London: T&T Clark, 2003.

Childs, Brevard S. *Isaiah*. Old Testament Library. Louisville: Westminster John Knox, 2001.

Ciampa, Roy E. *The Presence and Function of Scripture in Galatians 1 and 2*. Wissenschaftliche Untersuchungen zum Neuen Testament 2.102. Tübingen: Mohr, 1998.

Clines, David. *I, He, We, and They—A Literary Approach to Isaiah 53*. Journal for the Study of the Old Testament Supplement 1. Sheffield: JSOT Press, 1976.

Dinter, Paul E. "Paul and the Prophet Isaiah." *Biblical Theology Bulletin* 13.2 (1983) 48–52.

Fee, Gordon D. *Galatians*. Pentecostal Commentary Series. Dorset, UK: Deo, 2011.

Fredriksen, Paula. "Paul and Augustine: Conversion Narratives, Orthodox Traditions, and the Retrospective Self." *Journal of Theological Studies* 37 (1986) 3–34.

Fringer, Rob A. *Paul's Corporate Christophany: An Evaluation of Paul's Christophanic References in Their Epistolary Contexts*. Eugene, OR: Pickwick, 2019.

Garland, David E. *Colossians and Philemon*. NIV Application Commentary. Grand Rapids: Zondervan, 1998.

Gaventa, Beverley. "Paul's Conversion: A Critical Sifting of the Epistolary Evidence." PhD diss., Duke University, 1978.

Gignilliat, Mark S. *Paul and Isaiah's Servants: Paul's Theological Reading of Isaiah 40–66 in 2 Corinthians 5:14–6:10*. Library of New Testament Studies 330. London: T&T Clark, 2007.

———. "Who is Isaiah's Servant? Narrative Identity and Theological Potentiality." *Scottish Journal of Theology* 61.2 (2008) 125–36.

Goldingay, John. "The Arrangement of Isaiah XLI–XLV." *Vetus Testamentum* 29 (1979) 289–99.

Gorman, Michael J. *Inhabiting the Cruciform God: Kenosis, Justification, and Theosis in Paul's Narrative Soteriology*. Grand Raids: Eerdmans, 2009.

Harmon, Matthew S. *She Must and Shall Go Free: Paul's Isaianic Gospel in Galatians*. Beihefte zur Zeitschrift für die Neutestamentliche Wissenschaft 168. Berlin: de Gruyter, 2010.

Haybron, Dan. *Happiness: A Very Short Introduction*. Oxford: Oxford University Press, 2013.

Hays, Richard B. *The Conversion of the Imagination: Paul as Interpreter of Israel's Scripture*. Grand Rapids: Eerdmans, 2005.

———. *The Faith of Jesus Christ: The Narrative Substructure of Galatians 3:1—4:11*. 2nd ed. Biblical Resource Series. Grand Rapids: Eerdmans, 2002.

———. "Galatians." In *New Interpreter's Bible*, vol. 11, 181–348. Nashville: Abingdon, 2000.

Hofius, Otfried. "The Fourth Servant Song in the New Testament Letters." In *The Suffering Servant: Isaiah 53 in Jewish and Christian Sources*, edited by Bernd Janowski and Peter Stuhlmacher, translated by Daniel P. Bailey, 163–88. Grand Rapids: Eerdmans, 2004.

Hurka, Thomas. "The Three Faces of Flourishing." *Social Philosophy & Policy* 16.1 (1999) 44–71.

Hussey, Ian. *The Soteriological Use of Call by Paul and Luke*. Australian College of Theology Monograph Series. Eugene, OR: Wipf & Stock, 2018.

Jervis, Ann. *Galatians*. New International Biblical Commentary on the New Testament. Peabody, MA: Hendrickson, 1999.

Kim, Seyoon. *The Origin of Paul's Gospel*. Wissenschaftliche Untersuchungen zum Neuen Testament 4. Tübingen: Mohr Siebeck, 1981. Reprint, Eugene, OR: Wipf & Stock, 2007.

Koch, Dietrich-Alex. *Die Schrift als Zeuge des Evangeliums: Untersuchungen zur Verwendung und zum Verständnis der Schrift bei Paulus*. Beiträge zur historischen Theologie 69. Tübingen: Mohr Siebeck, 1986.

Longenecker, Richard. *Galatians*. WBC 41. Dallas: Word, 1990.

———. "A Realized Hope, a New Commitment, and a Developed Proclamation: Paul and Jesus." In *The Road from Damascus: The Impact of Paul's Conversion on His Life, Thought, and Ministry*, edited by Richard N. Longenecker, 18–42. Grand Rapids: Eerdmans, 1997.

McFarland, Orrey. "The One Who Calls in Grace: Paul's Rhetorical and Theological Identification with the Galatians." *Horizons in Biblical Theology* 35 (2013) 151–65.

McKenzie, John L. *Second Isaiah: A New Translation with Introduction and Commentary*. Anchor Bible 20. Garden City, NY: Doubleday, 1968.

Moyise, Steve, and Maarten J. J. Menken, eds. *Isaiah in the New Testament*. New York: T&T Clark, 2005.

Newman, Carey C. *Paul's Glory-Christology: Tradition and Rhetoric*. Supplements to Novum Testamentum 69. Leiden: Brill, 1992.

Pennington, Jonathan T. "A Biblical Theology of Human Flourishing." *Institute for Faith, Work & Economics*, 4 March 2015. https://tifwe.org/wp-content/uploads/2015/03/A-Biblical-Theology-of-Human-Flourishing-Pennington.pdf.

———. *The Sermon on the Mount and Human Flourishing: A Theological Commentary*. Grand Rapids: Baker Academic, 2017.

Ramsey, Michael. *Glory Descending: Michael Ramsey and His Writings*. Edited by Douglas Dales et al. Grand Rapids: Eerdmans, 2005.

Rohde, Joachim. *Der Brief des Paulus an die Galater*. Theologischer Handkommentar zum Neuen Testament 9. Berlin: Evangelische Verlagsanstalt, 1989.

Sandnes, Karl Olav. *Paul—One of the Prophets? A Contribution to the Apostle's Self-Understanding*. Wissenschaftliche Untersuchungen zum Neuen Testament 2.43. Tübingen: Mohr, 1991.

Scharbert, Josef. "Stellvertretendes Sühneleiden in den Ebed-Jahwe-Liedern und in altorientalischen Ritualtexten." *Biblische Zeitschrift* 2 (1958) 190–213.

Segal, Alan. *Paul the Convert: The Apostolate and Apostasy of Saul the Pharisee*. New Haven: Yale University Press, 1990.

Seitz, Christopher. "The Book of Isaiah 40–66: Introduction, Commentary, and Reflections." In *The New Interpreter's Bible*, vol. 6, 309–552. Nashville: Abingdon, 2001.

———. "How is the Prophet Isaiah Present in the Latter Half of the Book? The Logic of Chapters 40–66 within the Book of Isaiah." *Journal of Biblical Literature* 115.2 (1996) 219–40. .

Shum, Shiu-Lun. *Paul's Use of Isaiah in Romans: A Comparative Study of Paul's Letter to the Romans and the Sybilline and Qumran Sectarian Texts*. Wissenschaftliche Untersuchungen zum Neuen Testament 2.156. Tübingen: Mohr Siebeck, 2002.

Silva, Moisés. "Old Testament in Paul." In *Dictionary of Paul and His Letters*, edited by Gerald F. Hawthorne et al., 630–42. Downers Grove, IL: InterVarsity, 1993.

Spieckermann, Hermann. "The Conception and Prehistory of the Idea of Vicarious Suffering in the Old Testament." In *The Suffering Servant: Isaiah 53 in Jewish and Christian Sources*, edited by Bernd Janowski and Peter Stuhlmacher, translated by Daniel P. Bailey, 1–15. Grand Rapids: Eerdmans, 2004.

Stanley, David M. "The Theme of the Servant of Yahweh in Primitive Christian Soteriology, and its Transposition by St. Paul." *Catholic Biblical Quarterly* 17 (1954) 385–425

Stendahl, Krister. *Paul among Jews and Gentiles*. London: SCM, 1977.

Stuhlmacher, Peter. "Isaiah 53 in the Gospels and Acts." In *The Suffering Servant: Isaiah 53 in Jewish and Christian Sources*, edited by Bernd Janowski and Peter Stuhlmacher, translated by Daniel P. Bailey, 147–62. Grand Rapids: Eerdmans, 2004.

Sturm, Ricard E. "An Exegetical Study of the Apostle Paul's Use of the Words *Apokalyptō/Apokalypsis*: The Gospel as God's Apocalypse." PhD thesis, Union Theological Seminary, 1983.

Wagner, J. Ross. *Heralds of the Good News: Isaiah and Paul "in Concert" in the Letter to the Romans*. Leiden: Brill, 2003.

Ware, James P. *Paul and the Mission of the Church: Philippians in Ancient Jewish Context*. Grand Rapids: Baker Academic, 2011.

Westermann, Claus. *Isaiah 40–66*. OTL. Philadelphia: Westminster, 1969.

Wilcox, Peter, and David Paton-Williams. "The Servant Songs in Deutero-Isaiah." *Journal for the Study of the Old Testament* 42 (1988) 79–102.

Wilk, Florian. *Die Bedeutung des Jesajabuches für Paulus.* Forschungen zur Religion und Literatur des Alten und Neuen Testaments 179. Göttingen: Vandenhoeck & Ruprecht, 1998.

Witherington, Ben, III. *Grace in Galatia: A Commentary on St Paul's Letter to the Galatians.* Edinburgh: T&T Clark, 1998.

Wright, N. T. *Paul and the Faithfulness of God: Parts III and IV.* Christian Origins and the Question of God 4. London: SPCK, 2013.

www.ingramcontent.com/pod-product-compliance
Lightning Source LLC
Chambersburg PA
CBHW070938240426
43667CB00036B/2307